BLACK'S NEW TESTAMENT COMMENTARIES
General Editor: Henry Chadwick, DD, FBA

THE REVELATION OF ST JOHN

THE

REVELATION OF SAINT JOHN

G. B. CAIRD

HENDRICKSON
PUBLISHERS
PEABODY, MASSACHUSETTS 01961-3473

First published 1966

A & C Black (Publishers) Limited, London

Copyright © 1966 George Bradford Caird

Hendrickson Publishers, Inc. Edition

ISBN 1-56563-018-1

Reprinted by arrangement with A & C Black (Publishers) Limited.

The mosaic fretwork on the cover comes from the Galla Placidia
Mausoleum in Ravenna and is used courtesy of ITALCARDS, Bologna, Italy.

PREFACE

I F we make adequate allowance for vast technological change, the times John lived in were astonishingly like our own, perhaps more like than any of the intervening centuries. The purpose of this commentary is to carry the reader back to the end of the first century A.D. to hear what the Spirit was then saying to the churches, so that, returning to the present, he may be the better able to hear what the Spirit is saying to the churches of our own day.

The Greek text of Revelation fortunately raises few major problems, and I have drawn attention to textual variants only where they make a real difference to the meaning. The translation is my own; I have tried to be independent of other versions, but not so independent as to forego what was obviously the most felicitous rendering. Translation is itself a form of interpretation, and I have not thought it necessary to comment in the notes on every word of the text, if the translation seemed to make John's intention sufficiently clear.

Every commentator on a book of the Bible is aware of his debt to his predecessors, not least to those with whom he disagrees. I make no claim to have read all the vast literature on this subject, but it is proper that I should acknowledge my indebtedness to those writers from whom I have learned the most. Like others, I have found the vast erudition of R. H. Charles indispensable, even though I have wanted to dissent from many of his conclusions. From W. M. Ramsay I have learnt to see John's world through the eyes of a Roman historian; from E. Stauffer I have learnt the true significance of myth; and from S. B. Frost I received my first clue to the meaning of apocalyptic. But above all my thanks are due to A. M. Farrer, who first opened my eyes to John's use of the imagination and taught me to see in him both an exegete and a supreme literary artist.

Some of the material in this commentary has already appeared in a different form in four articles, 'On Deciphering the Book of Revelation', which I wrote for the *Expository Times* (Oct.

v

THE REVELATION OF ST. JOHN THE DIVINE

1962–Jan. 1963). I must thank Miss A. W. Hastings for her genial pertinacity in extracting these articles from me, and for agreeing that I should be free to use any part of them again in the commentary on which I was already engaged.

Finally, I am grateful to Professor Henry Chadwick for giving me the opportunity and the encouragement to write this book, for the patience with which he has waited for it, and for a number of constructive suggestions, including the proposal that I should add to the end of the commentary a brief summary of John's theology.

G. B. C.

CONTENTS

BIBLIOGRAPHY

Barclay, W., *Letters to the Seven Churches*. London: S.C.M. Press, 1957.

Beckwith, I. T., *The Apocalypse of John*. New York: Macmillan, 1920.

Bousset, W., *Die Offenbarung Johannis* ('Meyer's Kommentar'). 6th ed. Göttingen: Vandenhoeck & Ruprecht, 1906.

Bowman, J. W., *The Drama of the Book of Revelation*. Philadelphia: Westminster Press, 1955.

— 'Book of Revelation' in *The Interpreter's Dictionary of the Bible*. New York: Abingdon Press, 1962.

Caird, G. B., *Principalities and Powers*. Oxford: Clarendon Press, 1956.

Charles, R. H., *A Critical and Exegetical Commentary on the Revelation of St. John* ('The International Critical Commentary'). Edinburgh: T. & T. Clark, 1920 (2 vols.).

Farrer, A. M., *A Rebirth of Images*. Westminster: Dacre Press, 1949.

— *The Revelation of St. John the Divine*. Oxford: Clarendon Press, 1964.

Feuillet, A., *L'Apocalypse: l'état de la question*. Paris: Desclée de Brouwer, 1963.

Frost, S. B., *Old Testament Apocalyptic*. London: Epworth Press, 1952.

Glasson, T. F., *The Revelation of John* ('The Cambridge Bible Commentary'). Cambridge University Press, 1965.

Hanson, A. T., *The Wrath of the Lamb*. London: S.P.C.K., 1957.

Holtz, T., *Die Christologie der Apokalypse des Johannes*. Berlin: Akademie Verlag, 1962.

Hoskier, H. C., *Concerning the Text of the Apocalypse*. London: Bernard Quaritch, 1929 (2 vols.).

Kepler, T. S., *The Book of Revelation*. New York: Oxford University Press, 1957.

Kiddle, M., *The Revelation of St. John* ('The Moffatt New Testament Commentary'). London: Hodder & Stoughton, 1940.

Lilje H., *The Last Book of the Bible*. (Tr. O. Wyon.) Philadelphia: Muhlenberg Press, 1957.

Lohmeyer, E., *Die Offenbarung des Johannes* ('Handbuch zum Neuen Testament'). Tübingen: J. C. B. Mohr, 1953.

Lohse, E., *Die Offenbarung des Johannes* ('Das Neue Testament Deutsch'). Göttingen: Vandenhoeck & Ruprecht, 1960.

Minear, P. S., 'The Cosmology of the Apocalypse' in *Current Issues*

THE REVELATION OF ST. JOHN THE DIVINE

in New Testament Interpretation, ed. W. Klassen and G. F. Snyder. London: S.C.M. Press, 1962.

Niles, D. T., *As Seeing the Invisible*. London: S.C.M. Press, 1962.

Oman, J., *The Book of Revelation*. Cambridge University Press, 1923.

Peake, A. S., *The Revelation of John*. London: Holborn Press, 1920.

Preston, R. H. and Hanson, A. T., *The Revelation of St. John the Divine*. ('The Torch Bible Commentaries'). London: S.C.M. Press, 1949.

Ramsay, W. M., *The Letters to the Seven Churches of Asia*. London: Hodder & Stoughton, 1904.

Rissi, M., *Zeit und Geschichte in der Offenbarung des Johannes*. Zürich, 1952.

Rist, M., *Revelation* ('The Interpreter's Bible'). New York: Abingdon Press, 1957.

Scott, C. A. Anderson, *Revelation* ('The Century Bible'). Edinburgh: T. C. & E. C. Jack, 1902.

Scott, E. F., *The Book of Revelation*. London: S.C.M. Press, 1939.

Stauffer, E., *Christ and the Caesars*. (Tr. K. and R. Gregor Smith.) London: S.C.M. Press, 1955.

For a more detailed bibliography see the works by A. Feuillet and T. Holtz.

INTRODUCTION

I F an intelligent reader, hitherto unfamiliar with the Bible, were set to read St. Matthew's Gospel or the Epistle to the Romans, he would certainly be puzzled by some of the details, but he would be in no serious doubt about the general drift of what he was reading; and summaries of either, given by two such readers, might be expected to be recognizably accounts of the same book. But could this be said of the Revelation of St. John? Is not the untutored reader bound to end with the question, 'What on earth is this all about?' In one sense, of course, it is perfectly obvious what the book is about: it is about an exile and the visions which he describes for the benefit of seven churches, about a throne and a scroll, seals, trumpets, and bowls, horsemen, locusts, and scorpions, a dragon and a monster, two women, one clothed in heavenly, the other in earthly finery, and two cities, the one worldly and the other not of this world. But what *on earth* is it all about? For these are heavenly symbols. Do they correspond to anything, past, present, or future, in the experience of ordinary men and women? No sooner is this question asked than others follow. How did this book find its way into the New Testament? Is it a really Christian book? Can the heavenly figure it portrays be identified with Jesus of Nazareth? It is even a moral book? Does not its author take altogether too much delight in gloating over the doom of the wicked? The prophet Jeremiah, though he predicted disaster, protested that he had never wanted the fatal day to come (Jer. xvii. 16); but John seems to welcome a whole succession of catastrophic events. The Romans denounced the early Christians as enemies of the human race, partly at least because they suspected them of praying for the downfall of civilization. Does not the Revelation justify their suspicions?

The mystified reader may derive some consolation, though little help, from the discovery that his difficulties have been shared throughout the centuries by humble believer and scholar alike. The great Jerome wrote to Paulinus, bishop of Nola:

'The Apocalypse of John has as many secrets as words. I am saying less than the book deserves. It is beyond all praise; for multiple meanings lie hidden in each single word.' (*Ep.* liii. 9) Others of equal eminence have considered it beyond the possibility of praise. 'My spirit,' wrote Martin Luther in his 1522 Preface, 'cannot accommodate itself to this book. There is one sufficient reason for the small esteem in which I hold it—that Christ is neither taught in it nor recognized.' No other book can have aroused such equally passionate love and hatred. It has been the inspiration of poetry, music, and art, the fountain of worship and devotion, the comfort of the bereaved, and the strength of the persecuted. But it has also been roundly denounced by more critics than Luther as a work of vindictive and unchristian spirit. In the second century Justin Martyr (*Tryph.* 81), Melito of Sardis (Eusebius, *H.E.* iv. 26. 2), the author of the Muratorian Canon, Irenaeus (*Haer.* iii. 11. 1; iv. 20. 11; v. 35. 2), and Tertullian (*Marc.* iii. 14. 24) all accepted Revelation as scripture and attributed it to the apostle John; but there were others who called it 'unintelligible and illogical' and thought that its author must have been John's traditional enemy, Cerinthus (Eus. *H.E.* vii. 25. 1-2). From the time of the millenarian Papias to the present day it has been the paradise of fanatics and sectarians, each using it to justify his own peculiar doctrine and so adding to the misgivings of the orthodox. And in modern times scores of commentaries have been written on it so diverse as to make the reader wonder whether they are discussing the same book.

It might appear, then, that the reader's plight is even worse than he had supposed. He is faced not only with a bewildering book, but with an even more bewildering array of interpretations. Now it would be theoretically possible to write a very long introduction, in which all these theories were classified and debated, until by a process of exhaustion, both of the subject and of the reader, one solution only was left.[1] But there are at least two excellent reasons for not adopting this procedure. The first has been succinctly put by A. M. Farrer: 'An exposition of the Revelation is at the same time an argument. And it is one

---

[1] For an admirably concise survey see A. Feuillet, *L'Apocalypse: l'état de la question.*

of those arguments in which nothing short of the whole story proves the case.'[1] It is better therefore to postpone all argument until we come to the commentary, where the whole story can be told, and to allow John to unfold his theme in his own way. The other reason is still more cogent. John was not compiling a week-end problem book. Whatever else he may have intended, he cannot have set out to mystify. Even the implausible theory that he wrote in code to deceive the secret police is belied by the open reference in xvii. 9 to the seven hills of Rome. John was a pastor, writing with a passionate concern that ordinary men and women should understand what he had been charged to tell them, and, rightly or wrongly, he must have believed that they would be able to understand. No doubt an effort of comprehension was required of them, for a revelation would not be worth communicating if it did not transcend their previous knowledge; but the effort must have been within the competence of the ordinary members of the churches of Asia. Whoever had ears to hear might hear what the Spirit was saying to the churches. If only we can learn to put ourselves in the place of those Asiatic Christians, we may expect to find that John has said exactly what he means and that he is his own best interpreter.

The one question therefore which we need to ask before beginning to read is this: what did those early Christians know about this book which we do not know? If we can be clear about that, we can measure the full extent of the advantage which they had over us and make the necessary allowances. What is required of us is that we shall turn historians. For it is the task of the historian by the exercise of an informed and sympathetic imagination to enter into the experience of a past generation and so to bring it to life that it becomes meaningful for his own time.

The recipients of the Revelation knew the identity of the author, and we do not. But there are three distinct points involved here. As we have seen, there was a strong tradition from the time of Justin Martyr, whose debate with the Jew Trypho is located in Ephesus c. A.D. 135, that the author was John the apostle, though some vigorously denied this. The evidence of a man who lived in Ephesus only forty years after the probable date of the writing of Revelation might seem to be unassailable.

[1] *The Revelation of St. John the Divine*, p. 19.

But in fact second-century traditions about the apostles are demonstrably unreliable. Irenaeus undoubtedly confused James the apostle with James the Lord's brother (*Haer.* iii. 12. 14 f.), and wrongly supposed that Papias had been a disciple of the apostle John (Eus. *H.E.* iii. 39. 1). Polycrates, bishop of Ephesus, in a letter to Victor, bishop of Rome, written *c*. A.D. 190, confused Philip the apostle with Philip the evangelist (Eus. *H.E.* iii. 31. 3); and this mistake appears to have been shared by Papias, who was bishop of Hierapolis, the very town in which Philip the evangelist was living with his prophetic daughters at the time of his death (Eus. *H.E.* iii. 39. 9). Moreover, the John who wrote Revelation does not give the impression of being an apostle; he does not appeal to apostolic authority, and he speaks of the twelve apostles in a way hard to understand if he were one of them (xxi. 14). It would be interesting to have our curiosity on this point satisfied once and for all, but nothing more than curiosity is involved. The apostles were eyewitnesses of the ministry of Jesus, and in matters of historic fact their authority was of supreme importance. But the authority of a prophetic vision lies wholly in its content. The little that we know of the apostle John would add nothing to our ability to interpret the Revelation, and its authority would be neither increased if his authorship of it could be proved nor diminished if it were disproved.

A much more important question is whether John of Patmos also wrote the Gospel and Epistles of John, since this would give us a very deep insight into the working of his mind. There are striking similarities between the five Johannine writings, as well as striking differences, and it is certain that they all came from the same geographical, cultural, and theological setting, if not from the one hand. The chief reason for ascribing Revelation to a different author is the character of the Greek in which it is written, as Dionysius of Alexandria pointed out in the third century. The Gospel and Epistle, he claimed, were written in flawless Greek, free from barbarism, solecism, or vulgarism; whereas the Apocalypse was written in inaccurate Greek, full of barbarous idioms and solecisms (Eus. *H.E.* vii. 25. 24-27). To most modern scholars this argument still appears decisive, though some have wanted to add that there are equally impressive differences in theology. There is, however, a growing consensus that both these arguments have been somewhat overstated. It is, indeed, possible so to interpret the Revelation that the author of the Fourth Gospel could not conceivably have written it; but this, as we shall see, is not the only, nor even the most natural, way of interpreting it. R. H. Charles has argued most persuasively that John's Greek, for all its idiosyncrasy, is not ungrammatical, but has a grammar of its own, unparalleled in any other ancient writing, but none the less real and consistent, the hybrid grammar of a man thinking in Hebrew while he wrote in Greek.[1] But because a man writes in Hebraic Greek, it does not inevitably follow that this is the only Greek he is capable of writing. He may have adopted this style quite deliberately for reasons of his own, as Luke appears to have imitated the style of the Septuagint in his nativity stories, and as the Jew Aquila, in a much more pedantic fashion, chose to reproduce the details of Hebrew idiom in his Greek translation of the Old Testament. John's Greek may be all his own, but it is not the product of incompetence, for he handles it with brilliant lucidity and compelling power, so that it cannot be held accountable for any of our difficulties of comprehension. It is thus possible to put up a case for common authorship, though the balance of probability is still against it. What must be said is that the closer together we date these documents the less likely it is that they all came from the same hand. In any case it is worth while to remember that we are not here at any disadvantage compared with the first readers of the Revelation. For if one man wrote both Revelation and Gospel, it is certain that the Revelation came first. The Gospel could conceivably be earlier, but not if it came from the same author. Thus, when the Revelation was read in the churches of Asia, the congregations either knew the Fourth Gospel and were aware that John of Patmos was not its author, or, more probably, they were still unacquainted with it.

The first readers of the Revelation knew the date at which it was written. This is a far more serious gap in our knowledge

---

[1] *The International Critical Commentary*, pp. cxvii-clix. Charles, however, went too far when he reduced this grammar to strict rules, which he thought could then be used to detect the interpolations of a later and bungling editor.

than our ignorance of the identity of the author. We cannot expect to decipher the book unless we know what happened to account for John's visionary experience and what he expected to happen in the imminent future; and certainty about its precise historical setting would carry us a long way. The only early evidence comes from Irenaeus, who assigns John's visions to the closing years of the reign of Domitian (A.D. 81–96). The majority of scholars, ancient and modern, have been prepared to accept this statement. But there are some passages in the book which have been thought to require an earlier date. It has been argued, for example, that xi. 1-2 implies a date in the reign of Nero, when the Jerusalem temple was still standing; and that the description of the seven heads of the monster in xvii. 10 can only have been written in the reign of Vespasian. Three courses are open to us: we may accept an early date, we may accept the Domitianic date with the qualification that John used earlier material which he very imperfectly assimilated, or we may accept the Domitianic date and find some other explanation for the apparently conflicting evidence. The first proposal may be discounted, because no two pieces of evidence point to the same early date, and because the demand for emperor-worship reflected in the chapter on the monster was openly made for the first time by Domitian. Our choice between the second and third courses will depend largely on our opinion of John's literary abilities, since the second would commit us to the view that he was an exceedingly slovenly craftsman. Clearly the only wise procedure is to start with the hypothesis that the date of writing was c. A.D. 95 and see where it leads us.

The first readers were almost certainly well versed in the sort of symbolic language and imagery in which the book is written. Whether they had formerly been Jews or pagans, they would read the language of myth as fluently as any modern reader of the daily papers reads the conventional symbols of a political cartoon. Much of this language we can reconstruct for ourselves from the Old Testament and the Jewish apocalyptic writings on the one hand and from Greek and Roman literature, inscriptions, and coinage on the other.[1] Our difficulties begin when we try to decide how far to take this picture language

[1] See esp. E. Stauffer, *Christ and the Caesars.*

literally and how far to take it figuratively. When John echoes the Roman legend that the dead Nero was about to return, how literally does he mean it? Does he believe that Nero was not in fact dead, or that he would be resurrected, or that another paranoiac would come to fill his empty shoes? When he uses images from the Old Testament does he give them their exact Old Testament value, or are they baptized with a Christian spirit and meaning? Are his numbers part of a system of numerology and his astrological references integral to the structure of his work, or are they but passing allusions to things that everybody took for granted? Does he use a code, in which each symbol has a precise translation value (which is a kind of literalism), or are his images of the deep, evocative kind to be found in great poetry? Is he the slave or the master of his sources and models? Is he a painstaking stitcher of patchwork traditions or an artist handling his material with creative originality? We have all known times when a contemporary of ours has left us wondering whether to take him literally or not. Only if we know the speaker personally can we be sure that this will not happen. The great advantage that the Christians of Asia had over us was that John was their personal friend. He might write things that were strange to them, but they must have had a pretty shrewd idea how his mind worked. Where they walked with confidence, we can only grope our way.

In other respects the first readers were no better off than we are. If they wanted to ask questions about the nature of John's experience, the structure of his book, or the meaning of his warning message, they had to look for their answers exactly where we must look, in the book itself. And if they asked the last and vital question, whether this book is the word of God, whether God had indeed spoken through John to their immediate condition and beyond them to the church of all time— that is a question which every man must answer for himself.

Then I saw in my Dream that the Interpreter took Christian by the hand, and led him into a place where was a Fire burning against a wall, and one standing by it alway casting much Water upon it to quench it; yet did the Fire burn higher and hotter. Then said Christian, What means this? . . . So he had him about to the backside of the wall, where he saw a man with a Vessel of Oil in his hand, of the which he did also continually cast (but secretly) into the Fire.

JOHN BUNYAN

'I appoint you this day over nations and kingdoms,
  To uproot and to overturn, to smash and to demolish, to
      build and to plant.'
          'Is not my word like a fire, says the Lord,
          Like a hammer that shatters the rocks.'

JEREMIAH

Thou art where'er the proud
In humbleness melts down;
Where self itself yields up;
Where martyrs win their crown;
Where faithful souls possess
Themselves in perfect peace.

Not throned above the skies,
Nor golden-walled afar,
But where Christ's two or three
In His name gathered are,
Be in the midst of them,
God's own Jerusalem.

F. T. PALGRAVE

The victory that conquers the world is our faith.

I JOHN

THE REVELATION
OF ST. JOHN THE DIVINE
I
THE PROPHET'S CALL
i. 1-3. THE TITLE

(1) The Apocalypse of Jesus Christ,
given him by God, to show his servants what is bound to
happen soon. He made it known by sending his angel to
his servant John, (2) who hereby bears witness to all that
he saw—the purpose declared by God and attested by
Jesus Christ. (3) Blessed is the reader, and blessed are the
congregation who listen to the words of this prophecy
and heed what is written in it. For the crisis is near.

John calls his book an **apocalypse** or revelation, and this 1
title not only describes its content, but classifies it as a recognized
type of literature. During the three hundred years between the
persecution of the Jews by Antiochus Epiphanes (167 B.C.) and
the destruction of the Jewish nation by Hadrian (A.D. 135)
Jewish writers produced a series of apocalypses—of which the
first and greatest was the Book of Daniel—to encourage Jewish
resistance to the encroachments of paganism, by showing that
the national suffering was foreseen and provided for in the
cosmic purpose of God and would issue in ultimate vindication.
It is characteristic of these writings that they portray the present
crisis, whether it be the persecution of Antiochus or the fall of
Jerusalem, against a background of world history, the present
struggle as part of the agelong struggle between the kingdom
of light and the kingdom of darkness, and victory over the immediate enemy as the embodiment of the final victory of God.
It is also characteristic of them that they are written in symbolic
language. The writers believed that every earthly person, in-
stitution, and event had a heavenly equivalent, so that a seer,
transported to heaven in an ecstatic rapture, could see enacted
in the symbols of heavenly drama the counterpart of earthly

9

events, past, present, and future. He would thus be able, for the benefit of his fellows in distress, to interpret the past and predict the future. For example, in Daniel we hear of a battle between the Prince of Greece and the Prince of Persia (Dan. x. 20). The earthly event is the invasion of Persia by Alexander the Great. Yet the two princes are not Alexander and Darius III, but the angelic rulers and representatives of the two empires, whose meeting in heavenly battle is the counterpart of the earthly battles of Granicus, Issus, and Gaugamela. It follows, therefore, that, in order to explain an apocalypse, we must first identify the earthly realities to which the heavenly symbols correspond, and then see how by the use of this symbolism the author has tried to interpret earthly history.

When we begin to ask what John's symbolism means, we shall rightly expect guidance from the Jewish apocalyptists and from the Old Testament, which was his Bible as well as theirs. But we shall do well to be cautious. John's apocalypse is unlike the others. For one thing, all Jewish apocalypses are pseudonymous; that is, they purport to have been written by some ancient worthy—Noah, Lamech, Enoch, Baruch, Shealtiel, Daniel, Ezra—who sealed up the message until the time when it should become relevant, the time of the actual author. But John writes openly in his own name for his own contemporaries, and is explicitly told not to seal his book. These works also cover a very wide range of literary and religious worth. The Jewish rabbis who were responsible for putting Daniel into the canon of Old Testament scripture and excluding the others were men of sound judgment. For Daniel is the product of an original mind, but the others are for the most part imitative and pedestrian. *The Book of Enoch* has been justly called one of the world's six worst books. The *Ezra Apocalypse*, which somehow found its way into the Vulgate, and so into the Apocrypha under the title of 2 Esdras, is responsible for many of the most deplorable features of mediaeval theology. It is therefore quite unjust to John to insist that he must be judged by such company as this. For John, though he adopts the apocalyptic form, claims over and over again to be a prophet. If Old Testament scholars are right in drawing a sharp distinction between apocalypse and prophecy, John would insist that his book was

prophecy. But the most important difference is that his book is **the apocalypse of Jesus Christ.** The gospel of Jesus was new wine which could not be contained within the old leather bottles of Judaism, yeast which kept working until nothing was left unleavened. Whatever he touched he transfigured, and not least the language and imagery of religious thought. We shall expect, then, to find that John's symbols do not mean exactly what they would have meant to a Jewish writer. We shall expect what Farrer has called 'a rebirth of images'.

In his opening sentence John tells us in general terms what his book is about. It has to do with current events: God has instructed him to warn his fellow Christians about an impending **crisis;** and if his book is still relevant to our critical times, this is because it was first relevant to them as they faced their imminent ordeal. **What is bound to happen** is an echo of Daniel ii. 28, and John clearly expected his readers to know their Old Testament well enough to pick up his frequent allusions to it. Sometimes, no doubt, he uses biblical phrases, much as the Puritans did, simply because the language of the Bible came naturally to his mind and was the natural vehicle for his self-expression. But here something more seems to be involved. For this phrase comes from Daniel's prediction of the end of the four tyrannical world empires and the establishment of a new empire under the sovereignty of God, and this prophecy is to play a substantive part in John's later visions. Thus by this allusion John is indicating that his prophecy gathers up all the threads of Old Testament hope; the crisis is sure to come, not for any merely political reason, but because it has been written by God in the scroll of the world's destiny and prefigured in the scriptures (cf. iv. 1, where the phrase is repeated).

The content of his message is, in fact, **the purpose declared 2 by God.** Here, as in John i. 1-14, 'word' is a quite inadequate rendering of the Greek *logos.* God never speaks simply to convey information, but always to achieve results. 'He spoke and it happened; he commanded and it came into being' (Ps. xxxiii. 9). 'My word shall not return to me empty-handed, but shall accomplish what I purpose and succeed in the task I sent it to do' (Isa. lv. 11). The word which came to the prophets was always a statement of God's intentions, combined with a demand for man's co-operation. 'Surely the Lord God does nothing without revealing his secret plan to his servants the prophets' (Amos iii. 7). It is just such a plan that John has seen dramatically disclosed in his heavenly vision—rather it is *the* plan, **the purpose** of God for all mankind, for all creation, already **attested by Jesus Christ** in his life and teaching, when 'the Purpose took human flesh' (John i. 14). How John conceived this absolute and ultimate **purpose** to be related to the immediate **crisis** we shall see as the narrative unfolds.

What then was it that John expected to happen **soon?** There is a general agreement that he expected persecution of the church by the Roman Empire. But like the other apocalyptic writers he has set this threat against a background of world history, and his prophecy carries us from a vision of God the Creator at one extreme to a vision of the Last Judgment and the eternal city of God at the other. We cannot, however, do justice to his very plain opening statement (cf. i. 3; iv. 1; xxii. 10) by saying that he foresaw a long series of events covering centuries, which could be described as imminent because they were to *begin* shortly. Whatever earthly realities correspond to John's symbols, he expected them to be accomplished quickly *in their entirety*. We must choose between two answers to our question. The one answer, which would have the support of a majority of modern scholars, is that John expected the End, the final crisis of world history, the return of Christ in victory and judgment; and that everything else in his vision, the last plagues, the emergence of Antichrist, the great martyrdom of the church, and the fall of Babylon, are only premonitory signs heralding the great day of God. The other answer, which I believe to be the true one, is that John's coming **crisis** was simply the persecution of the church, and that all the varied imagery of his book has no other purpose than this, to disclose to the prospective martyrs the real nature of their suffering and its place in the eternal purposes of God, or, in Bunyan's language, to take them about to the backside of the wall.

John's instructions are to write to the churches **all that he saw.** An older generation of commentators doubted whether John's claim to be a visionary could really be taken seriously. They believed that, while prophecy was the product of spon-

taneity and inspiration, apocalyptic was an artificial and purely
literary affair, and that John was no exception to the general
rule. Visions would not spontaneously arrange themselves in
elaborately balanced groups of seven, nor would angelic choirs
quote extensively from the Old Testament. In any case, many
of the things John claims to have seen, e.g. living creatures full
of eyes inside and out (iv. 8), and a city 1,500 miles high, are
incapable of being visualized, and therefore cannot have been
communicated to John in vision. These objections will appear
less impressive to a generation which has accepted surrealist art
and has become familiar with the kaleidoscopic quality of
dream imagery. For the rest, we must remember that John
never supposed that vision could be communicated without the
intervening medium of art. What he offers us may be regarded
as vision recollected in tranquillity; but, as Farrer has pointed
out, it reads much more like a continuous meditation on the Old
Testament, and John was told to write before he began to see.[1]
He was a man who thought with his pen, and whose meditations
bodied forth into fresh vision as he wrote, so that vision and art
were not two processes but one. It is some indication of his
consummate artistry and of the validity of his claim to inspiration that he never fails to make a profound impression even on
those who imperfectly apprehend his meaning. Much of the
New Testament is written for those who have ears to hear,
but this book is written for those who have eyes to see; and for
a generation whose mental eye has been starved of imagery it is
in some ways the most important book in the New Testament.

John expected his book to be read publicly in church to a   3
congregation, and so he couched it in the form of a letter. Here
and there he uses a phrase which suggests that he may have
known some of the letters of Paul, and this may have influenced
his choice of literary form, though he shows little trace of any
other Pauline influence. E. J. Goodspeed has propounded an
interesting theory, which has had considerable popularity, that
Paul's letters had already been collected, to form a corpus of
letters to seven churches, of which John's sevenfold letter was a
deliberate imitation—a theory which neatly reverses that of the

[1] *Op. cit.* pp. 23-29.

Muratorian Canon.[1] But we shall find shortly that there are
other and more obvious reasons for John's use of the number
seven.

The recipients of the letter do not have to be told who the
author is, for they know him. Unfortunately we do not have
their advantage. It is improbable that he was John the son of
Zebedee; for the only authority he claims is that of a prophet,
and he speaks of the twelve apostles as though they belonged to
a bygone age (xxi. 14). It is improbable, though not impossible,
that he was the author of the Fourth Gospel (see Introduction).
The two books could conceivably have come from a single
author if they could be assigned to separate periods of his life.
But all the evidence goes to show that they were written during
the same decade. According to Irenaeus (*Haer.* v. 30. 3), John
wrote the Revelation at the end of the reign of Domitian, who
was emperor from A.D. 81 to 96, and this accords well with the
internal evidence.

i. 4-8. THE ADDRESS

**(4) From John to the seven churches in the province of
Asia. Grace to you and peace from Who is and was and is
coming, from the seven spirits before his throne, (5) and
from Jesus Christ, the faithful witness, the firstborn of the
dead, the ruler of earthly kings. To him who loves us
and has released us from our sins with his own life-blood,
(6) who has appointed us to be a royal house of priests to
his God and Father—to him be glory and dominion for
ever and ever. Amen. (7) Behold he comes with the
clouds, and every eye shall see him, everyone who
pierced him, and all the tribes on earth shall lament for
him. So be it, Amen. (8) 'I am Alpha and Omega,' says
the Lord God, 'who is and was and is coming, the Omnipotent.'**

4   John uses the number **seven** as a symbol for completeness or
wholeness. He has a pastor's concern for individual congregations and writes to them by name, showing a knowledge of local

[1] *New Solutions of New Testament Problems* (1927).

conditions. But there were more churches in the Roman
province of Asia than those he names, certainly at Troas
(Acts xx. 5-12), Colossae (Col. i. 2), and Hierapolis (Col. iv. 13),
and almost certainly at Magnesia and Tralles where the churches
were well established when Ignatius wrote to them not more
than twenty years later. John chooses **seven** of the **churches**
to indicate that his message is really addressed to the church at
large. Each of the separate letters that follows contains 'what
the Spirit is saying to the churches'. Similarly **the seven
spirits** represent the Spirit of God in the fulness of his activity
and power. Possibly John had in mind the sevenfold spirit with
which the Messiah was to be endowed (Isa. xi. 2). But a more
important source of his ideas is Zechariah iv, where the prophet
describes a candelabra (Israel) with seven lamps ('the eyes of the
Lord which range over the whole earth'); and the burden of his
vision is, ' "Not by might or power, but by my Spirit," says the
Lord of hosts.' We have here the first example of John's
kaleidoscopic variations on Old Testament imagery; for in his
vision the church is symbolized as an earthly reality by seven
lampstands, and as a heavenly reality by seven stars in the right
hand of Christ (i. 20), but it draws its life and power from the
seven lamps or spirits before the throne (iv. 5), which are also
said to be held by Christ (iii. 1) and are identified with the
seven eyes of the Lamb (v. 6). At all these points Zechariah was
John's primary source. But he may also have been aware of the
part played by the seven planets in pagan mythology and
politics. Coins from the early part of Domitian's reign portray
the emperor's heir, who had died in childhood, as an infant
Zeus playing with the stars, as though he had been compensated
by a cosmic dominion for the earthly empire he was never to
inherit. The use that John makes of the seven spirits, lamps, or
stars was a direct challenge to the imperial myth of the divine
ruler, and, since defiance of emperor-worship was one of the
main themes of his vision, it is reasonable to suppose that the
challenge was intended.[1]

[1] See E. Stauffer, *Christ and the Caesars*, p. 152. The idea that the Menorah
or seven-branched lamp represented the seven planets must have been
in the air, for it is found also in Philo (*Q.R.D.H.* 221 f.; *Vit. Mos.* ii. 102 f.;
Quaest. in Exod. ii. 75 f.).

The title of God, **Who is and was and is coming,** is a Christian elaboration of that found in the Septuagint translation of Exodus iii. 14, where the name Yahweh is rendered 'He who is' (cf. Jer. i. 6; xiv. 13; xxxix (xxxii). 17). It sets the church's coming ordeal against a background of God's eternity, but it also brings God down into the arena of history. He is Lord of past, present, and future. But the order of the tenses is significant. The temporal order is meaningful to God, for it is the scene where he is working out his purpose. Yet at all times past and future are embraced in his eternal present. This is a theme of paramount importance for John's theology, and he will expound it in greater detail in a moment. Although he uses a preposition which takes the genitive, John keeps the divine title in the nominative. God is, so to speak, always in the nominative, always the subject; he always holds the initiative, and things happen because he chooses, not because men force his hand and so put him into the accusative (cf. Rom. ix. 15-18; John x. 18).

The titles of Christ are equally carefully chosen for John's pastoral purpose. His friends are called to bear the costly witness of martyrdom, trusting that in his death Christ has been a **faithful witness** to God's way of overcoming evil; to look into the open jaws of death, remembering that he has risen as **the firstborn** of many brothers; to defy the authority of Imperial Rome in the name of a **ruler** to whom Caesar himself must bow. However exalted the terms he uses, John's thinking about Christ is from first to last rooted in earthly fact. As we shall see even more clearly and forcibly in chapter v, all Christ's heavenly authority is grounded in his earthly existence and the subsequent earthly existence of his church. Because on earth he was **the faithful witness** (cf. 1 Tim. vi. 13), he has become the risen head of the church, **firstborn of the dead;** and in so far as the church of which he is head continues his witness, he can exercise his authority over **earthly kings.** John is here adapting the promise made in Psalm lxxxix. 27 to the Davidic Messiah:

'I will appoint him firstborn,
Highest of the kings of earth.'

By two small adjustments he has given a profoundly Christian application to the words of scripture. It is in virtue of his death and resurrection that the Messiah has entered on his promised reign; and so for him **firstborn,** instead of being an honorific title, is the guarantee that others will pass with him through death to kingship. The same thought is put in a different way in the doxology which follows. The love of Christ is an eternal love, as the present tense indicates; but it has shown itself in the once-for-all, historic act of redemption through which the church has been constituted **a royal house of priests.** This 6 is the first of many instances in which John applies to the church Old Testament descriptions of Israel (Exod. xix. 6), and so expresses the belief, which he shares with other New Testament writers, that the church is the true people of God. But his quotation raises a very important theological question of a different kind. What is involved in being **a royal house of priests?** Is theirs purely a Godward function, or do they have a manward function as well? Is their sole task to offer to God that sacrifice of obedience and worship which the world is incapable of offering, or do they have the further task of mediating God's blessing to the world? When the author of Exodus xix. 1-6 called Israel 'a kingdom of priests', it is unlikely that he had any thought of a world-wide mission. They were a kingdom because they belonged to God the King; and they were priests because they had been set apart out of all nations for a special vocation of holiness, just as within Israel the tribe of Levi was chosen to offer to God a representative holiness. But John is not necessarily bound by the limitations of the Old Testament. He believed that those whom Christ had released from their sins were called to be **a royal house,** not merely because he reigned over them as King, but because they were to share his regal authority over the nations (cf. ii. 26; iii. 21; v. 10; xx. 6). Ought we not therefore to expect that they are to share his priestly office also, and be a body through which he can exercise his redemptive as well as his regal power?

The repeated use of the words 'witness' and 'testimony' is one of the many points of resemblance between the Revelation and the Fourth Gospel. In Greek as in English these words could be treated as dead metaphors, without any conscious reference to the lawcourt, which was their primary setting. But both these books use the words in their primary, forensic sense.

The author of the Fourth Gospel, perhaps inspired by the example of Second Isaiah, presents his argument in the form of a lawcourt debate, in which one witness after another is summoned, until God's advocate, the Paraclete, has all the evidence he needs to convince the world that Jesus is the Son of God, and so to win his case. In the Revelation the courtroom setting is even more realistic; for Jesus had borne his testimony before Pilate's tribunal, and the martyrs must face a Roman judge. What they have to remember as they give their evidence is that that evidence is being heard in a court of more ultimate authority, where judgments which are just and true issue from the great white throne.

The **earthly kings** and their subjects are not as yet aware of the sovereignty of Christ. John's object in writing is to help his friends to discern behind the throne of Caesar the superior authority of Christ, so that they may 'endure as seeing the Invisible' (Heb. xi. 27). But what they now see with the eyes of faith will one day become open and incontrovertible fact, which the enemies of Christ will recognize with sorrow. John's description of the Parousia or Advent of Christ is a combination of phrases from Daniel vii. 13 and Zechariah xii. 10-xiii. 1; and, since the same combination of texts occurs also in Matthew xxiv. 30, it is likely that both writers were drawing on an older tradition of scriptural exegesis. In the Zechariah passage the mourning is quite evidently said to be penitential grief, which is followed by divine pardon, cleansing, and restoration. It is commonly assumed that John used the scriptural words with a different intention, to describe the futile remorse with which the world will grieve over its own prospective doom.[1] What John
7 in fact says is that men will **see** the pierced but triumphant Christ and will **lament,** not for themselves, but **for him.** This can only mean that they will have compunction for the wounds they have caused him. Whether this grief will amount to a true repentance John does not for the present discuss (but see the notes on iii. 8-9 and xi. 13), for he is here concerned, not with the ultimate fate of men, but with the ultimate vindication of

---

[1] This may be the correct interpretation of Matt. xxiv. 30, where the words *ep' auton* are omitted. For *koptesthai epi* with acc., meaning to 'to grieve for', cf. Rev. xviii. 9, 11; Luke xxiii. 28.

Christian faith. Nor is it true to say that John is preoccupied
with the idea of the Parousia. For the Christ who will come one
day in the sight of all comes constantly to those who have the
faith to perceive him (iii. 20). He is 'the same yesterday, today,
and for ever' (Heb. xiii. 8), and his coming is the coming of
God, **who is and was and is coming.** For this reason John 8
can speak of his final advent in the present tense. Only to the
faithless is the Parousia of paramount importance; for he who
is **Alpha and Omega** is also the great **I am,** in whose presence
Christians are perpetually confronted with the Beginning and
the End.[1] **The Omnipotent** (*Pantokrator*) is one of the several
Septuagint translations of *Yahweh Sebaoth* (Lord of hosts),
but like all other Old Testament terms John uses it with a
difference; for he has learned from Christ that the omnipotence
of God is not the power of unlimited coercion but the power of
invincible love.

i. 9-11. THE EXILE

**(9) I John, your brother and partner in the ordeal and
sovereignty and endurance which are ours in Jesus, was
on the island called Patmos because of the word spoken
by God and attested by Jesus. (10) On the Lord's day I fell
into a trance and heard behind me a great voice like a
trumpet. (11) 'What you see write in a scroll and send it to
the seven churches, to Ephesus, Smyrna, Pergamum,
Thyatira, Sardis, Philadelphia, and Laodicea.'**

Nothing that John wrote gives us a clearer insight into the
working of his mind than his description of the Christian calling
which he shares with his friends: **the ordeal and sovereignty** 9
and endurance which are ours in Jesus. Like the fourth
evangelist (John xii. 23 ff.; xiii. 31) and unlike other New Testament writers (Luke xxiv. 26; 1 Pet. i. 11) he does not think of the
suffering of Christ as the prelude to kingly glory; Christ reigns
from the Cross (v. 6). So too for his followers the coming **ordeal**

[1] For I AM as a divine title see C. H. Dodd, *The Interpretation of the
Fourth Gospel*, pp. 93-96.

is not a qualifying test through which they must pass in order
to enter upon their promised reign with Christ. **Ordeal** and
sovereignty are obverse and reverse of the one calling; for those
who endure with Christ also reign with him, and reign in the
very midst of their **ordeal**. **Endurance** is, as Charles puts it,
'the spiritual alchemy which transmutes suffering into royal
dignity'.

By **the ordeal** John means the persecution of the church
which he expected to happen shortly. But this does not mean
that we are entitled to use the Revelation as evidence that a
major persecution actually occurred in Domitian's reign.
Before the end of the second century a strong Christian legend
had sprung up that Domitian had been the second great persecutor of the church, 'the replica of Nero's cruelty' (Tertullian,
Apol. 5); but it does not seem to have been based on any genuine
evidence. All we may properly glean from the Revelation is that
Antipas had been put to death at Pergamum—and it would
surely be a strange thing to single him out for special mention
if he had been one of a great host of martyrs—and that John
himself had been exiled. From Pliny's letter to Trajan in A.D.
112 (*Ep.* x. 96) we learn that Pliny was unacquainted with the
customary procedure in legal cases involving Christians, which
implies that there had in the past been occasional, though not
necessarily frequent, instances of Christians being taken to
court on a criminal charge; and that some of those who were
accused of being Christians claimed that they had abandoned
their Christian faith twenty years before, which suggests that
there was some kind of severe social pressure at work in A.D. 92.
In Rome a number of leading citizens fell victim to the neurotic
suspicions of the emperor, but there were at least as many
Stoics among them as Christians. Domitian had a deep sense of
inferiority, the result, no doubt, of being constantly over-
shadowed by a dominant father and a brilliant elder brother;
and he lived in morbid terror of being supplanted. It was to
offset this sense of insecurity that he began to demand towards
the end of his reign that his subjects should worship him as
Lord and God (*Dominus et Deus*: see Dio Cassius lxvii. 13;
Suetonius, *Dom.* 13; Martial v. 8). In the last year of his life he
ordered the execution of the consul, Titus Flavius Clemens, and

the banishment of his wife, Domitilla, who were his own cousin and niece, and whose eldest son was his designated heir. Suetonius describes Clemens as 'a man of most despicable sloth', but admits that he was put to death 'on very slender suspicion' (*Dom.* 15). Dio Cassius gives the charge as 'atheism', and adds that other eminent Romans, including a former consul, Manlius Acilius Glabrio, were executed on the same charge (lxvii. 14). It is likely that Clemens and Domitilla were Christians, and that 'sloth' and 'atheism' are two different ways of describing a refusal to join in the imperial cult, which a consul could achieve only by studied inactivity. But it was their high rank that drew the emperor's attention to them and cost them life and liberty. There is no evidence that, at the time when John wrote, there had been any open and systematic persecution of Christians since the days of Nero.

Patmos was one of the group of islands off the coast of Asia Minor called Sporades, and there is ample evidence in Roman literature that the Sporades and Cyclades (round Delos) were regularly used for the banishment of political offenders (Tacitus, *Ann.* iii. 68; iv. 30; xv. 71; Juvenal, *Sat.* i. 73; vi. 563 f.; x. 170). All these were cases of *deportatio in insulam*, a penalty which involved confiscation of property and loss of civil rights, and which corresponded to the *aquae et ignis interdictio* of Republican times (*Digest*, xlviii. 13. 3). Sir William Ramsay argued that this penalty cannot have been applied to John, (*a*) because it 'was reserved for persons of good standing and some wealth', and (*b*) because 'it is impossible to suppose that the crime of Christianity could have been punished so leniently at that period'.[1] He therefore conjectured (without any further evidence) that Patmos must have been a penal settlement, where John was sentenced to hard labour in the quarries; and this conjecture has been widely adopted by others as though it were a well attested fact.[2] The first of Ramsay's objections is sound enough as far as it goes, but the second rests, as we shall see, on a misrepresentation of the legal status of Christians. On the first point Ramsay seems to have overlooked the fact that there was

[1] *The Letters to the Seven Churches of Asia*, p. 84.
[2] Many commentaries invoke the authority of Pliny; but all that Pliny has to say about Patmos is that it is thirty miles round (*Hist. Nat.* iv. 69).

another and more lenient form of banishment, *relegatio in insulam*, which involved loss of neither property nor rights. Only the emperor could pronounce a sentence of *deportatio*, but a provincial governor could sentence a man to *relegatio*, provided that he had a suitable island within his jurisdiction (*Digest*, xlviii. 22. 6-7). Tertullian, who was a lawyer and can be trusted to use legal terms accurately, tells us that this was the sentence John had incurred: '*Ioannes . . . in insulam relegatur*' (*De Praescript. Haer.* 36).

What then was the legal standing of Christians, which made such a sentence possible? In Roman law religion was regarded as a department of state, so that the only legal religion was the officially approved cult, and participation in state religion was regarded as a sign of political loyalty. In practice foreign religions were tolerated, provided that they did not interfere with the local cult or with public order; and, since most of the subjects of the empire were polytheists, the adherents of one religion could take part in the ceremonies of another without any violence to conscience. An exception had been made in favour of the Jews, who were allowed to practise their religion in any part of the empire and were exempted from all forms of official religion. As long as Christians were officially regarded by the Romans as a sect of Judaism, they benefited from this tolerance (see, e.g., Acts xviii. 12-17). During the investigations that followed the fire of Rome in A.D. 64 it was discovered that Christianity was in fact a new and, from the Roman point of view, pernicious religion. It does not, however, follow that Christianity automatically became a crime meriting a death penalty, as Ramsay seems to have supposed. Christians had lost their legal security, but what happened to them depended on two unpredictable factors. In the provinces the administration of justice lay wholly within the *imperium* of the governor, unrestricted by any rules of procedure or any legal code, other than the laws which gave special privileges to Roman citizens and those which required the governor to submit to scrutiny at the close of his tenure of office.[1] As judge he could make his own rules and assess his own penalties. The one thing he must

---

[1] See A. N. Sherwin-White, *Roman Society and Roman Law in the New Testament*, pp. 1-23.

not do, except in cases of breach of the peace, was to initiate procedure; there must be an accuser (*delator*).[1] After A.D. 64, then, the fate of the Christians depended firstly on their ability to keep on such sufficiently good terms with their neighbours that nobody would lay an accusation against them; and secondly on the personal attitude of the Roman governor. John must have been unlucky in the first respect and comparatively fortunate in the second.

It was not, therefore, his own experience of exile that led John to expect widespread martyrdom. It must have been Domitian's new insistence on the worship of the reigning emperor that provided the stimulus for his visions. Emperor-worship had been conducted in Asia since the days of Augustus. But John must have seen in Domitian's edict the emergence of a new totalitarianism which Christians were bound to resist, and which would therefore result in war to the death between church and state, between Lamb and Monster. The persecution did not actually come at that time, because within a year Domitian had died by an assassin's knife. But that fact deprives John's vision of none of its depth and power.

i. 12-20. THE SON OF MAN

(12) I turned to see whose voice was speaking to me, and having turned I saw seven gold lamps, (13) and among the lamps one like a son of man, dressed in a long robe, with a gold girdle round his breast. (14) The hair of his head was white as snow-white wool, and his eyes flamed like fire; (15) his feet were like pure bronze fresh from the furnace, and his voice was like the roar of many waters. (16) In his right hand he had seven stars, and out of his mouth came a sharp two-edged sword; and his face was like the sun shining in its strength. (17) When I saw him I fell like a dead man at his feet, but he laid his right hand on me, and said, 'Do not be afraid. I am the first and the last, (18) the living one who was dead; now I am alive for ever and hold the keys of death and the grave. (19) Write down

[1] See Trajan's reply to Pliny's letter about the Christians (Pliny, *Ep.* x. 97).

therefore what you see, what now is and what is to happen hereafter. (20) Here is the secret of the seven stars
which you saw in my right hand and of the seven gold
lamps: the seven stars are the angels of the seven
churches, and the seven lamps are the seven churches.'

The churches to which John is told to write are represented in
his vision by a double symbolism, which illustrates what we have
already said about the correspondence between the heavenly
12 and the earthly in apocalyptic thought. **The seven gold lamps**
are the empirical, earthly churches, **the seven stars** their
heavenly counterpart. The imagery of the lamps is derived
from Zechariah's vision of the seven-branched candelabra of
Israel, a passage which would be well known to anyone who had
regularly attended the synagogue, because it was one of the
readings for the Feast of Lights. Once again John is asserting
that the church is the new Israel, the true people of God, but
with this difference: whereas Israel was represented by a single
candelabra with seven lamps, the churches are represented by
seven separate standing lamps; for according to the teaching of
the New Testament each local congregation of Christians is the
church universal in all its fulness. The unity of the church is to
be found only 'in Jesus', in him who holds **the seven stars.**
The angels are not to be identified with bishops or pastors.
The Jews had long since become accustomed to the idea that
each nation had its angelic representative in heaven, who
presided over its fortunes and was held accountable for its misdeeds,[1] and John is simply adapting this familiar notion to a
new situation. We must not confuse John's apocalyptic way of
thinking with Platonic idealism, and suppose that the angel
symbolizes the perfect heavenly pattern of which the earthly
church is only a shadowy and imperfect reproduction. For John
addresses his letters not to the earthly churches but to the
angels, and holds them responsible for the faults of the communities they represent. If we are to understand John's mind,
we must rid our own minds of the presupposition that earth is
the place of faults and failings and heaven the place of perfection. In John's world heaven and earth are equally parts of
the physical universe which God created, they belong in-

[1] See G. B. Caird, *Principalities and Powers*, pp. 1-30.

24

separably together, and everything on earth, including its evil,
has its equivalent in heaven.[1] When the old order is finally
destroyed, John sees a new heaven as well as a new earth, for the
former heaven and earth together, along with their contaminating evil, have been removed. The angels, then, are the 'spiritual
counterparts of human individuals or communities, dwelling in
heaven, but subject to changes depending on the good or evil
behaviour of their complementary beings on earth'.[2] But the
stars which symbolize **the angels** are no doubt also the seven
planets, pictured as a necklace of glittering jewels hanging from
the hand of the Son of Man.

It is of the utmost importance for John's theology that the
first statement he makes about the heavenly Christ is that he saw
him **among the lamps.** He is no absentee, who has withdrawn 13
from earth at his Ascension, to return only at his Parousia,
meanwhile exercising his authority over the churches by remote
control through their heavenly representatives, the angels. The
first characteristic of Christ revealed to John in his vision is that
he is present among the earthly congregations of his people, and
whatever John has later to say about the coming of Christ must
be interpreted in the light of this salient fact.

The description of the Son of Man is full of Old Testament
phrases, which we may track down to their various sources. The
figure bears a general resemblance to the angel of Daniel's
vision (Dan. x. 5-6). The **robe** and **girdle** are the garb of the
high priest (Exod. xxviii. 4; xxxix. 29), the **white hair** is the 14
mark of the Ancient of Days (Dan. vii. 9), the **bronze feet** 15
remind us of Ezekiel's cherubim (Ezek. i. 7), and the **voice** of
the returning glory (Ezek. xliii. 2). But to compile such a
catalogue is to unweave the rainbow. John uses his allusions not
as a code in which each symbol requires separate and exact
translation, but rather for their evocative and emotive power.
This is not photographic art. His aim is to set the echoes of
memory and association ringing. The humbling sense of the
sublime and the majestic which men experience at the sight of a

[1] See notes on iv. 6. and xii. 7, and cf. also Heb. ix. 23. For John's cosmology see P. S. Minear, 'The Cosmology of the Apocalypse' in *Current
Issues in New Testament Interpretation*, ed. W. Klassen and G. F. Snyder,
pp. 23-37.
[2] J. H. Moulton, 'It is his Angel', *J.T.S.* III, p. 514.

16 roaring cataract or the midday **sun** is the nearest equivalent to
   the awe evoked by a vision of the divine. John has seen the risen
   Christ, clothed in all the attributes of deity, and he wishes to call
   forth from his readers the same response of overwhelming and
   annihilating wonder which he experienced in his prophetic trance.

17   None but the pure in heart may see God and live. John falls
   like a dead man, and is revived from his death-like swoon by

18 the assurance that **the living one** himself had laid aside his immortality to undergo the sharpness of death. By the resurrection
   he had not just resumed the eternal life which he had with the
   Father before the world began; he had entered upon a new,
   victorious life in which death was for ever conquered. Not only
   had he burst out of the prison, he had carried away **the keys.**
   His followers may pass confidently into the dungeons **of death
   and the grave,** knowing that he holds the authority to unlock
   the gates and set them free. **The grave** is a translation of the
   Greek *Hades,* which itself stands for the Hebrew *Sheol.* But
   nothing is gained by retaining either of these proper names in
   English, except in vi. 8, where Death and Hades are personified.
   Hades to the Greek and Sheol to the Jew were nothing other
   than the common grave, the long home of all men which had
   many entrances.

19   John is instructed to write to the churches **what you see,
   what now is and what is to happen hereafter.** Those
   scholars who believe that the imminent crisis John expected
   was the Parousia have tended to see here a threefold division
   corresponding to a threefold literary structure of the book: thus
   what you see denotes the present vision of chapter i, **what now
   is** covers the analysis of the condition of the churches in
   chapters ii and iii, and chapters iv-xxii are concerned with **what
   is to happen hereafter,** i.e. the Parousia and its premonitory
   signs. But this is a grotesque over-simplification. Chapters ii
   and iii, though mainly appraisal, contain both threats and
   promises; and the remaining chapters include many tableaux
   which can only denote events already past or present at the time
   when John was writing. It is better therefore to take the words
   what you see to mean the whole of John's vision, which in all
   its parts is equally concerned with the interpretation of past and
   present and the anticipation of the future.

II
THE LETTERS TO THE CHURCHES

THE seven letters are written according to a common fourfold plan. First comes a recitation of the qualities of Christ, drawn for the most part from the description in the first chapter; and we can see that in many cases these qualities are chosen because of their peculiar relevance to the local situation. Next comes praise for the church's good record, then censure for its deficiencies (except that in Laodicea there is nothing to praise, and in Smyrna and Philadelphia nothing to blame). Finally there are the promises: four churches receive a general promise, but all the letters end with a promise to the Conqueror. Together the letters constitute a visitation of the churches to see whether they are in a fit state to face the coming crisis. We have already raised the question whether the crisis John expected was the Parousia or persecution, but we must raise it again. Are the churches being investigated to see whether they are fit to meet their Lord, or to see whether they are strong enough to survive a thorough-going persecution? There are four reasons why we ought to adopt the second alternative. (a) The examination is conducted by Christ himself, who repeatedly affirms that he knows their strengths and weaknesses; they are being prepared by him, not for him. (b) In four of the letters there is a conditional threat that, if there is not repentance or watchfulness, Christ will come in judgment; and this seems strangely out of keeping with a belief in an imminent Parousia. (c) The virtues most frequently praised are patience, endurance, constancy, and loyalty, which in normal times would not rank first among the Christian virtues, whereas there is no mention of joy and hardly a mention of love. The stern virtues may be of supreme importance when the church is facing a struggle for survival. But John can hardly have thought that they would be the only ones to matter at the last assize. (d) The character of the letters is determined by the promises to the Conqueror which form their climax. But the Conqueror is the Christian who by martyrdom

bears his witness to Christ and so wins the victory over temptation and death (cf. iii. 21).

Ramsay has put forward the suggestion that the order in
which the churches are named indicates the route to be followed by the courier charged with the delivery of the letter.
Starting from Ephesus he would travel forty miles north to
Smyrna, and forty miles further north to Pergamum, then
forty-five miles south-east to Thyatira, thirty miles south to
Sardis, thirty miles east-south-east to Philadelphia, and another
forty miles south-east to Laodicea. Much more interesting,
however, is his theory, backed by a wealth of evidence which
seems conclusive for Laodicea and impressive for the other six,
that the letters betray John's intimate knowledge, not only of
the churches, but of the history, topography, and economics of
the cities in which they were set.

ii. 1-7. EPHESUS

**(1) 'To the angel of the church at Ephesus write: This is
the message of the One who holds the seven stars in his
right hand, who walks among the seven gold lamps:
(2) "I know what you have done, your hard work and
endurance. I know you cannot tolerate evil men and have
tested those who claim to be apostles, though they are
not, and have found them liars. (3) Endurance you have:
you have borne the burden of my cause without flagging.
(4) But I have this against you: you have lost the love you
had at first. (5) Remember then how far you have fallen;
repent, and do as you did before. Otherwise, if you do not
repent, I shall come and move your lamp from its place.
(6) Yet you have this to your credit: you hate what the
Nicolaitans are doing, as I do. (7) Hear, if you have ears
to hear, what the Spirit is saying to the churches! To the
Conqueror I will give the right to eat from the tree of
life, which is in the Garden of God." '**

1   Ancient **Ephesus** stood on a broad inlet at the mouth of the
river Cayster, its natural harbour protected from the Aegean

Sea by a range of hills to the west. When the first Ionian colonists arrived, the sea reached right up to the temple of Artemis at the extreme northern end of the plain. (Pliny, *Hist. Nat.* ii. 201). Today, after thirty centuries of silting, it has receded eight miles southwards, leaving the ancient gulf of **Ephesus** a swampy plain. Already in the sixth century B.C. the walls of the Greek city were almost a mile south of the temple, and the Roman harbour was further south still. The last pre-Roman ruler, Attalus III of Pergamum, made a disastrous attempt to deepen the harbour (Strabo xiv. 641), and a more successful attempt was made by the Roman governor in A.D. 65 (Tacitus, *Ann.* xvi. 23). In spite of these vicissitudes **Ephesus** was still in Roman times the most important seaport in Asia Minor. The seat of government of the province of Asia was at Pergamum, but Ephesus had the right of *cataplous* or first landing, which meant that senatorial governors must land there when they arrived to enter on their year of office. Through **Ephesus** also passed a large part of the trade and travel between east and west. The shortest route to the east lay up the steep valley of the Cayster, but the easier and more commonly used route up the valleys of the Meander and Lycus could be reached quite quickly from Ephesus by a short climb over the pass to Magnesia.

The Mother Goddess had been worshipped at **Ephesus** long before the coming of the Greeks, who simply identified her with the Artemis of their Olympic pantheon (Pausanias vii. 2. 6). She became Greek only in name and in all other respects remained Asiatic. Her huge temple, built with the help of contributions from the whole of Asia to replace an older building burnt in 356 B.C., was reckoned among the wonders of the ancient world and undoubtedly helped the city to maintain its position of leadership. In 29 B.C. part of her precinct was dedicated to the worship of the goddess Roma and the divine Julius (Dio Cass. li. 20), and from that time on the worship of Artemis was closely associated with the Roman imperial cult.

John begins his tour of the churches with the church at **Ephesus,** not only for geographical and political reasons, but also because this was the most important church in the province. Forty years earlier Paul had spent there three whole years of his ministry (Acts xx. 31). In the closing decade of the first century it seems to have been the literary centre of Asiatic Christianity, from which emanated not only the Revelation, but also the Gospel and Letters of John, and perhaps also at a slightly later date the Pastoral Epistles. Twenty years later Ignatius was to write to **Ephesus** his first and longest letter, full of unqualified approbation for the 'deservedly happy church', which is known for its good deeds and harmonious love, and for living in blameless unity and good discipline under that 'man of inexpressible love', their bishop Onesimus.

Under the scrutiny of their Lord, who keeps all the churches in his active care and is intimately aware of their faults and merits, the Ephesians at first show up well. They have strenuously resisted all threats to the purity of their faith, both from without and from within. From outside have come men claim-
2 ing to be **apostles.** Later John tells us that the foundations of the heavenly Jerusalem bear 'the twelve names of the twelve apostles of the Lamb' (xxi. 14), which has suggested to some commentators that to John the word 'apostle' always meant one of the Twelve. It is hard to believe, however, that, even in an age of imposture, anyone ever went about pretending to be one of the Twelve. It would have been small credit to the church of Ephesus to see through that pretence. Nor is it likely that the impostors were claiming merely to be 'apostles of the churches', like those mentioned in 2 Corinthians viii. 23. They must have been claiming to belong to that group of **apostles** of Christ which was wider than the Twelve, and which included James the Just, Barnabas, Paul, Silas, Andronicus, and Junias (1 Cor. xv. 7; Gal. i. 19; Acts xiv. 14; 1 Thess. ii. 6; Rom. xvi. 7). When men came to Corinth who claimed to be **apostles** and produced impressive credentials, Paul dismissed them scathingly as 'super-apostles', insisting that the only valid criterion of apostleship was whether 'the works of an apostle' had been performed (2 Cor. xii. 11 ff.). By some such standard the *soi-disant* **apostles** at Ephesus had been **tested** and found to be **liars,** because they proved unable to live up to their pretensions. It says much for the integrity of the Ephesians that they were able to apply such a test. Nor was this an isolated incident, for Ignatius learnt from Onesimus that no sect could win a foothold in Ephesus, and that, when anyone tried to introduce any

harmful teaching, the people closed their ears and would not
allow it to be disseminated (Ign. *Eph.* vi. 2; ix. 1).

The internal threat came from **the Nicolaitans.** According 6
to Irenaeus (*Haer.* i. 26. 3; cf. iii. 11. 1) these were followers of
Nicolas of Antioch (Acts vi. 5). Hippolytus (*Refutat.* vii. 36)
adds that Nicolas had lapsed from true doctrine. Clement of
Alexandria attempts to rehabilitate Nicolas by arguing that **the
Nicolaitans** misunderstood a story about him in which he was
recorded to have said that one 'ought to despise the flesh'
(*Strom.* iii. 4. 25). It is unlikely that any of these writers
possessed any information about **the Nicolaitans** apart from
what they could read in the Revelation, for Eusebius tells us
that the sect lasted only 'a very short time' (*H.E.* iii. 29. 1).
It has been suggested that, since Nicolaitan = Balaamite (ii.
14-15), Nicolas is simply the Greek counterpart of Balaam,
arrived at by a fanciful etymology; for, according to the Talmud
(*Sanh.* 105ᵃ), Balaam is derived from two Hebrew words (*bala'*
and *'am*), meaning 'he has consumed the people', and a similar
Greek etymology can be given for Nicolas (from *nikan* and
laos).[1] The only solid information we have about these people is
contained in the letters to Pergamum and Thyatira, and we
must postpone discussion of them until the evidence is before us.

The one charge against the Ephesians is that their intolerance
of imposture, their unflagging loyalty, and their hatred of
heresy had bred an inquisitorial spirit which left no room for
love. They had set out to be defenders of the faith, arming 4
themselves with the heroic virtues of truth and courage, only to
discover that in the battle they had lost the one quality without
which all others are worthless. John has much to tell us about
the demonic process by which all that is noble and good can be
distorted into opposition to God, but nothing more eloquent
than this simple statement that zeal for Christian truth may
obliterate the one truth that matters, that God is love. John is a
rigorist who shares the hatred of heresy which he attributes both
to the church of Ephesus and to the church's Lord; but he
recognizes the appalling danger of a religion prompted more by
hate than by **love.** The only legitimate hatred is a revulsion
against all that thwarts the operations of love; and how easily

[1] For a comparable use of Hebrew cf. ix. 11, xiii. 18, and xvi. 16.

that hatred can turn into something less innocent! For all its apparent strength and vigour, this church is in danger of losing
5 its **lamp,** of ceasing to be a real church.

The coming of Christ in judgment is here said to be conditional: **if you do not repent** (cf. ii. 16; iii. 3). If we adopt the view that the apocalyptic visions predict an imminent, universal, and final coming of Christ, these passages in the letters clearly present a difficulty. It is quite unjustifiable to force an alien sense on them, as though they meant: 'I am coming shortly, whatever happens; but if you do not repent, my coming will bring judgment on you'. The writer of the letters has said as clearly as words can say that it is the coming itself, not the result of the coming, which is conditional on men's failure to repent. The threatened coming of Christ would not, in fact, be a worldwide crisis, but a crisis private to the churches concerned. Partly for this reason, and partly because the letters seem to reflect no trace of universal martyrdom (but see iii. 10) or of the imperial cult, Charles conjectured that they had been written by John during the reign of Vespasian and were subsequently incorporated in his later book without any attempt to remove discrepancies. A better way of dealing with the difficulty is to recognize that John writes sometimes in apocalyptic and sometimes in non-apocalyptic language, and to accept the non-apocalyptic passages as a key which he has provided for the decoding of his apocalyptic imagery (see esp. xiv. 12-13 and xvi. 15, which on any other theory have to be treated as irrelevant intrusions). If we take this view, we shall take the conditional threats to Ephesus, Pergamum, and Sardis as evidence that an imminent Parousia was *not* one of the events which John believed were 'bound to happen soon' (i. 1), and that even in the apocalyptic visions his immediate concern is with martyrdom rather than the End.

This letter closes, like the other six, with a promise of heavenly
7 bliss **to the Conqueror**; the imagery changes from letter to letter, but the substance of it remains the same, as we can see when it is gathered up in the one comprehensive vision of the celestial city. But who is **the Conqueror?** To what battle is he summoned? And by what weapons is he to win his victory? John introduces this mysterious, almost numinous, term over

and over again without any attempt at definition, for it is the purpose of his whole book to answer these questions. Only slowly
does the character of **the Conqueror** take shape as we read.
He is one who perseveres to the end in doing the will of Christ
(ii. 26), whose victory is analogous to the victory of Christ
(iii. 21), who has come through the great ordeal and washed his
robe white in the life-blood of the Lamb (vii. 14). He has
conquered the accusing Satan by the sacrificial death of Christ
and his own testimony, not counting his life too dear to surrender (xii. 11). He has conquered the monster and its image
and the number of its name (xv. 2). **The Conqueror,** in other
words, is the victim of persecution, whose martyr's death is his
victory, just as the Cross was the victory of Christ. He is the
Christian in whom Christ wins afresh with the weapons of love
the victory of Calvary.

John's promises to **the Conqueror** do not imply that he
expected all Christians to undergo martyrdom or that only the
martyrs would enter the joys of Paradise. Four of his letters
include a general promise to all Christians which is independent
of the promise to **the Conqueror**: at Smyrna the faithful who
are to receive the crown of life are distinguished from the few
who are to be imprisoned; the unstained few at Sardis, as well as
the Conqueror, are worthy to walk with Christ in white
robes; the whole church at Philadelphia is to be kept safe in
the hour of trial; and even in Laodicea those who repent and
open the door to the knocking Christ will sit at table with him.
Moreover, when the promises to the Conqueror are made good
in the heavenly city, all those are allowed to enter whose names
are written in the book of life. Why then does John promise
specifically to the martyrs that which is to be the destiny of all,
and why does he end every letter with this promise, reinforced
in each case by the sonorous call to **hear what the Spirit is
saying to the churches?** Surely the plain answer is that this
is what John's book is about. He is not an armchair theologian
working out a philosophy of history, nor a fantastic visionary
losing all touch with reality in dreams of the future; he is a
pastor deeply absorbed in the task of preparing his friends for an
imminent ordeal and helping them to see, by the light of the
Cross, that this ordeal is in fact the victory which is both theirs

and God's. He himself does not know who the martyrs will be; not all Christians will suffer martyrdom, but all must face the prospect of it.

ii. 8-11. SMYRNA

(8) 'To the angel of the church at Smyrna write: This is the message of the first and the last, who was dead and came to life: (9) "I know your suffering and your poverty (yet you are rich) and the slander of those who claim to be Jews and are not—they are Satan's synagogue. (10) Do not fear what you are about to suffer. The Devil indeed is going to throw some of you into prison, to put you to the test; and for ten days you will be hard pressed. Be loyal, even if you die for it; and I will give you the crown of life. (11) Hear, if you have ears to hear, what the Spirit is saying to the churches! The Conqueror shall not be harmed by the second death."'

8   Roman **Smyrna** was a seaport great enough to rival Ephesus, which it ultimately supplanted. The ancient Greek city, built as a fortress two or three miles inland, was destroyed by the Lydians about 600 B.C. and never rebuilt. The new city on the coast was planned by Alexander the Great and built by his successors. **Smyrna** was one of the oldest allies of Rome, and as early as 195 B.C. had built a temple to the goddess Roma. When in A.D. 26 eleven cities of Asia were competing for the right to build a temple to Tiberius, Rome decided in favour of **Smyrna** in recognition of her long loyalty (Tac. *Ann.* iv. 55-56). **Smyrna** had therefore some claim to the title of 'first city of Asia', which she disputed with Ephesus and Pergamum. Ramsay has pointed out that the description of Christ as the first and the last, who was dead and came to life is well suited to a city which had also been dead and come to life, and which now claimed to be 'first'.

Nothing is known of the origin of the church in **Smyrna**. Twenty years after the writing of Revelation Ignatius stayed there and wrote four of his letters. A little later, from Troas, he wrote two letters to **Smyrna,** one to the church and the other to its bishop, Polycarp. At that time, it appears, the church was seriously divided by the Docetic heresy (*Smyrn.* ii-v). But of this there is no hint when John wrote, for **the church at Smyrna** is one of the two for which he has unqualified praise. We may judge from what John says that there has been as yet no official action taken by the Roman government against the church. Even when Polycarp was burnt alive some sixty or seventy years later,[1] he was only twelfth in the combined roll of martyrs for Smyrna and Philadelphia (*Mart. Polyc.* xix. 1). The Christians have been subjected to active hostility from the community, instigated by the **Jews.** Their **poverty** must have 9 been due in part to mob violence and looting (cf. Heb. x. 35), in part to the difficulty of making a living in an antagonistic environment. Christians in other cities had long been familiar with Jewish resentment, occasioned by the conversion of Jews and 'God-fearers' to Christianity; but at Smyrna and Philadelphia it was apparently more than usually virulent. Whatever the reason for this, John will allow no excuses: by rejecting their Messiah and attacking his followers they have forfeited the right to be called **Jews,** and by their slanderous accusations they have made themselves agents of **Satan,** the Great Accuser (cf. xii. 10). John expects that before long Satan will for a short limited period **(ten days)** intensify his campaign against the 10 church and, presumably using the same agents, will lay before the authorities information leading to criminal charges against some Christians. It would be anachronistic to suppose that, when John predicts that **some of you** will be thrown **into prison,** he has in mind a milder penalty than other churches had to face. **Prison** in the ancient world was not a punishment, but merely a place of detention pending trial; and **prison** for a Christian meant that he had to be prepared to **die for** his faith. But whether he dies for his faith or not, his loyalty will be rewarded with **the crown of life.**

John prepares his friends for persecution in a number of ways. First of all, they are to recognize the attack as the work of

---

[1] The commonly accepted date is A.D. 155, but Eusebius (*H.E.* iv. 15. 1) puts the martyrdom in the reign of Marcus Aurelius.

the Devil. If a sympathetic Roman tries to persuade them to save their lives, as later the governor Statius Quadratus suggested to Polycarp, by a trifling concession, such as offering a pinch of incense before the emperor's statue or taking an oath by the fortune of Caesar, they will recognize that this is a Satanic onslaught on their integrity, and will be loyal, **even if they die for it.** But their ordeal will also be a divinely ordained **test** of their faith; for what Satan intends as a temptation, God uses as a **test.** Throughout his book John is constantly trying to show how Satan's hand may be detected in the affairs of this world; but he is equally insistent that Satan can do nothing except by permission of God, who uses Satan's grimmest machinations to further his own bright designs. Finally he

11 promises that **the Conqueror shall not be harmed by the second death.** He cannot promise immunity from the death which kills the body, but he can promise immunity from that which annihilates the soul (cf. xx. 6, 14; xxi. 8; Matt. x. 28; Luke xii. 4 f.; and see Charles *ad loc.* for frequent Rabbinic parallels).

ii. 12-17. PERGAMUM

(12) 'To the angel of the church at Pergamum write: This is the message of the One who has the sharp two-edged sword. **(13)** "I know where you live, where Satan has his throne; and yet you are true to my cause. You did not deny your faith in me even in the time when Antipas, my faithful witness, was killed in that city of yours which Satan has made his home. **(14)** But I have one or two things against you: you have there adherents of the teaching of Balaam, who taught Balak how to set a pitfall for the Israelites. He tempted them to eat meat sacrificed to idols and commit fornication; **(15)** and in the same way you too have some who adhere to the teaching of the Nicolaitans. **(16)** So repent! Otherwise I shall come soon and make war on you with the sword of my mouth. **(17)** Hear, if you have ears to hear, what the Spirit is

saying to the churches! To the Conqueror I will give a
share of the hidden manna; I will give him also a white
stone, and written on the stone will be a new name,
known only to him who receives it."'

The city of **Pergamum** came to prominence only after the 12
death of Alexander the Great, when it became the capital of a
new, independent state. The last king of **Pergamum**, Attalus
III, died in 133 B.C. and bequeathed his territory to Rome,
and in this way the city became the seat of government of the
Roman province of Asia. The first temple of the imperial cult
was built there in 29 B.C. in honour of Rome and Augustus. This
is the primary reason why John speaks of **Pergamum** as the
place **where Satan has his throne**. As we shall see later, it is
not quite true to say that John identifies Rome with **Satan**,
or even with Satan's emissary, the monster. But he does believe
that, in his decisive battle against the church, **Satan** is using
Rome and **has made his home** at the seat of Roman power.
But John pictured **Satan** as the ancient serpent (xii. 9), and he
could hardly have mentioned **Satan** in a letter addressed to
Pergamum without remembering that that city was the centre
for the worship of Asclepius, the serpent-god who presided
over the art of healing, and whose serpents were one of the
city's emblems. Another of the city's patron gods was Zeus
Soter, whose huge altar dominated the city from the middle of
the acropolis. Here was a perfect symbol of the fusion of
western and eastern religion and culture, which was the un-
intended result of Alexander's conquests; for the simple Ionic
pillars of the colonnade stood on a plinth decorated with a
sculptured representation of the battle between gods and giants,
in which Greek restraint had given way to oriental luxuriance.
John believed that Rome was the latest and greatest agent of
Satan, not only because of her totalitarian demand for that
absolute allegiance which is due to God alone, but also because
he saw in her the epitome of all paganism and worldliness; and
no better expression of this could have been found than in the
religious monuments of Pergamum.

The senatorial governor of Asia was a proconsul and therefore possessed for the period of his office an almost unlimited

imperium, of which the symbol was a **sword** (Rom. xiii. 4).[1] This explains the choice of imagery in the opening sentence. The Christians are reminded that, though they live under the authority of one who holds the sword of imperial justice, they are citizens also of the greater empire of him who needs no other weapon than the spoken word, **the sword** of his **mouth,** which is the word of God. If a Christian should be called to confess his faith before a Roman court of justice, he must remember that it is Christ, not the proconsul, who **has the sharp two-edged sword.**

13   **You did not deny your faith in me** might suggest that some members of the church had actually been asked to do so. From Pliny's letter to Trajan (*Ep.* x. 96) and from the story of the martyrdom of Polycarp we know that in the second century it was part of lawcourt procedure that those accused of being Christians should be invited to exculpate themselves by cursing Christ. But the fact that **Antipas** is singled out for special mention must mean that he had been the only martyr **(my faithful witness),** and it is by no means clear that even he was killed by judicial sentence rather than by mob violence. For other Christians the pressure to deny their faith came not from legal jeopardy but from popular antipathy. Peter denied his Master without being charged in a lawcourt, and there must have been many occasions in the public life of **Pergamum** when it was safer not to be openly recognized as a Christian. The words **even in the time when** indicate that the temptation was an ever-present one, not confined to the brief crisis in which **Antipas** met his death.

As we have already seen,[2] there is no information available about **the Nicolaitans** except what can be inferred from this letter and the one to Thyatira. Since the rest of this letter is
13   about the proper behaviour of Christians in a city **where Satan has his throne,** we may reasonably assume that John's quarrel with **the Nicolaitans** was over their attitude to pagan society and religion. The first point to notice is that there were not
14-
15   two types of error in Pergamum, only one: **the teaching of**

---

[1] During the first two centuries A.D. it was not strictly accurate to equate this power with the *ius gladii*, which was the legal right to pronounce the death sentence on a Roman citizen—see Sherwin-White, *op. cit.* pp. 8-10.
[2] Cf. ii. 6.

Balaam is merely John's opprobrious name for **the teaching of the Nicolaitans.** Whether or not they claimed to be followers of Nicolas, they certainly did not claim to be followers of **Balaam,** and would have resented the imputation. We must not make the mistake of attributing to them the sensuality of the antinomian group attacked in Jude and 2 Peter, of whom it is said that they copied Balaam's error by doing wrong for pay (cf. *Pirke Aboth* v. 21-22). The Balaam saga had been developed into a cautionary tale in the Jewish midrash for two quite distinct purposes: his acceptance of Balak's bribe made him a typical example of the mercenary spirit, and his supposed responsibility for the episode at Baal-peor (Numb. xxv. 1-2; xxxi. 16; cf. Philo, *Vit. Mos.* i. 53-55; Jos. *Ant.* iv. 6. 6) made him the father of religious syncretism. It is the second of these traditions only that John is following. But is he ascribing to Balaam two errors or only one, idolatry and sexual licence or only idolatry? This is a difficult question, because the verb *porneuein* (to **commit fornication**) is regularly used in both Old and New Testaments to mean either sexual licence or religious infidelity; and since pagan religion frequently involved sexual immorality, it could sometimes be used in both senses at once. A good example of this is found in the story of Baal-peor, where the Israelites had intercourse with Moabite women; for the real offence of this action was that they were *foreign* women, who enticed them to eat meat which had been offered in sacrifice to pagan gods. On the basis of that story John could obviously use the word in either or both of its senses. But in every other case except one in which he uses the verb *porneuein* or the noun *porneia* he uses them metaphorically, and it is best to assume that this is his intention here. There might indeed be some doubt about those at Pergamum whom John calls **adherents of the teaching of Balaam,** but there can be no doubt about the woman at Thyatira whom he calls Jezebel, and to whom he ascribes the same teaching; for nobody ever accused Ahab's wife of harlotry except in a metaphorical sense (2 Kings ix. 22). The sum total of the Nicolaitans' offence, then, is that they took a laxer attitude than John to pagan society and religion. Because we hear only one side of the argument, it is easy for us simply to accept John's verdict without considering whether his opponents might have had a defensible point of view. We are here admittedly in the realm of conjecture; yet, if we are to do justice to John's teaching, it is worth while trying to see what alternative policy was open to the church of his day. Let us suppose then that the Nicolaitans wished to avoid a headlong clash with Rome and believed that it was possible without disloyalty to maintain a peaceful coexistence. They would have had no difficulty in producing arguments to support their case. Had not Jesus himself attacked the separatism of the Pharisees, broken down the barriers between Jew and Gentile, and declared that it was possible to be loyal at the same time both to God and to Caesar? When a controversy arose in Corinth over the eating of meat that had been offered in a pagan sacrifice, the one side claiming that, since the pagan gods did not exist, the ritual of their worship could make no difference to good meat, the others that to eat such meat was to be a participant in the idolatrous cult, had not Paul shown his sympathy with those he called 'the strong', urging them only to bear the infirmities of the weak? (1 Cor. viii-x; cf. Rom. xiv. 13-23). Had not Paul taught that the Roman authorities were ordained ministers of God? (Rom. xiii. 1-7). And even when insisting on the purity of the Christian community, had he not explicitly said that this did not involve the total avoidance of sinful company, since that would mean leaving the world altogether? (1 Cor. v. 10). Was it not in fact totally unrealistic to suppose that anyone in this world could avoid all contact with paganism, whether in Corinth or in Pergamum, when the meat sold in the open market or served at a banquet was likely to have come there by way of the pagan altar, when pagan rites accompanied the meetings of clubs and trade guilds, as well as public ceremonies, and when the coins in daily use bore the image of the emperor with his head irradiated like the sun-god? But the man who believed in the one true God need not be upset by all this. He could recognize that what the Romans really wanted was a gesture of political loyalty, an open acceptance of Roman *imperium*. No educated Roman took the emperor's claim to divine status as anything more than a constitutional fiction. Even Domitian, who seemed to take his own divinity more literally than others, was in fact only bolstering his own sense of insecurity, because he had no heir and suspected everyone of trying to supplant him. The Stoics had suffered more from his tyranny than the Christians, because they wanted the principate to be elective, not hereditary. The revolution seven years ago (A.D. 88), led by the governor of Upper Germany and involving the governor of Asia, had showed that the imperial claims were essentially political. In other words, the Nicolaitans agreed with the strong party at Corinth that the pagan gods do not exist, and that a Christian may therefore without scruple or fear of contamination enter fully into the social life, commerce, and politics of a great pagan city.

The very plausibility of the case explains the violent and abusive language John uses to refute it. The pagan gods may not be real gods, but that does not mean that they do not exist, that their power is not a real power. If the state claims to be divine, though its claim is false, its power is real, the Satanic distortion of the genuine authority given to it by God. As long as Caesar keeps his proper and limited place in God's created order, men may obey both him and God; but if Caesar claims what is due to God alone, this means open war in which there can be no neutrality, a war which is part of the age-long struggle between God and Satan.

Not all the church members are **Nicolaitans,** but all are warned to **repent** of the indifference which has allowed the **16** Nicolaitan error to go unchecked. The fault of Pergamum is the opposite of the fault of Ephesus; and how narrow is the safe path between the sin of tolerance and the sin of intolerance! The call to repentance, here as at Smyrna, is followed by a threat of a conditional coming of Christ in judgment. What form of punishment the church is to expect if it fails to repent we are not told. Perhaps it is to undergo one of the plagues from which the martyrs are protected by the seal of the Lamb (vii. 1-3). Perhaps John is thinking of physical illness, which seems to be the fate in store for the prophetess Jezebel (ii. 22). The one thing clear is that, when John speaks of an imminent coming of Christ, he is not necessarily thinking of the Parousia.

The promise **to the Conqueror** picks up the main theme of **17** the letter. Those who refuse to win safety by making themselves at home in the banquets of the pagan world will find themselves at home in the messianic banquet, feasting on the heavenly **manna.** According to Rabbinic legend the manna given in the wilderness had been preserved in a golden jar in the Holy of holies, was **hidden** by Jeremiah at the destruction of the temple in 586 B.C., and would reappear from heaven at the coming of the messianic age (Heb. ix. 4; 2 Macc. ii. 4-8; 2 *Bar.* xxix. 8; *Ḥag.* 12ᵇ). The **white stone** is probably the Conqueror's ticket of admission to the heavenly banquet, a very permanent ticket to an eternal feast. It has no precise analogy in ancient social custom. But pebbles (not necessarily white, and without inscription) were used, among many other purposes, as tokens of admission to public occasions. This pebble is **white** because it symbolizes the Conqueror's victory, which is his real title to a place at the banquet, and it bears the secret **name** of Christ, which no one can learn without sharing his suffering (cf. iii. 12; xiv. 3).

ii. 18-29. THYATIRA

(18) 'To the angel of the church at Thyatira write: This is the message of the Son of God, who has eyes like flaming fire and feet like pure bronze: (19) "I know what you have done, your love and loyalty, your service and your fortitude. I know that lately you have done better than at first. (20) But I have this against you: you tolerate that Jezebel, the woman who calls herself a prophetess, whose teaching misleads my servants into fornication and eating meat sacrificed to idols. (21) I have given her time for repentance, but she refuses to repent of her fornication. (22) So I am making her take to her bed and bringing severe pain on her lovers, unless they renounce what she is doing; (23) and I will strike her children dead with plague. All the churches shall know that I am the searcher of heart and mind and that I will give to each of you what your conduct deserves. (24) But this is my word to the rest of you in Thyatira, all who do not accept this teaching and have no experience of what they call

the profundities of Satan: on you I am laying no further
burden; (25) only keep what you have, until I come.
(26) To the Conqueror who perseveres to the end at the
work he does for me I will give authority over the
nations, as I myself have received authority from my
Father—(27) to smash them with an iron bar, the way
earthenware jars are broken; (28) and I will give him
the morning star. (29) Hear, if you have ears to hear,
what the Spirit is saying to the churches." '

The city of **Thyatira** was founded by Seleucus I as a frontier 18
post to guard one of the western approaches to his straggling
empire. But its site had no military strength, and, after its in-
corporation into the Roman empire, it owed its importance
entirely to trade. The evidence of inscriptions shows that it
was the home of an unusually large number of trade guilds, and
we know that the Purple Cloth Company of Thyatira had its
representative in Philippi in the time of Paul (Acts xvi. 14). It
has been conjectured that the local guild of bronze-smiths may
have known the precise meaning of the word *chalcolibanon*
(pure bronze), which occurs nowhere else in Greek literature.
The tutelary god of the city, Tyrimnos, had been identified
with the Greek sun-god, Apollo, and appears on the city's coins
grasping the hand of the Roman emperor. It is possible that
John's picture of **the Son of God who has eyes like flaming
fire** was put forward in deliberate opposition to this combination
of local and imperial religion. The title **Son of God** prepares
the way for the quotation from Psalm ii, the psalm in which the
Messiah is addressed by God as 'my Son'.

The letter opens with generous praise for a record of in-
creasingly effective **service**; the **fortitude** of this church has 19
not been tainted by the loveless inquisitions of Ephesus. The
one fault is the tolerated presence of the **prophetess**. In view
of the prominence accorded to her it is likely that this woman 23
was accepted on the grounds of her charismatic gifts as leader
of the community; and since the charge against her so closely
resembles that against the Nicolaitans of Pergamum, she may
had been the leader of that movement also. From the First
Epistle of John we know that at about this time in Asia another

sect, which split off from the church and formed a separatist movement, based its teaching on the authority of prophetic inspiration (1 John ii. 19; iv 1-3). They were forerunners of the later Gnostics, yet without being guilty of the sensuality and libertinism which characterized some forms of Gnosticism; for the author of the epistle believed that their denial of the Incarnation had led them into moral failing, but the only moral charge he brought against them was a neglect of the claims of Christian love. Not even this charge could be levelled against the prophetess of Thyatira, for the church under her leadership had actually made progress in **love** and **service. The searcher of heart and mind** had detected no flaw in that aspect of the church's life. It is highly improbable that a church in such a healthy condition would have tolerated the preaching of sexual immorality, even by one who claimed the authority of the Spirit. The word **fornication,** here as in the previous letter, means religious infidelity, and the woman's **lovers** and **children** are the devotees and disciples of her teaching. This interpretation gains support from the name **Jezebel,** by which John attempts to undermine her influence. For the original Jezebel earned the hatred of Elijah solely for attempting to seduce Israel from the worship of Yahweh to that of Baal (or more probably for attempting to combine the two religions, for we must not make her more of a monotheist than Elijah), and it was for this alone that she was accused of harlotry (2 Kings ix. 22).

24   The policy of Jezebel involves, according to John, **experience of . . . the profundities of Satan.** This phrase may be explained in two different ways. One possibility is that the followers of **Jezebel** actually claimed, in so many words, to have such **experience.** They believed that it was their Christian duty to participate as fully as possible in the pagan society around them, to identify themselves with the common life of their city. They recognized that pagan social life was an open field for the operations of **Satan,** and that those who entered it did so at their peril. But they were confident that their baptism gave them supernatural protection from the onslaughts of **Satan,** so that they could touch pitch without being defiled and handle fire without being burnt. One must experience at first

hand the full depth of the mystery of evil in order to appreciate to the full the grace by which evil is rendered innocuous. Alternatively, it may be that the followers of **Jezebel** claimed only, like Paul (1 Cor. ii. 10), to know the deep secret of God, and that it is John who contemptuously retorts that their deep secrets are in fact the secrets of **Satan**; they claim that their policy of conformity introduces them into the secret place of the Most High, but in fact it only gives them a deeper acquaintance with **Satan**. In that case we should translate the clause: 'all who . . . have no experience of what they call the profundities (profundities of Satan!)'.

It is John's role to play Elijah to this woman's **Jezebel**. Just as Elijah on Mount Carmel accused Israel of limping on two opinions, in their attempt to combine the worship of Yahweh with that of Baal, and compelled them to decide which of the two was truly God, so John demands that the church shall choose between Christ and Caesar. Christians may render to Caesar what is Caesar's, but not what is God's. We shall find John reverting to this imagery later with new applications. For the mantle of Elijah descends on those witnesses who testify with their lives to the truth of the gospel (xi. 6), and the great city in which they die turns out to be the great Jezebel, the mother of harlotry (xvii. 4-5).

The promise **to the Conqueror** presents two problems, one linguistic and one theological. It contains an echo—John never quotes verbatim—of Psalm ii. 9, which in the Hebrew runs: 'you shall smash them with an iron bar and crush them like an earthenware pot'. In the place of the verb 'smash' the Septuagint uses *poimainein*, which means either 'to be a shepherd' or 'to govern'; and John uses this same verb. If we adopt the obvious explanation that John was here using the Septuagint, we should have to conclude that he intended *poimainein* to have one of its normal meanings in Greek usage. But it makes singularly poor sense to say that the Conqueror is 'to rule the nations with an iron bar the way earthenware pots are broken', and in any case John does not commonly use the Septuagint, but makes his own, often erratic, translation from the Hebrew. The preferable theory is that John, independently of the Septuagint, made the same mistake which the Septuagint

26-
28

translator had made before him—a perfectly understandable mistake for one to whom Greek was a foreign language—of supposing that, because the Hebrew r'h can mean both to pasture and to destroy, its Greek equivalent must be capable of bearing both meanings also (cf. xii. 5; xix. 15).[1] **The Conqueror,** then, is to be given the right **to smash** the pagan nations, a right which belongs in the first instance to Christ himself. But when? And how? And to what end? The promises to **the Conqueror** in the other three letters we have read are all to be made good in the life beyond death, where, safe from the second death, he will eat the fruit of the tree of life and the hidden manna. The promise in this letter that the Conqueror will be given **the morning star,** which is Christ himself (xxii. 16), is another promise of the same order. But in the heavenly city, into which nothing unclean is allowed to enter, and in which the tree of life stands for the healing of the nations, it will surely be out of place **to smash** the nations **with an iron bar.** Are we then to suppose that the promise refers to the millennial kingdom of chapter xx, in which the martyrs are raised to reign with Christ for a thousand years? This can hardly be; for before the millennium the enemies of God have been finally overcome and Satan himself confined in the abyss. We are compelled therefore to look for the fulfilment of this promise *within the present order*; and since the Christian becomes a **Conqueror** in this world only in the moment of his leaving it, the fulfilment must be the actual death of the martyrs. Martyrdom is for **the Conqueror** a personal victory over temptation and death, but it is also the victory that overcomes the world (cf. 1 John v. 4). The psalmist had looked forward to the day when God's Messiah would **smash** all resistance to God's kingly rule and assume **authority over the nations.** John sees this ancient hope transfigured in the light of the Cross. Pagan resistance will indeed be smashed, but God will use no other **iron bar** than the death of his Son and the martyrdom of his saints.

[1] The Hebrew word *tr'm* in Ps. ii. 9 almost certainly comes from *r"*, (to break), but by a different vocalization it could be derived from *r'h*.

(1) 'To the angel of the church at Sardis write: This is the message of the One who holds the seven spirits of God, the seven stars: "I know what you are doing; you have the name of being alive, though you are dead. (2) Wake up and put strength into what is surviving and likely to die! For I have found that nothing you do is ever completed in the eyes of my God. (3) So remember the tradition you received, heed it, and repent. If you do not wake up, I shall come upon you like a thief, and you will not know the hour of my coming. (4) Yet I can name a few of you in Sardis who have not stained their clothes. They shall walk with me in white, as they deserve. (5) Like them, the Conqueror shall be robed in white. I will never strike his name from the book of life, but will acknowledge him before my Father and his angels. (6) Hear, if you have ears to hear, what the Spirit is saying to the churches!"'

Roman **Sardis** was a prosperous centre of trade and industry, with an almost impregnable acropolis to remind its citizens of a departed glory. For **Sardis** had been the capital of the Lydian kingdom of Croesus, and subsequently the greatest Persian city in Asia Minor, the western terminus of the Great King's highway from Susa. The acropolis, accessible only by a narrow approach from the south, had never been captured by assault; but twice it had been captured by stealth without resistance, once by Cyrus in 546 B.C. and once by Antiochus the Great in 218 B.C. On both occasions the invader had come **like a thief** in the night, and the defenders had not known **the hour of** his **coming**. At **Sardis,** as in the other cities of Asia, the imperial cult had been grafted into the local religion. The Asiatic Cybele had been identified by the Greeks either with Persephone or, more often, with Demeter (Mother Earth); and on a coin of **Sardis** from the reign of Tiberius the deified empress Livia is depicted sitting like Demeter with a sheaf of grain in her hand, the new dispenser of prosperity.

John's letter, however, is silent about any pressure on this church from pagan religion. Here no outward signs betray the activity of Satan. Here there are no Jewish accusers, no apostolic impostors, no fraternizing Nicolaitans, no prophetic ecstasy. This is a church which everyone speaks well of, the perfect model of inoffensive Christianity, unable to distinguish between the peace of well-being and the peace of death. The church is **dead;** and it is therefore fittingly addressed by Christ as **the One who holds the seven spirits;** for only the life-giving Spirit of God in all its fulness can bring the dead to life. It is important for our understanding of John's kaleidoscopic imagery to notice that **the seven stars** do not mean in this letter what they meant in the letter to Ephesus. There they were the angels of the churches, here they are the sevenfold Spirit of God; and since the Spirit, in speaking to the churches, addresses the angels of the churches, the two are clearly not to be identified. The one symbol does double service.

But what does John mean by death? It would be quite wrong to picture **the church at Sardis** as an elderly and dwindling congregation, unable either to maintain its previous activities or to make new converts. The church had **the name of being alive.** Its moribund condition was not visible to outward sight.

2 The phrase **what is surviving** (*ta loipa*) refers not to a numerical remnant but to a residue of spiritual vitality. Death is a spiritual state which the undiscriminating may mistake for life; and John analyses for us three of its symptoms. It is a lack of vigilance, like that which cost Croesus his kingdom, and the church must **wake up** before it is too late. It is a stain upon the white robe of faith; and since the Conquerors are later said to have washed their robes and made them white in the life-blood of the Lamb (vii. 14), we may conclude that the stain is anything which qualifies or dilutes the church's faith in the saving grace of God. But above all death means that **nothing you do is ever completed.** Small wonder that neither controversy nor persecution has disturbed this church's superficial prosperity. Content with mediocrity, lacking both the enthusiasm to entertain a heresy and the depth of conviction which provokes intolerance, it was too innocuous to be worth persecuting.

3   The threat of judgment—**I shall come upon you like a**

thief—is couched in imagery traditionally associated with the Day of the Lord (cf. Matt. xxiv. 43; Luke xii. 39; 1 Thess. v. 2; 2 Pet. iii. 10), and it has been commonly assumed that John shared with the rest of the early church a belief in the imminent Advent of Christ. Charles, for example, comments: 'it is implied that the Church of Sardis will be caught off their guard by the suddenness of Christ's Advent'. But this is to force the text into a preconceived pattern. If we allow John to speak for himself, he is clearly saying that the coming itself is contingent on the church's refusal to repent: **if you do not wake up, I shall come.** The obvious conclusion is that John's attitude to eschatology was not so naïve as that of his modern commentators, and that he expected the final coming of Christ to be anticipated in more limited but no less decisive visitations. In this sense the coming of Christ is always imminent, and the church must keep constant watch for it, since it is always liable to be embodied in some immediate historic crisis.

The promise to the **few** who **have not stained their clothes** 4 is proof that John did not expect all faithful Christians to undergo martyrdom. Like the Conquerors they are to be **robed in white,** the symbol at once of purity and of victory. But **the Conqueror,** here as in the other churches, needs the special assurance which will carry him through his approaching ordeal.

All ancient cities kept a civic register in which the names of the citizens were inscribed, and **the book of life** is the register 5 of citizens of the heavenly city (xxi. 27). But it is more than that; for the names it contains were inscribed in it at 'the foundation of the world' (xvii. 8). This is one of the many ways in which John expresses his belief in predestination. If a man is a citizen of the heavenly Jerusalem, it is not because he has earned his place, but because Christ has loved him and released him from his sins with his own life-blood (i. 5); and what Christ has done is the fulfilment of an age-long purpose—the purpose declared by God and attested by Jesus Christ (i. 2). Before all human faith or striving there lies the divine choice and the divine initiative. Yet the predestination in which John believes is a conditional predestination. A man cannot earn the right to have his name on the citizen roll, but he can forfeit it; Christ may **strike his name**

from the book of life. The decrees of God are not irreversible, but wait on the acceptance or rejection of man.

The scene changes from City Hall to lawcourt. At the Great Assize Christ the Advocate **will acknowledge** as his colleagues in sovereignty those who have been his colleagues in suffering. This is the second time in this one short letter that we have had an echo of the Synoptic teaching of Jesus. 'Everyone who acknowledges me before men, the Son of Man will acknowledge before the angels of God; but whoever disowns me before men will be disowned before the angels of God' (Luke xii. 8-9). John is a prophet, and the words which he speaks in the name of Christ are the words of the heavenly Lord, not necessarily part of the tradition of the earthly words of Jesus; but he knew that tradition and was prepared to draw on it when it seemed to

6 him to express **what the Spirit** was **saying to the churches.** As John the evangelist would have put it, the function of the Spirit of truth was to take what belonged to the earthly Jesus and expound it to the contemporary church (John xvi. 14).

iii. 7-13. PHILADELPHIA

(7) 'To the angel of the church at Philadelphia write: This is the message of the true Holy One, who holds the key of David, who opens and none may shut, who shuts and none may open: (8) "I know what you are doing. See, I have opened a door in front of you, which no one can shut. Though your strength is small, you have kept my word and not disowned my name. (9) So I am causing men from Satan's synagogue, liars who claim to be Jews when they are not—I am making them come and do homage at your feet; they shall know that I love you. (10) Because you have kept my call to endurance, I in turn will keep you safe through the hour of ordeal which is about to fall on the whole earth to test its inhabitants. (11) I am coming soon; keep what you have, and let no one deprive you of your crown. (12) I will make the

Conqueror a pillar in the temple of my God; he shall never leave it. I will write on him the name of my God, the name of the city of my God, the new Jerusalem which comes down out of heaven from my God, and my own new name. (13) Hear, if you have ears to hear, what the Spirit is saying to the churches!"'

Philadelphia was the newest of all the cities addressed in 7 John's letters. It had been founded by and named after Attalus II Philadelphus of Pergamum (159–138 B.C.), who intended it to be a missionary centre for the spread of Greek language and culture in the backward highlands of Lydia. It stood in a region where earthquakes were common and had been totally destroyed, along with Sardis and ten other cities, by the great earthquake of A.D. 17 (Strabo xii. 579; xiii. 628; Tac. *Ann.* ii. 47). The city was rebuilt with generous help from Tiberius, and in gratitude changed its name to Neocaesarea. But even then many of the citizens were apprehensive of a fresh disaster and continued to live in the surrounding country. Under Vespasian the name of the city was changed again to Flavia, but the old name persisted through all attempts at change.

Because this letter is primarily concerned with the church's relation to the Jews, it opens with Christ's claim to be the true Messiah, **who holds the key of David.** John echoes here the language of Isaiah xxii. 22, in which the key of the house of David is entrusted to a new steward, Eliakim, as a symbol of his complete control over the royal household and of his authority to grant or refuse access to the king's presence. We might therefore have expected that in the hand of Christ **the key of David** would be symbolic of his right to grant or refuse access to God. But in fact, as the sequel shows, John has chosen to develop the imagery of the key in quite a different direction. Paul had more than once spoken of a new missionary opportunity as 'an open door' (1 Cor. xvi. 9; 2 Cor. ii. 12). So here Christ has **opened a door in front of** the Philadelphian Christians, by 8 giving them an opportunity for the conversion of the Jews, with every expectation of success, since he **opens and none may shut.**

Some commentators have argued that John envisages no

conversion, but only the ultimate humiliation of the Jews and their reluctant, unrepentant admission that Christ is God's **true Holy One** and the church his holy, beloved people. There is no indication that the Jews at Philadelphia were any better than the Jews in other parts of Asia: they have rejected the Messiah, thereby forfeiting their right to be called Jews; and by their slanderous accusations of the Christians they have con-

9 stituted themselves **Satan's synagogue**. For Satan is at once the Great Accuser (xii. 10) and the presiding genius of imperial tyranny (xiii. 4). How could John have entertained any hope for the salvation of those who had enlisted in the army of the Enemy? There are, however, two very good reasons why we should not submit to this gloomier interpretation. The first is John's use of Old Testament allusion. Ever since the Exile the Jews, taught by Ezekiel and Deutero-Isaiah, had looked forward to the day when God would bring about a reversal in world affairs, when Israel, 'ransomed, healed, restored, forgiven', would be vindicated in the eyes of the world, and the heathen nations would acknowledge her as the chosen servant of the one true God. 'The nations will know that I am the Lord, says the Lord God, when through you I prove myself holy before their eyes' (Ezek. xxxvi. 23). 'My dwelling shall be with them; I will be their God, and they shall be my people. Then the nations shall know that I the Lord make Israel holy, when my sanctuary is in their midst for ever.' (Ezek. xxxvii. 27-28). 'They shall bow down to you as suppliants, saying: "God is with you and there is no other, no other God but he."' (Isa. xlv. 14). 'The sons of your oppressors shall come to do you homage, and all who abused you shall bow down at your feet; they shall call you the City of the Lord, the Zion of the Holy One of Israel' (Isa. lx. 14). Admittedly in the prophecies of Ezekiel it is not plain that the knowledge of God to which the heathen are to be brought is a saving knowledge, but in the Isaianic prophecies there is no doubt at all; for there Israel is depicted as the servant of the Lord, 'a light to the nations, that my salvation may reach to the ends of the earth' (Isa. xlix. 6). It is these Isaianic prophecies that John echoes here: **I am making them come and do homage at your feet; they shall know that I love you** (cf. Isa. xliii. 4). We can be sure,

too, that he understood them to be predictions of the conversion
and redemption of the Gentile nations; for in his picture of the
heavenly city he draws on these same passages again, to describe the entry of the Gentile kings, bringing the tribute of their
national wealth and glory (xxi. 23-26). In the present context
he has taken this Jewish hope and turned it upside down. It is
not the Gentile oppressors of Israel who must be brought to
recognize Israel's primacy in the kingdom of God; it is the
Jewish persecutors of the church who must come to see that the
church is the true Israel, because Christ, **the true Holy One**
of Israel, has loved her in giving his life as her ransom.

The second reason is John's boundless confidence in the
power of Christ. Humanly speaking the conversion of the Jews
is indeed impossible, but what is impossible with men is
possible with God. The church at Philadelphia is **small** in
strength, but Christ works best through human weakness; all
he needs is their loyal proclamation of the gospel. If he opens
the door, **no one can shut it,** not even Satan. Repeatedly in the
letters we have heard the heavenly Christ issue his summons to
repentance, even where the church seemed hopelessly compromised or sunk in lethargy, and the same possibility of
renewal is open to the church's Jewish and Gentile enemies. If
they respond to the invitation, it will not be for any merit of
their own, but because Christ is making them come, as in
former days he had transferred both Peter and Paul from the
service of Satan to the service of God. Yet, though he does not
need human strength, he will not act without human agents;
he has **opened a door** in front of his loyal followers, not
in the first instance in front of the Jews. Christ holds the key to
earthly opportunity as well as to heavenly glory.

There follows the only explicit reference in the letters to the
approaching worldwide **ordeal** which is the main theme of the 10
rest of the book. Charles, convinced that the letters were written
in the reign of Vespasian, when John was not yet expecting
general persecution, treats verse 10 as a later editorial addition.
There are far too many cross-references between the letters and
the apocalyptic visions, particularly in the promises to the
Conqueror, to make this theory at all probable; and it is surely
highly improbable that an artist as competent as John would

have incorporated into his final work an earlier document incompatible with his later purpose. Nevertheless, Charles has
drawn attention to a real problem, the remarkable difference of
atmosphere between the two parts of a book which otherwise
makes an impression of tightly-knit unity. The letters are
addressed to a critical situation, but do not give any hint that
the author felt himself to be living on the eve of the final
crisis of history. The church is under attack from inside and
outside, and the attack will shortly be drastically intensified.
For those who are unprepared for the testing period ahead there
is the added menace of Christ's coming in judgment, but that
coming is contingent and may not prove to be necessary; and,
if it does happen, it will be an event in the spiritual life of the
particular church, not the final event of world history. Even in
11 the present letter the promise **'I am coming soon'** is best taken
with what precedes: the Christians will be kept **safe through
the ordeal,** because this is the moment at which Christ will
make good to them his promise to come again. In short, the
atmosphere in the letters is practical, pastoral, and personal.
How different it is when we move into the world of cosmic
symbol, where everything is larger than life, where the imperfections of the churches are forgotten and everything is seen in
clear-cut black and white, where events move with inexorable
certainty to the destined climax, the seventh seal, the last
trumpet, the final battle on the field of Armageddon! Is it
possible that John should have written both the letters and the
visions at the same time and for the same purpose, and have
intended them to be mutually complementary parts of a single
artistic whole? It is possible only if we can attribute to him the
sophistication to use, consciously and deliberately, two different types of language to depict the same basic facts. The literary problems of Revelation are insoluble so long as we suppose
that John was a literalist, unable to distinguish between myth and
fact.

12   The promise to **the Conqueror** forms a fitting conclusion to
this letter to the missionary church: he is to be **a pillar in the
temple of my God.** In those Old Testament prophecies which
looked forward to the drawing of the Gentiles into the spiritual
empire of Israel, the great attraction by which they were to be

drawn was the conviction that God's sanctuary was to be found
only in Israel, that Jerusalem was the City of the Lord (cf.
Isa. ii. 2-4; Zech. viii. 23; xiv. 16; Rev. xxi. 3). So the Conqueror, through whose faithful witness the Jews are to be drawn
to submission and faith, is to have a permanent place in the new
living temple and to bear the name of **the new Jerusalem.**
We are reminded that in the final vision of Ezekiel, to which
John makes frequent reference, the name of the holy city was
'The Lord is there'. There is no more than a verbal conflict
between this promise and xxi. 22, where John tells us that there
was no temple to be seen in **the new Jerusalem;** for there he is
denying that in heaven there is any more need for the distinction
between the sacred and the secular or for the mediation of the
divine presence, and here he is asserting that the new temple,
like the new city, is composed of the lives of the redeemed.
Ramsay has suggested that this promise of stability and per-
manence **(he shall never leave it)** would have had a
peculiar appeal in the city of many earthquakes.

The city of God is described as **the new Jerusalem which
comes down out of heaven from my God.** John uses this
same description twice more in his account of his vision of the
new heaven and earth (xxi. 2, 10). We might therefore conclude
that he regarded the descent of the city as a wholly future event,
destined to happen only at the end of time. In that case we must
take the present participle in the context before us as a futuristic
present. But this is by no means the most obvious or natural
way of taking it. The natural way is to treat it as an iterative
present, denoting a permanent attribute of **the new Jerusalem.**
Wherever a man lives by faith in Christ and bears witness to
that faith without counting the cost, there is the holy city
coming down out of heaven from God. We shall find
cumulative evidence that this is what John meant.

iii. 14-22. LAODICEA

**(14) 'To the angel of the church at Laodicea write: This
is the message of the Amen, the faithful and true witness,**

the beginning of God's creation: (15) "I know what you
are doing; you are neither cold nor hot. How I wish you
were either cold or hot! (16) But because you are lukewarm, neither hot nor cold, I intend to spit you out of my
mouth. (17) You say, 'I am rich, I have made my fortune,
I have all I want'—not knowing what a pitiful wretch you
are, poor, blind, and naked. (18) My advice is that you buy
from me gold refined in the fire to make you rich,
white robes to put on to hide your shameful nakedness,
and ointment for your eyes to help you see. (19) Those
whom I love I reprove and discipline; so be in earnest
and repent. (20) Here I stand at the door knocking; if
anyone hears my voice and opens the door, I will come
in and have supper with him and he with me. (21) To the
Conqueror I will grant a seat beside me on my throne, as
I myself conquered and sat down beside my Father on his
throne. (22) Hear, if you have ears to hear, what the
Spirit is saying to the churches!"'

14   **Laodicea**[1] was founded by Antiochus II (261–246 B.C.),
but, because it was more strategically situated for commerce
than for war, rose to importance only under the peaceful rule
of Rome. It was known to Cicero as a banking centre (*Ep. ad
Fam.* iii. 5; *ad Att.* v. 15); but it was also famous for its textile
industry, which manufactured cloth and carpets from the
special glossy-black wool produced in the vicinity (Strabo, xii.
578), and for its medical school, which was noted for its ear
ointment and probably also for the 'Phrygian powder' used in
the making of eye salve (Galen, *De san. tuenda* vi. 439). The
city was proud of its financial independence and refused the
customary imperial aid to restore the damage caused by an earthquake in A.D. 60 (Tac. *Ann.* xiv. 27).

All this John must have known. Here, as in the other letters,
he identifies the church in some measure with the city in which
it is located, but in no other letter is his local knowledge so much
in evidence. This is the church in an affluent society, without

---

[1] This Laodicea, with its neighbours Colossae and Hierapolis (Col. iv. 13),
stood in the Lycus valley, and is to be distinguished from other towns of the
same name in Asia Minor. See W. M. Ramsay, *Cities and Bishoprics of
Phrygia.*

either **hot** enthusiasm or **cold** antagonism towards religious 15
matters. Even open hostility would be preferable to this **luke-** 16
warm and repulsive indifference, for it would at least suggest
that religion was something to **be in earnest** about. Spiritually
the church is **poor, blind, and naked,** and not all the banks, 17
pharmacies, and looms in Laodicea can provide for its need;
for it has failed to find in Christ the source of all true wealth,
splendour, and vision. Of this church alone the heavenly
scrutineer has nothing good to say.

The opening address helps us to see why John has chosen to
end his series of letters with what at first sight appears to be un-
relieved gloom. Christ is **the Amen . . . the beginning of
God's creation. Amen** is a Hebrew word derived from a
root meaning strength and firmness, and no doubt John uses it
partly with reference to its etymology, to proclaim that Christ
has all the consistency and fixity of purpose which the Laodiceans lack. But in the Revelation Amen is frequently used as a
liturgical response, a strong affirmative answer to the declara-
tions of God. Christ, we are to understand, in his earthly life
and above all in his character as **the faithful and true witness,**
was the Amen to God's purpose for man and therefore to his
purpose for the universe, of which man was designed to be the
crown (cf. 2 Cor. i. 20). He can be called **the beginning** (or
source) **of God's creation** because, when God set in motion
the creative process, what he intended to produce was Christ
and men like Christ who would respond to him with utter faith
and obedience. Wherever he is present, God's creative and
recreative power is at work. It is this Christ who addresses the
Laodiceans, summoning them to find their true strength and
wealth in the recreating love of God. The very harshness of his
censure is the proof of a love that is satisfied only with the best;
those whom I love I reprove and discipline. If they are to 19
come safely through the approaching ordeal, they must recognize their essential poverty and open their doors to the **knocking** Christ, whose 'power reaches its full strength in weakness'
(2 Cor. xii. 9). He stands **knocking,** not with the timid tap 20
that requests admission, but with the imperious hammering of
the divine initiative, loud enough to penetrate even the deaf
ears of Laodicea.

The promise that Christ **will come in and have supper**
has a eucharistic flavour about it. The mention of a **supper**
with Christ could hardly fail to conjure up pictures of the last
supper in the upper room and of subsequent occasions when
that meal had been re-enacted as the symbol of Christ's continuing presence. This reference to the Lord's Supper is of
peculiar importance for our understanding of John's theology:
for that sacrament is a clear indication that the early church
believed in a coming of Christ which was an anticipation of his
Parousia. Just as the Jews had kept the Passover as a memorial
of God's saving act at the Exodus and as a foretaste of the
messianic banquet in the kingdom of God, so Christians celebrated the Lord's Supper to 'proclaim the Lord's death until
he comes' (1 Cor. xi. 26). Week by week, past and future met
in the sacramental Now, in which the crucified and regnant
Lord made his presence known to his disciples in the breaking
of the bread. Yet for all that, it is not to the Lord's Supper that
John is directing the reader's attention. He is using language
resonant with eucharistic associations to describe a coming of
the Lord even more intimate and personal than that experienced
in the corporate worship of the church.

21 The final promise explicitly tells us at last what John means
by the mysterious title, **the Conqueror.** Christ owes his royal
authority to his own victory: **I myself conquered and sat
down beside my Father on his throne;** and the victory of
Christ was the Cross (v. 5-6). **The Conqueror** is one who
follows Christ along the road which leads to that victory; or
rather, because Christ comes in all his victorious power to
those who open the door to him, **the Conqueror** is one in
whom Christ wins afresh his own victory, which is also God's
victory. Christ shares the Father's throne because his victory
is the Father's victory also, and **the Conqueror** shares Christ's
throne because his victory is Christ's. It is the profound and
moving theme of the apocalyptic visions which follow that, in
the agelong battle between God and Satan, God knows no
other victory and needs no other victory than that which is won
by the Cross of Christ, faithfully proclaimed to the world in the
martyr witness of his church.

III

THE HEAVENLY COUNCIL

iv. 1-11. THE CREATOR

(1) After this I looked, and there in heaven was an open door ! And the voice that I had first heard speaking to me like a trumpet said: 'Come up here, and I will show you what must happen hereafter'. (2) At once I fell into a trance. There in heaven stood a throne with someone seated on it. (3) His appearance was like jasper or cornelian; and encircling the throne was a rainbow, bright as an emerald. (4) Round the throne were twenty-four other thrones, and on them sat twenty-four elders, robed in white and wearing gold crowns. (5) From the throne came flashes of lightning and peals of thunder, and burning before it were seven blazing lamps, the seven spirits of God. (6) In front of the throne was what appeared to be a sea of glass, like crystal.

In the heart of the throne, all round it, were four living creatures, with eyes all over, back and front. (7) The first creature was like a lion, the second was like an ox, the third had a human face, and the fourth was like an eagle in flight. (8) These four creatures, each with six wings, had eyes all over, inside and out; and day and night they never ceased to sing:

'Holy, holy, holy is the Lord God Omnipotent, who was and is and is coming !'

(9) Whenever the creatures gave glory and honour and thanks to the One who was sitting on the throne, who lives for ever and ever, (10) the twenty-four elders fell down before the One who was sitting on the throne and worshipped him who lives for ever and ever; they laid their crowns before the throne and said:

(11) 'You are worthy, our Lord and God, to receive glory, honour, and power; for you have created the universe, by your will it was created and came into being.'

59

We have now come to the apocalypse proper, and John in-
1 dicates this by the simple literary device of recalling **the
voice that I had first heard speaking to me**. For when **the
voice** first spoke, it said: 'What you see write in a scroll and
send it to the seven churches'. Structurally the first three
chapters are a covering letter to accompany and introduce the
account of John's apocalyptic visions, which begins here in
chapter iv. But John intended his readers to come to the
visions with their minds prepared by what they had read in
the letters. From the warnings, from the scrutiny of their
strengths and weaknesses, and above all from the promises to
the Conqueror, they now knew that the church faced an imminent ordeal; and they could expect that the apocalypse
would disclose to them the true nature of this coming conflict.

John sees **an open door** in **heaven** (not to be confused with
the open door on earth which was set before the church of
Philadelphia), hears **the voice** summon him to enter it, and is
transported from earth to heaven in a prophetic rapture. None
of this would seem at all strange to readers of the Old Testament. In a prophetic **trance** Micaiah ben-Imlah had seen the
Lord on his heavenly throne, surrounded by his angelic coun-
sellors, and consulting them about ways and means of making
his purpose effective in earthly history (1 Kings xxii. 19 ff.).
Amos had declared that the Lord of history would never put
his secret plan into effect without revealing it to his servants the
prophets (Amos iii. 7). Jeremiah had given it as the criterion
for distinguishing true prophecy from false that the true
prophet 'has stood in the council of the Lord' (Jer. xxiii. 18).
The Old Testament prophet, in fact, may be regarded as a
privileged press-reporter admitted to sessions of the heavenly
Privy Council, in order that he may subsequently publish to
Israel what is God's secret policy, and what part Israel is to
play in implementing it. By the same token, John, believing
that the church faces an immediate life-and-death battle, which
is not theirs alone but God's, is summoned to the control room
at Supreme Headquarters.

Imagine a room lined with maps, in which someone has
placed clusters of little flags. A man in uniform is busy moving
some of the flags from one position to another. It is wartime,

and the flags represent units of a military command. The movement of flags may mean one of two things: either that changes
have taken place on the battlefield, with which the map must
be made to agree, or that an order is being issued for troop
movements, and the flags are being moved to the new positions
the units are expected to occupy. In the first case the movement
of flags is descriptive symbolism, in the second case determinative symbolism. The strange and complex symbols of John's
vision are, like the flags in this parable, the pictorial counterpart
of earthly realities; and these symbols too may be either determinative or descriptive. John sees some things happen in
heaven because God has determined that equivalent events
should shortly happen on earth, but other heavenly events take
place, as we shall see in the next chapter when the Lamb
breaks the seals of the scroll, because earthly events have made
them possible.

Military illustrations like this one are useful for the understanding of John's vision, in which the battle between the
kingdom of light and the kingdom of darkness occupies so large
a space; but they have their limitations. John himself frequently
uses military imagery, but mixes it freely with other types of
image, and makes no attempt at sustained metaphor or allegory.
In other books of the New Testament the Atonement is often
depicted as a victory, but also as an acquittal, an emancipation,
a sacrifice. Any one of these metaphors by itself is liable to mis-
interpretation and needs the others to balance and correct it. We
need not be surprised, then, to find that the **heaven** to which
John is summoned turns out to be more than a military headquarters—a throneroom where the heavenly King holds court
(iv. 2), a synagogue in which the scroll of God's word is
opened and read (v. 1), a temple with an altar on which the
incense of prayer is offered (viii. 3 f.), and a lawcourt from which
the Accuser is drummed out in disgrace (xii. 10). The very
fluidity of John's images strongly suggests that he was aware of
the inadequacy of all forms of religious language to express the
ineffable being of God.

Not only is the one reality expressed by many symbols, but
one symbol may also have a variety of meanings, as we have
already seen in the cases of the candelabra and the open door.

In particular there is an ambiguity attaching to John's use of the word *ouranos* **(heaven)**, which creates problems for the translator. If we imagine that he was the naïve inhabitant of a three-storey universe, who believed that bodily locomotion upwards would bring him to the floor above where God lived, and that bodily locomotion downwards would bring him to the floor below with its less desirable tenants, we shall find ourselves constantly in difficulties of our own making. The three-storey universe belongs to spiritual, not physical, geography, as the author of Solomon's prayer had made abundantly plain (1 Kings viii. 27). Sometimes John uses *ouranos* unmistakably to mean the sky, part of the physical, created universe (vi. 13, 14; viii. 10; xi. 6; xvi. 21). At other times he uses it to mean the uncreated realm which is the eternal dwelling of God (iii. 12; xxi. 2, 10). But in what category are we to place the **heaven** which is the scene of John's visions? In spite of the presence of God there, it cannot be simply identified with the eternal abode of God; for it contains symbols of the world's evil (iv. 6; xii. 7; xiii. 1) and in the end must vanish along with the old earth and its imperfections (xx. 11; xxi. 1). It is also difficult to decide whether the portents that John sees appeared in the sky or in **heaven** (cf. xii. 1 with xv. 1). The **heaven** which is the scene of John's visions, then, is part of the created universe, but a part which is entered by the opening of the spiritual eye rather than by any more literal form of transit.

2   The first thing that John sees in heaven is **a throne**. From first to last John's vision is dominated by this symbol of divine sovereignty. The final reality which will still be standing when heaven and earth have disappeared is the great white throne (xx. 11). To those who must live under the shadow of Caesar's throne, and find that that shadow is made darker by the shadow of Satan's throne (ii. 13), the one truth that matters above all others is that there is a greater **throne** above. As soon as we hear of the **throne**, we know that the secret plan of God, which is to be unfolded in John's apocalypse, is the plan that will make this heavenly fact an earthly reality also, and we are agog for the great announcement that 'the sovereignty of the world has passed to our Lord and to his Christ' (xi. 15). But for the moment the relevance of this theme to the pastoral needs of

the churches is held in abeyance. For the moment John is content simply to gaze in wonder and worship at the symbols of omnipotent majesty. If we are to know God at all, we must know him as the unfathomable mystery, a mystery to be explored only by the humility of worship.

Apart from the obscure and restrained mention of **jasper** and 3 **cornelian,** which conjure up a picture of luminous splendour, John makes no attempt to describe the figure **who was sitting on the throne.** His model is Ezekiel i. 26-28, but unlike Ezekiel he does not ascribe to God a human form. With evocative language he hints at what is beyond description, but that is all. Yet the whole chapter is numinous with the divine presence. John knows that to ordinary mortals the presence of God becomes real not through direct vision, even in the mind's eye, but through the impact of those to whom God is the supreme reality. So he allows his readers to look on the Eternal Light through the mirror of the worshipping host of heaven.

With every new sentence John deliberately deepens our sense of mystery. Overarching **the throne** is **a rainbow,** a reminder of God's covenant with Noah, with its guarantee that 'his mercy is as great as his majesty' (Ecclus. ii. 18). But this is no prismatic bow in the sky; it is like an emerald—a statement which teases the imagination out of all thought. This **rainbow** is second in importance only to the throne. It tells us that there is to be no triumph for God's sovereignty at the expense of his mercy, and it warns us not to interpret the visions of disaster that follow as though God had forgotten his promise to Noah.

Round **the throne** sit **twenty-four elders,** the heavenly 4 council of angels. The word 'elder' is not used in the Old Testament to denote an angel, but there is one passage where it might be taken to have this meaning (Isa. xxiv. 23), and it is possibly the source of John's usage. Many theories have been proposed to explain the number **twenty-four.** It has been suggested that they represent the twelve patriarchs and the twelve apostles, whose names were written on the gates and foundations of the holy city (xxi. 12-14); or that they are the twenty-four star gods of the Babylonian pantheon (Diod. Sic. ii. 31. 4); or that they correspond to the twenty-four courses of priests, led by the 'heads of fathers' houses' (1 Chron. xxiv. 1-6). All these suggestions have a certain plausibility. John's symbolism is always undergoing kaleidoscopic change, and there is no reason why the elders of the present passage should not become the gates and foundations of the New Jerusalem. The heavenly council of the Old Testament is frequently called 'the host of heaven', and so identified with the stars (cf. Job xxxviii. 7). And the elders are undoubtedly both kings and priests, and therefore fitting representatives of the people of God, which Christ has made 'a royal house of priests to his God and Father' (i. 6). We need not, however, delay over a question to which John himself may not have known the answer, for the number is an incidental detail of the scene of which he makes no significant use. The **elders** are here in this vision of heaven solely in order that they may lay **their crowns before the throne** of the King of kings. They are but pointers to the central majesty.

6-8   The same may be said of the even more mysterious **creatures.** The details of John's description are clearly drawn from Isaiah's vision of the seraphim, who stood before the throne of God (Isa. vi. 2), combined with Ezekiel's vision of the cherubim, who were the supporters of the cosmic throne and chariot (Ezek. i. 4-21). Behind these two prophetic visions we can trace their ancestry to the cherubim depicted on the sides of the ark (1 Sam. iv. 4; 2 Sam. vi. 2; Ps. lxxx. 1; xcix. 1)—probably because the ark itself was designed as a representation of God's heavenly throne—and to the cherub-wind on which God is said to have flown to the relief of his servant the psalmist (2 Sam. xxii. 11; Ps. xviii. 10). The cherubim were apparently the four winds, and therefore the four corners of the earth, the supporters of the firmament, and therefore the bearers of God's throne. It is safe to assume that in John's vision they represent the whole created cosmos of heaven and earth. What is not clear is whether the details that John takes over from the earlier prophets are used simply for their associative value or are intended by him to convey some precise symbolic idea. The lion, ox, man, and eagle may well have had their ultimate origin in the study of the constellations (but not, as is some- times said, in the Zodiac, for Aquila was never one of the signs of the Zodiac); but did John intend his readers to see here a reference to the stars, or was he merely copying from Ezekiel?

All we can say is that **the creatures** have no astrological significance which is consistently developed in the rest of the book,
and that here their sole function is to lead the worship of
heaven.

In all the heavenly harmony there is one discordant element—
a sea of glass like crystal. This **sea** has been interpreted in a
bewildering variety of ways. Some commentators have regarded
it as the counterpart of the lavers in Solomon's temple, a
symbol of that purity without which no man may approach God
(1 Kings vii. 38). They thus ignore the distinction between the
lavers and the bronze sea (1 Kings vii. 23), which was a cosmic
symbol representing the primaeval ocean of the creation myth,
but they have at least this much justification, that the confusion
was as old as the Chronicler (2 Chron. iv. 6). Others have
treated it as purely descriptive detail, designed to enhance the
splendour of the heavenly scene, although, unlike the other
symbols, it does not obviously direct attention to the central
figure. Others again have supposed that John was here drawing
on a traditional fund of imagery, the origin and meaning of
which had long since been forgotten. In fact, however, this is
one symbol which John has been at some pains to interpret for
us. The **sea of glass** is the reservoir of evil out of which arises
the monster (xiii. 1). It is the barrier which the redeemed must
pass in a new Exodus, if they are to win access to the promised
land (xv. 2-3). And in the new heaven and earth there is no more
sea (xxi. 1). This last passage reminds us that in John's cosmology heaven and earth belong inseparably together. When
God created the universe, he created heaven and earth (Gen.
i. 1), and heaven as well as earth is part of the transient and
temporal order; the one cannot pass away without the other
(Isa. lxv. 17; lxvi. 22; Mark xiii. 31; 2 Pet. iii. 13). It is significant
that, when John comes to speak of the new heaven and earth, the
first thing he has to say is that 'the sea was no more'. The **sea,**
whether on earth or in heaven, belongs essentially to the old
order, and within that order it stands for everything that is
recalcitrant to the will of God.

The origin of this symbol is to be found in the Babylonian
creation myth. There we are told that Marduk, the god of light
and order, went to battle with Tiamat, the primaeval ocean

monster, goddess of darkness and chaos, and, having killed her, split her body into two like a flat fish and made heaven out of one half and earth out of the other. From the Ras Shamra tablets we know that this myth was current also in Canaan, where the part of Tiamat was played by Lotan (Leviathan), the seven-headed monster. In the biblical account of creation in Genesis 1 the pagan story has been demythologized in the interests of a thoroughgoing monotheism, but traces of its original shape remain in the victory of light over chaos, in the name Tehom (the Deep) which is a recognizable variant of Tiamat, and in the separation of the waters above the firmament from the waters under the earth. Elsewhere in the Old Testament other echoes of the myth are found: there are references to Yahweh's primordial victory over the ocean monsters Rahab and Leviathan (Job ix. 13; Ps. lxxiv. 13-14; lxxxix. 10; Isa. xxvii. 1; li. 9), and to the creative act of power by which he confined the rebellious waters of the sea within their prescribed limits (Job xxxviii. 8-11; Ps. civ. 5-9; Prov. viii. 27-29; Ecclus. xxxix. 17).

None of those who used the ancient creation myth as a framework for their thinking about the meaning of existence, whether they were Babylonians, Canaanites, or Israelites, ever supposed that the victory of light over darkness had been achieved once for all, before the dawn of time. To suppose that they did is totally to misunderstand the character of myth. All myths are indeed stories about the remote past, but they are not to be regarded as primaeval history, still less as primitive and outmoded science. To be a myth a story must have three characteristics: it must be told in order to explain facts, practices, beliefs, or experiences of the present; it must embody some ultimate truth about human existence or some universal aspiration; and it must provide imagery by which men in every generation can interpret and express their own experience. In other words, a myth must be capable of being re-enacted in every succeeding age by those whose imagination has been awakened and illuminated by its truth.

The Babylonians had a New Year festival in which the victory of Marduk over Tiamat was annually re-enacted in a ritual battle. It is now considered unlikely that there was ever a similar festival in pre-exilic Israel, at which Yahweh was enthroned as king over the tumultuous waters of the flood (Ps. xciii), and therefore over all his enemies. But there can be no doubt about Israel's belief that the initial victory of Yahweh over the forces of chaos at creation needed to be repeated again and again, until his final victory at the Day of Yahweh; or that they therefore used the imagery of the creation myth to describe the triumph of Yahweh in the outstanding events of their own history. When the psalmist says,

> 'By your power you divided the sea,
> You broke the heads of the dragons as they reared from
> the water,
> You crushed the heads of Leviathan' (Ps. lxxiv. 13-14),

he is probably describing the Exodus rather than the creation, and he is certainly reminding the Almighty of a victory which he hopes will be repeated in the present. Similarly the prophet, recognizing that the God who divided the ocean at the creation has achieved a second victory over chaos and evil by dividing the sea at the Exodus, prays to God for a new Exodus from Babylon, which will be a new victory for the kingdom of God:

> 'Awake, awake, put on strength, O arm of the Lord!
> Awake as in ancient times, the days of long ago.
> Was it not you who cut Rahab in pieces and pierced the
> dragon?
> Was it not you who dried up the sea, the waters of the great
> deep,
> And made the depths of the sea a path for the ransomed to
> cross?'
>
>   (Isa. li. 9-10).

Israel believed that her national history was the scene where God was continuing to wage war on the powers of evil until the day of final victory. 'On that day the Lord with his great, strong, relentless sword will punish Leviathan the fleeing serpent, Leviathan the twisting serpent, and will kill the dragon in the sea.' (Isa. xxvii. 1).

These passages are found for the most part in the later strands of Old Testament writings, so that it cannot be maintained that the mythological way of thinking was a primitive survival, which

the Hebrew people outgrew in the days of their theological
maturity. It was still part of the living language of theology when
the author of Daniel described his vision of four great beasts
rising out of the great sea (Dan. vii. 2-3), and it is probable that
it was still a living language less than three centuries later when
John wrote. Indeed, it could hardly fail to be a living language
to anyone who knew the Old Testament as well as John did
and who moved about its imagery with his masterful freedom.
We need therefore have no hesitation in accepting the evidence
that the creation myth was one of the major sources of John's
symbolism.

There is thus a dualism in John's theology, as there must be
in the theology of anyone who takes seriously the fact of evil;
but it is not an ultimate dualism. For God is the Creator, and
everything that exists, including the sea of glass, owes its
11 existence to his sovereign will: **'for you have created the
universe, and by your will it was created and came into
being'.** This might in another context be taken to mean that
God is beyond good and evil and the Creator of both. But
John's vision has already excluded this possibility. Out of the
throne he has seen and heard **flashes of lightning and peals
of thunder,** and these reminiscences of Sinai are intended to
impress on us that the throne of God rests upon an immutable
and inexorable moral law; and the Trisagion of the living
creatures has attributed to God a holiness which cannot
ultimately tolerate the presence of evil. Evil things derive their
existence from God, but not their evil quality; for evil is the
corruption of that which God made good.

Thus by a collocation of symbols John's heavenly guide has
confronted him with the central problem of all theology. God's
holiness is such that in the end all evil must vanish into nothingness before it; there can be no place in the holy city for the
unclean or the false (xxi. 27). But what if the whole world be
unclean? The glassy sea stands before the throne as a mute
reminder that the whole creation is affected by the taint of evil.
Is God then to vindicate his holiness by destroying all that he
has made? Would not this be a confession of failure, a negation
of the will by which all things were made, and of the rainbow
arch with its covenant of mercy? How can God assert his

sovereign power over a sinful world without denying either his holiness or his creative purpose?

The answer to this question will be adumbrated in the next chapter in a vision of the redemptive work of God to which everything in all creation is to respond with worship. For the moment John is content to linger with the vision of God the Creator and to listen to the praises of heaven. For we shall be misled by the cumulative visions of destruction that follow unless we do full justice to this opening affirmation that the world is God's world and fundamentally good.

The voice which summoned John undertook to show him **what must happen hereafter,** and all that he has so far seen is the Creator in the splendour of his heavenly court. His readers are meant to perceive that the grim events which threaten them are not to be understood in isolation. Their coming ordeal will be part of the process by which the chaotic world is to be brought within the compass of the divine sovereignty, and the victory they are expected to achieve as Conquerors will be the earthly complement of God's own victory over the forces of darkness and disorder.

v. 1-14. THE SCROLL

(1) Then I saw in the right hand of the One who was sitting on the throne a scroll, with writing inside and on the back, sealed with seven seals. (2) I saw a mighty angel proclaim in a loud voice, 'Who is worthy to open the scroll and break its seals?' (3) But there was no one in heaven or on earth or under the earth able to open the scroll or to look inside it. (4) I began to weep bitterly because there was no one to be found who was worthy to open the scroll or to look inside it. (5) But one of the elders said to me, 'Do not weep; the Lion from the tribe of Judah, the Root of David, has conquered and has won the right to open the scroll and its seven seals'. (6) Then I saw standing between the throne with its four living creatures and the elders a Lamb bearing the marks of

slaughter. He had seven horns and seven eyes—the seven spirits of God sent out into all the world.

(7) The Lamb went and took the scroll from the right hand of the One who was sitting on the throne; (8) and as he took it, the four creatures and the twenty-four elders fell down before him. Each of them had a harp, and they were holding golden bowls full of incense, the prayers of God's people, (9) and they sang a new song:

'You are worthy to take the scroll and to break its seals, because you were slain and with your life-blood have ransomed for God men from every tribe, tongue, people, and nation; (10) you have made them a royal house of priests in God's service, and they shall reign on earth.'

(11) As I looked I heard the voices of many angels surrounding the throne and the creatures and the elders, myriad upon myriad, and thousand upon thousand, (12) singing aloud:

'Worthy is the Lamb that was slain to receive power and wealth, wisdom and might, honour and glory and blessing.'

(13) Then I heard the whole creation, everything in heaven and on earth and under the earth and in the sea, saying:

'Blessing and honour, glory and might, to him who sits on the throne and to the Lamb for ever and ever.'

(14) And the four living creatures said, 'Amen', and the elders fell down and worshipped.

1   There are four possible explanations of **the scroll** which John sees in the hand of God. The first identifies it with the Lamb's book of life (iii. 5; xiii. 8; xvii. 8; xx. 12, 15; xxi. 27). On this hypothesis the opening of **the scroll** is the disclosure of the names of the redeemed, which were written in it before the foundation of the world; and the **scroll** had **writing inside and on the back** because the redeemed were 'such a multitude that their names filled the scroll and ran over even on to the outside'.[1] But the arguments against this theory are

[1] D. T. Niles, *As Seeing the Invisible*, p. 55.

overwhelming. As each of the seven seals is broken, events happen; and the whole process of the breaking of the seals, with the accompanying events, is meaningless unless it is somehow related to the contents of the book. By opening the **scroll** the Lamb does not merely disclose its contents, but puts them into operation. There is a good parallel in Romans i. 17, where the revelation of God's righteousness is not merely the disclosure of the fact that he is righteous but the effective intervention of his power to right the wrongs of mankind. This is borne out further by the fact that John's description of the scroll is drawn from Ezekiel ii. 9-iii. 3, where the content of the scroll is God's judgment on Jerusalem, i.e. a forecast of coming events. John makes a second use of this same prophecy in his vision of the little scroll, which is said to contain 'the secret purpose of God' (x. 1-11). A second objection is that this episode is introduced by the solemn proclamation of a herald **angel,** who challenges all comers to offer themselves for the task of opening the **scroll.** In principle, if not in fact, any of God's creatures might qualify. But if the Lamb were the author of the **scroll,** the authority to open it would be his without question, and he would not have had to win by his passion **the right to open the scroll.** Finally, there is no suggestion here or elsewhere in the book that John's purpose was to reveal the identity of the redeemed (cf. ii. 17). His real purpose, constantly reiterated, is to tell the churches 'what is bound to happen soon' (i. 1).

This brings us to the second theory, that the **scroll** contains the revelation of those coming events which John has been charged to communicate. The book he has been told to write to the churches will then be nothing but a transcript of the **scroll with seven seals.** This theory is more in keeping with the evidence than the first one, and is generally adopted by those who suppose that the crisis which John expected was the end of the present world order. It is, however, considerably less satisfactory than it at first appears. For we are told that Christ **has conquered and won the right to open** (lit. conquered to open) **the scroll** by his death, and there is no very obvious reason why, having won the right in A.D. 30, he should have postponed the exercise of it until A.D. 95. The natural assumption is that the opening of the **scroll,** by which its contents are both revealed and put into effect, follows immediately on the victory by which he acquired **the right to open** it. This means that from John's standpoint some at least of the contents are already past; and for confirmation of this we need only turn to the vision introduced by the breaking of the fifth seal, in which John looks back on a past martyrdom as well as forward to a future one.

The third theory is that the **scroll** is the Old Testament. As on earth in the synagogue at Nazareth, so here in the heavenly synagogue Christ takes the scroll of prophecy and declares, 'Today this scripture is fulfilled in your hearing' (Luke iv. 21). He is the great expositor, who gathers up all the scattered prophecies into one comprehensive fulfilment. This theory has the merit that it fits the character of John's book, which is a sustained meditation on the Old Testament in the light of the Christian gospel. He believed as firmly as any other New Testament writer that Christ alone had opened for him the sacred book. Nevertheless, this theory has two defects. It overlooks John's dependence on Ezekiel, mentioned above; and it does not explain why the death of Christ should be the indispensable qualification for opening the **scroll**.

We turn therefore to the fourth theory, that the content of the **scroll** is God's redemptive plan, foreshadowed in the Old Testament, by which he means to assert his sovereignty over a sinful world and so to achieve the purpose of creation. John proposes to trace the whole operation of this plan from its beginnings in the Cross to its triumphal culmination in the new Jerusalem, not because he thinks that the whole process belongs to the imminent future, but because, without a vision of the process, the imminent future must remain a dark and unintelligible mystery. The redemptive plan, initiated by the archetypal victory of Christ, awaits a further fulfilment in the victory of the Conquerors, which will contribute to the final victory of God.

The **scroll,** then, contains the world's destiny, foreordained by the gracious purpose of God. The fact that the writing covers **the back** of the scroll as well as the **inside** is probably meant as an indication of the fulness and precision of the divine foreknowledge. But it is to be noted that God will not himself break the seals of his scroll and put its contents into operation. He has set this limit to his own omnipotence: man's destiny, and with it the destiny of all creation, must be achieved by man. The divine decree waits, **sealed with seven seals,** for the emergence of a human agent, willing and worthy to put it into effect, one who will place himself unreservedly at the disposal of God's sovereign will.

When no one in all creation is **able to open the scroll,** John 3-4 begins **to weep.** These are not the tears of the prophet, thwarted in his expectation of seeing into the future. His frustration goes deeper than that. Until the scroll is opened, God's purposes remain not merely unknown but unaccomplished. John has been brought up on the messianic hope of the Old Testament, which promised that one day God would assume his kingly power and reign openly on earth, punishing the wicked and redressing the wrongs of the oppressed. Especially in persecution God's people had longed for that day to bring an end to their sufferings, but also to vindicate their faith. For there is a limit to the capacity of faith to survive in the face of hostile fact; unless in the end right obviously triumphs over wrong, faith in a just God is utter illusion. God must 'vindicate his chosen who cry out to him day and night' (Luke xviii. 7). John weeps with disappointment because the hope of God's action appears to be indefinitely postponed for lack of an agent through whom God may act.

John's tears are checked by what he now hears and sees. It is always worth while to examine closely the connexion between what John hears and what he sees, and it is particularly unfortunate that in most editions and translations a paragraph break has been inserted between verses 5 and 6, so that we miss the full impact of the juxtaposition of images: **One of the 5 elders said, '. . . the Lion . . . has conquered . . . ' Then I saw . . . a Lamb.** What John hears is couched in the traditional messianic imagery of the Old Testament; what he sees constitutes the most impressive rebirth of images he anywhere achieves.

The Lion from the tribe of Judah is a title with an obviously martial ring, recalling the prophecy that 'the sceptre shall not depart from Judah . . . and the obedience of the nations shall be his' (Gen. xlix. 9-10). **The Root of David** reminds us of the ideal king who was to rise from the stock of Jesse to be an ensign to the nations:

'He shall strike the land with the rod of his mouth,
And with a breath from his lips he shall slay the wicked.'
(Isa. xi. 1-10; cf. Ecclus. xlvii. 22; Rev. xxii. 16)

This prophecy had been adapted by the Pharisaic author of the seventeenth Psalm of Solomon in his portrayal of the militant Messiah, who would drive out the tyrannical and impious Gentiles and establish the reign of God with Israel as the imperial nation. The words of the elder, therefore, encourage John to think that all the hopes and aspirations of the Old Testament are now on the point of fulfilment; and so they are, after being totally transformed by the alchemy of Christ. For John looks for **the Lion from the tribe of Judah** and sees **a Lamb.** We need not waste time searching through the Old Testament and other Jewish literature to find the meaning of this symbol, for
6 John has told us what he means by it. **The Lamb** bore **the marks of slaughter,** which were explained by the heavenly choir: **with** his **life-blood** he had **ransomed for God men from every tribe, tongue, people, and race. The Lamb** is the symbol of self-sacrificing and redemptive love.

By this one stroke of brilliant artistry John has given us the key to all his use of the Old Testament. He constantly echoes the Old Testament writings (without ever actually quoting them), partly because this was the language which came most naturally to him, partly because of the powerful emotive effect of familiar associations, and partly no doubt because his vision had actually taken its form, though not its content, from the permanent furniture of his well-stocked mind. But to all this we must add that he believed the Old Testament Scriptures to be the oracles of God, and that the same God who had spoken in partial and shadowy ways through the prophets had now spoken fully in his Son. The Old Testament was indispensable to the understanding of the character and purpose of God, but it must be read in the light of the fuller illumination of Christ. Throughout the welter of Old Testament images in the chapters that follow, almost without exception the only title for Christ is

the Lamb, and this title is meant to control and interpret all the rest of the symbolism. It is almost as if John were saying to us at one point after another: 'Wherever the Old Testament says **"Lion"**, read **"Lamb"**.' Wherever the Old Testament speaks of the victory of the Messiah or the overthrow of the enemies of God, we are to remember that the gospel recognizes no other way of achieving these ends than the way of the Cross.

The Lamb has **seven horns and seven eyes—the seven spirits of God sent out into all the world.** The horn is the symbol of strength, the eye of wisdom. Christ possesses in all their fulness the omnipotence and omniscience of God; he is 'the power of God and the wisdom of God' (1 Cor. i. 24). The **eyes** of the Lamb are a further elaboration of John's exegesis of Zechariah's candelabra, the seven lamps of which were said to be 'the eyes of the Lord which range over the whole earth' (Zech. iv. 10). In the previous chapter John was shown seven lamps burning before the throne, and understood them to be **the seven spirits of God** (iv. 5; cf. i. 4, 12; iii. 1). He saw the cherubim with their innumerable eyes, representing the divine omniscience, and heard them sing their psalm of praise to the Omnipotent. But the energies and wisdom of the Spirit of God were confined to heaven, barricaded from the life of men by the intervening sea of glass. They could be let loose into the world only by the unsealing of the scroll, which none even of the inhabitants of heaven was worthy to undertake. The Spirit of God in all its fulness could be sent out into all the world only as the **horns** and **eyes** of **the Lamb** (cf. John xv. 26; xvi. 7; Acts ii. 33). By this symbol John undoubtedly invests Christ with the attributes of deity, but he also does something more important still: he redefines omnipotence. Omnipotence is not to be understood as the power of unlimited coercion, but as the power of infinite persuasion, the invincible power of self-negating, self-sacrificing love.

The position of **the Lamb** when John first sees him is described with some ambiguity. A literal translation of the Greek would be: 'I saw standing in the middle of the throne and of the four creatures and in the middle of the elders'. This could mean that **the Lamb** was already standing on **the throne,** surrounded by an inner circle of the four **creatures** and an outer circle of **elders;** and this interpretation would agree with vii. 17, where **the Lamb** is 'in the heart of the throne', but it would be at odds with v. 7, where he goes up to **the throne** to receive **the scroll.** Alternatively, the construction may be a Hebraism (Where we say 'between A and B', Hebrew says 'between A and between B'). The meaning would then be that **the Lamb** was **standing between the throne** and **living creatures** on the one hand **and the** twenty-four **elders** on the other; and this is the interpretation adopted in the translation. Here, as in Ezekiel i, the **living creatures** are the supporters of the throne, though they also have a certain independence of action and movement.

7-9   As **the Lamb** receives **the scroll,** the heavenly choir breaks out into **a new song, new** because it is a response to the new covenant, of which the Lamb has now become the mediator. The phrase is taken from Psalm xcviii—a paean of exultation at the approaching world-wide victory of God (cf. vii. 10). Along with their own worship the elders present **the prayers of God's people,** because this is the moment to which all those **prayers** have been directed. The **song** begins with the same words as the hymn to the Creator in the previous chapter: **'You are worthy'.** The Lamb shares the worth of God and therefore the worship due to him.

The rest of the **song** illustrates a point made earlier about John's symbolism (see on iv. 1). Like the movement of flags on a military map, some of John's symbols are determinative, some descriptive. When the Lamb begins to break the seven seals, earthly events follow; the symbolism is determinative. But the taking and opening of the scroll has been made possible by what has happened on earth, so that the symbol is consequent on and descriptive of the earthly event: **'You are worthy... because you were slain'.** Thus at this point John's heavenly symbols are firmly anchored in historic fact (cf. the ejection of the dragon from heaven in xii. 7 ff.). But the once-for-all fact of the Cross is not for John an isolated incursion of the divine into history, with repercussions only in heaven. It has its factual continuation in the earthly life of the church.

10   Christ has **ransomed men for God** and made them **a royal**

house of priests in God's service (cf. i. 5-6). To be a Christian is to be both king and priest, but with a sovereignty and priesthood derived from Christ, as his were derived from God. John does not think of Christ as having withdrawn from the scene of his earthly victory, to return only at the Parousia. In and through his faithful followers he continues to exercise both his royal and his priestly functions.

In the closing phrase of the song some MSS. have a present tense instead of a future: 'they reign on earth'. Whichever reading we adopt, the sense will remain unchanged. For if we accept the future, it must be a future immediately consequent on the act of ransom and appointment as kings and priests. It is true that at the millenium we are told that the martyrs are to be resurrected to reign with Christ for a thousand years (xx. 6). But this is a special privilege for the martyrs, and here John is speaking of the whole church. It is true also that the inhabitants of the new Jerusalem are to reign for ever (xxii. 5), but that is not to be **on earth.** Any suggestion that the reign of the Christians belongs to an ultimate future is, however, beside the point, since we have now been twice told that they are already kings and priests.

The redemption of **men from every tribe, tongue, people, and race** is far from being the whole story of Christ's work of atonement as John understands it. For he hears the choirs of heaven joined by the voices of **the whole creation** in a final 13 outburst of praise. This should not be dismissed as mere hyperbole. John knows only too well that there is much **on earth and under the earth and in the sea** which has no inclination to join in the worship of Christ, and that these hostile elements are represented even **in heaven.** But such is his confidence in the universality of Christ's achievement that his vision cannot stop short of universal response. He agrees with Paul that God has already in the Cross reconciled the whole universe to himself (Col. i. 20), and that to make his act of amnesty and reconciliation known to the world is the royal and priestly task of the church, the success of which is already anticipated in the heavenly **Amen.**   14

IV

THE SEVEN SEALS

vi. 1-8. THE FOUR HORSEMEN

(1) I watched while the Lamb broke the first of the seven seals, and I heard the first of the four living creatures say in a voice like thunder, 'Come!' (2) And there as I watched was a white horse, its rider holding a bow; he was given a crown, and he rode out as a conqueror to win his victory. (3) When he broke the second seal, I heard the second creature say, 'Come!' (4) And out came another horse, fiery red. Its rider was given power to take peace from the earth and to make men slaughter each other; and he was given a great sword. (5) When he broke the third seal, I heard the third creature say, 'Come!' And there as I watched was a black horse, its rider holding in his hand a pair of scales. (6) And I heard what sounded like a voice from among the four creatures say, 'A day's wages for a quart of wheat, a day's wages for three quarts of barley! But do not harm the oil and the wine.' (7) When he broke the fourth seal, I heard the voice of the fourth creature say, 'Come!' (8) And there as I watched was a pale horse; its rider's name was Death, and Hades kept him company. They were given power over a quarter of the earth, to kill by sword and famine, by pestilence and wild beasts.

For all the haunting quality of John's poetry, the hymns sung by the heavenly choir in honour of the Lamb have not revealed any new truth. It was the common belief of the whole early church that the exalted Christ had taken his seat on the heavenly throne at God's right hand, there to reign as Messiah and Lord; and this belief was based on a psalm which declared that the Messiah was destined so to reign until God had put all his enemies under his feet (Ps. cx. 1; cf. Mark xii. 35-37; Acts ii. 33 ff.; v. 31; vii. 55 ff.; Rom. viii. 34; 1 Cor. xv. 25; Eph.

i. 20; Col. iii. 1; Heb. i. 3, 13; x. 12 f.; 1 Pet. iii. 22). If John
has something new to communicate about the reign of Christ,
it is because he insists on taking the traditional belief with the
utmost seriousness. It is not enough for him to assert that
Christ's reign is already established in heaven and will ultimately
be established on earth also at his Parousia; for heavenly events
must have here and now their earthly counterparts. It is not
enough for him to hold that the regnant Christ reigns over the
hearts of those who love him, that he reigns only in so far as
men by obedience and loyalty allow him the reign. He believes
that Christ is already the 'ruler of earthly kings' (i. 5). Unless
Christ can be said to reign over the world of hard facts in which
Christians must live their lives, he can hardly be said to reign
at all.

During the last thirty-five years of his life John has lived
through a series of grim events which might well seem a
challenge to the Christian belief in the kingship of Christ: the
earthquakes of A.D. 60 (Tac. *Ann.* xiv. 27); the humiliating
defeat of the Roman army on the eastern frontier by the Parthian
Vologeses in A.D. 62 (Tac. *Ann.* xv. 13-17); the persecution of
the Christians which followed the fire of Rome in A.D. 64 (Tac.
Ann. xv. 44); the four-year horror of the Jewish war which
ended in A.D. 70 with Jerusalem in ruins; the suicide of Nero in
A.D. 68 and the political chaos which ensued as four claimants
battled for the imperial throne, and for a whole year the
Roman world echoed to the tramp of marching armies; the
eruption of Vesuvius in A.D. 79 which had obliterated the
luxury resorts of the Bay of Naples and created a pall of darkness
so widespread that men feared the imminent dissolution of the
physical order (Pliny, *Ep.* vi. 16); and the serious grain famine
of A.D. 92 (Suet. *Dom.* 7). John's vision of the four horsemen is
intended to assert Christ's sovereignty over such a world as that.

The symbolism is drawn from the Old Testament, but modi-
fied to carry a radically new meaning. Zechariah had two
visions, one of four horsemen, one of four chariots, but both
were sent out only to patrol the earth and to report on its peaceful condition, and the different colours of the horses corresponded to the different winds or points of the compass (Zech.
i. 8-11; vi. 1-8). But in John's vision the four colours indicate a

difference of commission, and the emergence of each new rider betokens the release of a new disaster on earth: invasion, rebellion, famine, and pestilence. The identification of the first and fourth riders with invasion and pestilence, however, requires some justification, and it will be convenient to begin with the fourth. The Greek word *thanatos*, here translated **Death,** frequently also means pestilence (cf. ii. 23; xviii. 8), and this is the meaning implied by the colour of the horse. We are compelled, however, to take the word in its commoner sense, and to translate it as we have done, because the fourth rider is accompanied by **Hades** (cf. i. 18), who is the natural companion for the personified **Death.** John has made the fourth rider do double service, both as a symbol for pestilence and as an epitome of all four plagues.

2   Some scholars have claimed that the **rider** on the **white horse** represents the victorious course of the gospel, partly because of the similarity between this **rider** and the rider of xix. 11 ff., whose name is the Word of God, partly because the description of him as a conqueror is so closely akin to that of the martyr witnesses of the letters, and partly because, according to Mark xiii. 10, the preaching of the gospel to the whole world is, along with war, famine, and persecution, one of the inevitable preconditions of the coming of the End. But this theory is open to insurmountable objections. Mark's Apocalypse does not provide at this point such a close parallel to Revelation as does Luke xxi. 9-11, which mentioned 'wars and insurrections . . . famines and pestilences', but not the preaching of the gospel. The similarity between the **rider** of vi. 1 and the rider of xix. 11 is illusory, since the one is armed with **a bow** and the other with a sword, the traditional symbol of the Word of God (Wis. xviii. 16; Heb. iv. 12; Eph. vi. 17). The only mounted archers in the ancient world were the Parthians, and this is not the only place where John refers to the threat of eastern invasion (cf. ix. 14; xvi. 12). The similarity to the Conquerors becomes less impressive when we discover that the monster 'was allowed to wage war on God's people and to conquer them' (xiii. 7). We have already seen, too, that the fourth horseman is not only the last in the series, but is an epitome of all the others, whose common task it is **to kill by sword and famine, by**

pestilence and wild beasts. Moreover John explicitly distinguishes between these disasters and the last plagues which are the real precursors of the End (xv. 1). These plagues are preliminary and premonitory: the famine conditions are to be severe but not catastrophic, for **wheat** will be scarce but not unobtainable (a day's ration, **a quart of wheat,** will cost **a day's wages,** a *denarius*), and the luxury commodities, oil and wine, will not be affected; and only **a quarter of the earth** is to suffer from the horsemen's depredations. It would be strange to find the victorious preaching of the gospel ranked with such carefully qualified warnings. But the final and fatal objection to this theory is to be found in the repeated use of the word *edothe* **(was given).** John uses this word three times of a gracious gift of God which is in keeping with his purpose of redemption (vi. 11; xii. 14; xix. 8); but more frequently he uses it of the divine permission granted to evil powers to carry out their nefarious work—the denizens of the abyss (ix. 1, 3, 5), the monster (xiii. 5, 7), and the false prophet (xiii. 14, 15). The four uses in the present passage must be all homogeneous, and there can be no doubt to which class they belong. For the fourth rider, Death, and his companion, Hades, are beyond question evil powers. We may admit that, if we had to prove this out of the Old Testament and the Jewish literature, we should find the evidence disconcertingly divided. The author of Wisdom was convinced that 'God did not make death' and that it 'entered the world by the Devil's spite' (Wis. i. 13; ii. 24), and one of the Rabbis identified the Angel of Death with Satan (*Baba B.* 16ᵃ). On the other hand Ben Sira could write that 'fire and hail, famine and pestilence were all created for retribution' (Ecclus. xxxix. 29; cf. xl. 9-10). But the proof we need is to be found within the Revelation itself. For **Death** and **Hades** are destined in the end to be consigned to the lake of fire (xx. 14), along with the monster, the false prophet, and Satan. They cannot therefore be regarded as obedient angels, faithfully carrying out the task of retribution allotted them by God. It follows that all four riders represent evils which are not directly caused by the will of God, but only tolerated by his permission; and this excludes the possibility that one of them should signify the preaching of the gospel.

This brings us to the crux of the passage, which is also the crux of the interpretation of the whole book. At a first reading the account of the breaking of the **seals** leaves us with a sense of anticlimax. The choirs of heaven have sung their new song to acclaim a new act of God and to prepare us for the new revelation we can expect when the **seals** of the scroll are broken. Then on to the stage of history come only four horsemen representing disasters as old as the human race. Is this all that we are to receive from the regnant Christ? Has he after all nothing new to disclose, nothing new to achieve? Indeed, we may be pardoned for asking whether the Lamb who lets such horrors loose on the world is really the same person as the Jesus of the gospel story. But John has already given us the answer to all such doubts. It was by his death at Calvary that Jesus 'won the right to open the scroll' (v. 5). In the scroll is God's purpose for the world, but it cannot be put into operation, let loose into the world, except by a human agent who has won the right to do this. In other words, Christ's whole kingly power, his ability to control world history, has its source in the Cross. If we would ask in what sense the four horsemen represent the eternal purpose of God, we must first ask in what sense the Cross represents that purpose.

From one point of view the Cross was simply the product of the variegated turpitude of men: the bigotry of fanatics, the opportunism of corrupt priests, the moral astigmatism of lying witnesses, the vindictiveness of a nationalist mob demanding that an innocent man suffer the death penalty for a crime precisely because he had refused to commit it for them, the vacillation of a governor yielding against his judgment to popular frenzy, the treachery of one disciple, the denial of another, the cowardice of the rest, the taunts of callous bystanders. But because Jesus was content to accept the role of the Lamb assigned to him by his Father, he was able to transform all this into the signal triumph of divine love. He did not merely defeat the powers of evil; he made them agents of his own victory.

This is why John tells us that Jesus 'has won the right to open the scroll', and why the scroll, once open, lets loose upon the earth a series of disasters. He is not asking us to believe that

war, rebellion, famine, and disease are the deliberate creation of
Christ, or that, except in an indirect way, they are what God
wills for the men and women he has made. They are the result of
human sin; and it significant that, out of all the apocalyptic
disasters he could have chosen, John has at this point omitted
the natural ones, like earthquakes, and included only those in
which human agency has a part. The point is that, just where sin
and its effects are most in evidence, the kingship of the Crucified
is to be seen, turning human wickedness to the service of God's
purpose. The heavenly voice which says, **'Come !'** is not calling
disasters into existence. They are to be found in any case,
wherever there are cruelty, selfishness, ambition, lust, greed,
fear, and pride. Rather the voice is declaring that nothing can
now happen, not even the most fearsome evidence of man's disobedience and its nemesis, which cannot be woven into the
pattern of God's gracious purpose. Because Christ reigns from
the Cross, even when the four horsemen ride out on their de-
tructive missions, they do so as emissaries of his redemptive
love. In what way they can serve the purposes of the Lamb
remains to be seen. For the moment all we are told is that the
content of the scroll is God's redemptive plan, by which he
brings good out of evil and makes everything on earth subser-
vient to his sovereignty.

vi. 9-11. THE FIFTH SEAL

**(9) When he broke the fifth seal, I saw underneath the
altar the souls of those who had been slaughtered for
God's word and for holding to the testimony. (10) They
cried aloud, 'How long, sovereign Lord, holy and true,
is it to be before you pass sentence and avenge our
blood on the inhabitants of earth?' (11) Then each of
them was given a white robe, and they were told to wait
patiently for a little while longer, until the roll of their
brothers should be complete, those who were to be
killed in Christ's service as they had been.**

When a slaughtered beast was laid on the altar of burnt offering in the Jerusalem temple, its blood was allowed to run around the foot of the altar. John presumably has some such

9 analogy in mind when he says that **underneath the** heavenly **altar** he saw **the souls of** the martyrs; for 'the blood is the life' (Lev. xvii. 11). They are now **underneath the altar** because at some time in the past they have been offered in sacrifice on it. The heavenly **altar** is the counterpart of the earthly gibbet. The same divine alchemy which could turn the Cross into the victory of the Lamb and the four horsemen into ministers of grace can transmute a violent death into the sacrificial offering of a life in worship and service to God. The martyrs are said to have been **slaughtered for God's word and for holding to the testimony,** i.e. the testimony of Jesus. John has said of his own exile that it was 'because of the word spoken by God and attested by Jesus' (i. 9), and the martyrs have lost their lives in the same cause, not merely because they bore their own testimony to the word of God, but because in so doing they were giving new expression to **the testimony** which had brought Jesus to his death. Prominent among these martyrs would be those who had died in the persecution of Nero, but all others are included from Stephen to Antipas. Perhaps John meant also to include the martyrs of the Old Testament, for the

10 cry **'How long?'** had echoed down centuries of oppression (Ps. vi. 3; xiii. i. f; xxxv. 17; lxxiv. 9. f; lxxix. 5; lxxx. 4; lxxxix. 46; xc. 13; xciv. 3. f; Isa. vi. 11; Jer. xlvii. 6; Hab. i. 2; Zech. i. 12).

Charles (*ad loc.*) has argued that there is an element of personal vindictiveness in the prayer of the martyrs which is not to be found in the parallel passage in the teaching of Jesus (Luke xviii. 7-8). 'The *living* pray to God to free them from unjust oppression and secure them their just rights. On the other hand, the departed pray for vengeance for what they have suffered or lost.' It must be admitted that there is a *prima facie* embarrassment for the Christian reader in those prayers for vengeance which are found in both Old and New Testaments; it is difficult to entertain a passionate desire to see justice done without some sense of personal involvement. There are, however, reasons why in this instance we should not be too quick to assume the worst. John is here using the language not of private revenge but of public justice. In a Hebrew lawcourt there was no public prosecutor, charged with the suppression of crime. All cases were civil cases, in which a plaintiff must plead his own cause and the judge must decide whether he was in the right or in the wrong; so that any failure of the judge to vindicate the plaintiff was tantamount to a decision in favour of the defendant. The martyrs have been condemned in a human court of law, and that decision stands against them unless it is reversed in a higher court. But the heavenly judge cannot declare them to be in the right without at the same time declaring their persecutors to be in the wrong and passing sentence against them. Justice must not only be done; it must be seen to be done. We may still object that legal terminology is the wrong language to use, and that John would have done better to follow the examples of Jesus and Stephen by putting on the lips of the martyrs a prayer of forgiveness for their enemies. The blood of Jesus 'speaks better things than the blood of Abel' (Heb. xii. 24) precisely because it cries from the ground for mercy, not retribution. But such an objection misses the point of what John is saying. He cannot avoid legal language when he is dealing with men who have been condemned before a pagan tribunal and writing for the benefit of others who must face a like jeopardy. The point at issue here is not the personal relations of the martyrs with their accusers, but the validity of their faith. They have gone to their death in the confidence that God's word, attested in the life and death of Jesus, is the ultimate truth; but unless in the end tyranny and other forms of wickedness meet with retribution, that faith is an illusion. And not even Jesus could face death without some doubts about the rightness of the course he had chosen. We must remember too that, though John writes here about the dead, he does so in the interests of the living, for whom the validity of the martyrs' faith is a question of supreme moment, since they may shortly be required to make the same choice. The church expectant is made spokesman for the church militant, with which it has a solidarity of interest and destiny.

In answer to their plea the martyrs are first given the assurance of personal vindication: **each of them was given a white 11**

robe, the symbol of victory, purity, and bliss. White robes or robes of glory are mentioned several times in Jewish apocalyptic writings as tokens of heavenly existence (e.g. 1 *Enoch* lxii. 16; 2 *Enoch* xxii. 8). In three works, all probably written in the second half of the second century A.D., the white robes are explicitly identified with the body of glory which, according to Paul, is to be the outward form of the resurrection life (1 Cor. xv. 35 ff.; 2 Cor. v. 1 ff.; Phil. iii. 21). Ezra sees the saints in white robes and is told by an angel, 'these are they who have put off their mortal garment and have put on an immortal one' (2 Esdras ii. 39-44).[1] Another seer has a vision of the saints in heaven 'stripped of their fleshly garments' and clothed in 'garments of the world above' (*Asc. Isa.* ix. 9). In the Hymn of the Soul found in the Syriac *Acts of Thomas* the soul is made to leave behind its bright robe, when it descends to Egypt to charm the serpent and bring back the pearl which it guards. On its return the robe is brought out to it. 'On a sudden, as I faced it, the garment seemed to me like a mirror of myself. I saw it all in my whole self; moreover I faced my whole self in facing it. For we were two in distinction, and yet again one in one likeness.'[2] The last two of these works are certainly both Gnostic in origin, yet it is likely that they enshrine a genuine tradition of the meaning of this symbol in Jewish apocalyptic writing, and that John, following the same tradition, meant his readers to understand by the **white robe** a spiritual body which would replace the body of flesh. But it must be added that he shows singularly little trace of being interested in detailed speculations about the nature of life in the world to come and its relation to bodily existence.

The second part of the answer to the martyrs' question is of considerably more importance for the theology of the book as a whole: **they were told to wait patiently ... until the roll of their brothers should be complete.** This in itself could mean

[1] The central part of 2 Esdras is a Jewish apocalypse written *c.* A.D. 100, but the first two chapters are a later Christian addition.

[2] Lines 76 ff. Ed. A. A. Bevan, *Texts and Studies V*, No. 3 (1897), xx. The hymn is also preserved in one Greek MS. of the eleventh century, which may stand closer to the lost Syriac original than the extant Syriac recension. But the English translation of the Greek text given by M. R. James (*The Apocryphal New Testament*, p. 414) does not differ substantially from that quoted above.

any one of three things: that God has a limited number of vacancies in heaven, which he has determined to fill up with martyrs, and that the End will come when the full tally is made up; that salvation is here regarded as a corporate experience, so that John and his contemporaries could say about the martyrs of the past what the author of Hebrews said about the saints of the Old Testament—'only in our company were they to reach perfection' (Heb. xi. 40); or that the death of the martyrs is the means by which God is to win his victory over the powers of evil, and only total victory can bring about the consummation of God's purpose. The first interpretation is ruled out by the next chapter, in which John proves that he has no interest in mathematical computation: the number of the martyrs is 144,000, but this is a symbolic number, and the corresponding reality is 'a vast throng, which no one could count' (vii. 9). The second interpretation is incompatible with the gift of the white robe, which symbolizes personal immortality, already bestowed without even a little while of further delay. It is not the individual destiny of the martyrs which waits upon the completion of the roll of honour, but something infinitely bigger—the vindication of their faith in God's purpose as revealed in Jesus Christ. Only the third explanation does justice to the profundity of John's thought. He has already warned the churches that they face an imminent call to become Conquerors, men in whose martyr death Christ wins again the victory of the Cross (iii. 21). He has told them that only by the victory of the Cross has Christ won the right to open the scroll of God's purpose, both to disclose it and to put it into operation. It is not surprising then that the content of the scroll should include the story of continued martyrdom by which the final victory is to be won.

Here, as elsewhere in his book, John calls the persecutors of the church **the inhabitants of earth** (cf. iii. 10; viii. 13; xi. 10; xiii. 8, 12, 14; xvii. 2, 8). This is a qualitative, not a quantitative description. It does not imply that the majority of the earth's population are hostile to God and doomed to destruction. On the contrary the martyrs alone, to say nothing of the rest of the church, are a vast throng drawn from every country in the world. What John means is that, unlike Christians, whose citizenship is in heaven (Phil. iii. 20), and who have acknowledged that here

they have no lasting city, but are strangers on a journey through
the earth (Heb. xi. 13; xiii. 14), their opponents are at home
in the present world order, men of earthbound vision, trusting
in earthly security, unable to look beyond the things that are
seen and temporal. It follows therefore that, when John comes
to speak of the shaking of the earth, he is thinking not so much
of the dissolution of the physical universe as of that earth which
is the spiritual home of earthly men.

vi. 12-17. THE GREAT EARTHQUAKE

**(12) I watched while he broke the sixth seal. There was a
great earthquake; the sun turned black as sackcloth and
the moon red as blood; (13) the stars in the sky fell to the
earth, like unripe figs dropping from a fig-tree when it is
battered by a gale; (14) the sky split open and rolled up
like a scroll, and every mountain and island was dis-
lodged from its place. (15) Then the kings of earth,
courtiers and officers, the rich and the powerful, and all
men, slave or free, hid themselves in caves or among
the mountain crags, (16) and called to the mountains and
crags, 'Fall on us and hide us from the sight of the One
who sits on the throne and from the wrath of the Lamb;
(17) for the great day of their wrath has come, and who
can stand?'**

12   The **great earthquake** is not a local freak of nature, like the
earthquakes at Sardis, Philadelphia, and Laodicea; for it is
cosmic in its dimensions. On the other hand, it is not the final
collapse of the physical universe and the end of the world; for
after that had happened, the inhabitants of earth would hardly
still be hiding **in caves** and calling **to the mountains** to **fall
on** them. The sequence of events makes it plain that, like everything else in John's vision, the **earthquake** is a symbol. The
cosmic **earthquake** is indeed one of the most regular features
in the Jewish apocalyptic tradition. But this does not mean that
John has uncritically taken over a traditional symbol without

due attention to its meaning. He has carefully built up his picture out of Old Testament allusions, making particular use of five passages, each of which contributes something to the interpretation.

(a) The first Old Testament reference to the eschatological earthquake is found in an early prophecy of Isaiah, in which the prophet pictures men hiding **in caves** from the terror of the Lord; and here the **earthquake** is the symbol of the overthrow of human arrogance, which has built a corrupt political and economic system in defiance of the holiness of God.

> 'The Lord of hosts has a day in store against all that is proud and lofty,
> Against all that is lifted up and high;
> Against all the cedars of Lebanon, lofty and high, and all the oaks of Bashan;
> Against all high mountains and all lofty hills;
> Against all ships of Tarshish and all vessels of delight;
> And man's arrogance shall be humbled and his pride brought low,
> And the Lord alone shall be exalted in that day.'
>
> (Isa. ii. 12-17).

(b) With this John has combined an allusion to Hosea x. 1-8, a prediction of the utter destruction of Samaria, which will prompt the inhabitants to call **to the mountains** to cover their shame. (c) At a later date Israel came to believe that every nation had been set by God under the authority of an angel ruler or guardian, so that national punishment must involve the nation's angel as well as the nation's king:

> 'On that day the Lord will punish in heaven the host of heaven
> And on earth the kings of earth.'
>
> (Isa. xxiv. 21).

And since the phrase 'the host of heaven' could apply not only to angels but to stars, and in the ancient world the heavenly bodies were commonly regarded as living beings with a divine authority, the punishment of the principalities and powers who stood behind the authority of earthly kings could readily be

13 symbolized by the rolling up of **the sky** and the shaking of **the stars.**

> 'The Lord is enraged against all nations . . .
> All the host of heaven shall moulder away;
> The sky shall roll up like a scroll, all its host shall fall,
> As leaves fall from the vine or wither from the fig-tree.'
>
> (Isa. xxxiv. 2-4).

(*d*) In the prophecy of Joel the turning of **the sun** to darkness and **the moon** to **blood** portends the judgment of the nations which have oppressed Jerusalem and the restoration of the Jewish national fortunes (Joel ii. 28-iii. 3). (*e*) Finally, the question 'Who can stand?' is a quotation from Malachi iii. 2, from a prophecy of the Lord's coming in judgment to purge the national life, and in particular the worship and priesthood, of Judah.

We have every justification, then, for supposing that in John's imagery the **earthquake** stands for the overthrow of a worldly political order organized in hostility to God. If further confirmation is needed, we can turn to two passages of the New Testament which show that John did not stand alone in the use of these Old Testament allusions. Luke records a saying of Jesus, in which he quotes Hosea x. 8, applying the words not to some ultimate cosmic catastrophe but to the destruction of Jerusalem by Roman armies (Luke xxiii. 28-31). And the author of Hebrews explicitly tells his readers that the **earthquake** of Old Testament prophecy is a symbol, signifying 'the removal of all that can be shaken . . . in order that what cannot be shaken may remain' (Heb. xii. 27).

The one element in John's picture which is not drawn from
16 tradition is **the wrath of the Lamb.** This phrase is a deliberate paradox, by which John intends to goad his readers into theological alertness; and we ought not to blunt its point, either by treating the word **Lamb** as though it were a mere code equivalent for Christ, or by attributing to **the Lamb** the menacing attributes of the Lion of Judah. Neither literally nor as a metaphor for self-sacrificing love is a lamb naturally associated with **wrath.** It is too facile a resolution of the paradox to say that, because **the Lamb** breaks the seals of the

scroll, he may be deemed to have accepted responsibility for the retributive judgments of God which his action lets loose on the world. For the victory by which **the Lamb** won the right to open the scroll was the Cross; and, as we have already seen, we can as little hold him directly responsible for the activities of the four horsemen as for those of Judas, Caiaphas, and Pilate. This point has been well appreciated by A. T. Hanson in his valuable contribution to the study of John's vocabulary.[1] He argues that the wrath of God in the Revelation, as elsewhere in the Old and New Testaments, represents not the personal attitude of God towards sinners, but an impersonal process of retribution working itself out in the course of history; that the Lamb is at all times a symbol to be understood with reference to the Cross, so that the Cross itself is both the victory of God and the judgment of the world; and that therefore **the wrath of the Lamb** must be interpreted as 'the working out in history of the consequences of the rejection and crucifixion of the Messiah'. The two premises of this argument are, I believe, sound, and their soundness will be demonstrated as we follow the course of John's visions. It is also true that when John comes to describe the fall of Rome, he portrays that fall as the working out in history of the consequences of the persecution of the church by Babylon, which is also the city where the church's Lord was crucified. Yet even so Hanson's conclusion does not follow from his premises, for it involves a blurring of the distinctions between three ways in which the judgment of God may be linked to the Cross. We may say that, for those who participated in the actual historical events, the Cross was the judgment of God on the rejection and crucifixion of the Messiah, and that they may be regarded as representatives of mankind at large; but it should be noted that in this sense the Cross put the whole world under judgment, including those who were subsequently to see in it the instrument of their salvation. Alternatively, we may say that the Cross was the judgment of God on the sin of the world, inasmuch as Christ identified himself with men where they were, under God's judgment, and so bore the judgment in his own person (cf. John xii. 31-32). Finally, we may say that the Cross is not itself the judgment but the basis of judgment, since men

[1] *The Wrath of the Lamb*, pp. 159-180.

are judged by whether they accept or reject the forgiveness and restoration which it both makes possible and proclaims ('How shall we escape if we neglect so great a salvation?' (Heb. ii. 3). These three ideas are not of course mutually exclusive, but it is well to be clear which of them we are speaking about at any given time. Hanson recognizes that the theology of John points to the second of these ways of linking the Cross and judgment; for he insists that the Cross was a victory 'won not by killing others but by undergoing voluntary death', and that the Cross as judgment is analogous to the Cross as victory. But he finally settles for the third as an explanation of the present passage, because he sees that neither of the first two ways would justify the description of the Cross and its impact on men as the **wrath of the Lamb.** In so doing he has overlooked the fact that in the Revelation the judgment on which men's eternal destiny rests is in the sole hands of God (xx. 11 ff.). It seems probable therefore that, whenever John speaks of Christ as the Lamb, he thinks of him not as the dispenser but as the bearer of the world's judgment.

In view of all these complications it is best to make an entirely different approach to our present passage. There is no need to find a place in John's theology for any concept of **the wrath of the Lamb,** since it is not a phrase which he uses *propria persona*, but one which he puts on the lips of the terri-fied inhabitants of earth. It has its source not in the true nature of Christ, but in the tragic and paranoiac delusion to which they have surrendered themselves. Like Paul, John believes that the fundamental sin is the suppression of the truth, specifically the truth of God's sovereignty and man's dependence, which draws upon itself in nemesis a progressive darkening of the mind and an inability to see what ought to be self-evident (cf. Rom. i. 18 ff.). Satan, 'the deceiver of the whole world', has persuaded men to exchange the truth of God for a lie (xii. 9; cf. Rom. i. 25). His victims have for their king the monster, a travesty of Godhead, and for their home Babylon, a travesty of the church (xiii. 1 ff. and xvii. 1 ff.), and they bear a mark which is a parody of the seal of God (xiii. 16; cf. vii. 3). They are men to whom a lie has become second nature, so that, faced with the love and forgiveness of the sacrificed Lamb, they can see only a figure of inexorable vengeance. 'The wicked man runs though no one pursues' (Prov. xxviii. 1). To him no doubt the terror is real enough, perhaps even the only and ultimate reality; but it is nevertheless a travesty of the truth about Christ.

vii. 1-8. THE SEALING OF THE MARTYRS

(1) After this I saw four angels standing at the four corners of the earth, holding in check the four earthly winds to prevent any wind from blowing on land or sea or on any tree. (2) Then I saw another angel rising out of the east, holding the seal of the living God, and he cried aloud to the four angels who had been given power to make havoc of land and sea: (3) 'Do no damage to land or sea or trees until we set God's seal on the foreheads of his servants'. (4) I heard how many had received the seal. From all the tribes of Israel there were a hundred and forty-four thousand: (5) twelve thousand from the tribe of Judah, twelve thousand from the tribe of Reuben, twelve thousand from the tribe of Gad, (6) twelve thousand from the tribe of Asher, twelve thousand from the tribe of Naphtali, twelve thousand from the tribe of Manasseh, (7) twelve thousand from the tribe of Simeon, twelve thousand from the tribe of Levi, twelve thousand from the tribe of Issachar, (8) twelve thousand from the tribe of Zebulun, twelve thousand from the tribe of Joseph, and twelve thousand from the tribe of Benjamin.

The breaking of the first six seals has brought the whole rebellious world into a terror-stricken expectation of judgment, and all that now remains is for the Lamb to break the seventh seal, complete the opening of the scroll of destiny, and consummate the purpose of God. But first John interposes two further visions, which answer the frantic question of the self-deluded: 'Who can stand?' There are some who can stand, through all the shocks to which earth is exposed, and even in the

searching light of God's presence, because they bear **the seal of
1 the living God.** **The four earthly winds** of this new vision
are not a symbol for a further series of disasters which John
expected to follow in chronological succession on those depicted under the breaking of the first six seals; for the seventh
seal alone remains, and that is the End. Rather the **winds** are a
new symbol for the destructive powers already symbolized by
the four horsemen. The change of imagery was a perfectly
natural one to John, because in one of the Old Testament
sources of his vision the horsemen were explicitly identified
with **the four winds** of heaven (Zech. vi. 5; cf. Ps. xviii. 10;
lxviii. 17, 33; civ. 3; Isa. xix. 1; lxvi. 15; Hab. iii. 8; Deut.
xxxiii. 26). Indeed, it was probably because of their destructive
capacity as **winds** that John came to think of the horsemen as
destroyers in the first place (see e.g. Jer. iv. 11-12; xxiii. 19;
Nah. i. 3; Hos. xiii. 15). Moreover, the four living creatures, at
whose summons the horsemen were released, are related to the
cherub-winds of the Old Testament. It is to be noted, however,
that, where Zechariah speaks of **the four winds** of **heaven,**
John uses the curious expression **four winds** of *earth*. These
winds, although they are released by divine permission and
used as agents of a divine purpose, are in their essential nature
earthly, as **earthly** as the inhabitants of earth they destroy;
for they are evils which have their origin in human sin. The very
fact that they need to be held **in check** to prevent their pre-
mature activity is an indication of their rebellious and demonic
character. From all this it follows that John's vision carries us
back in time to a point before the release of the four horsemen or
winds, when they were still being held under restraint until the
servants of God should be sealed.

3   But who are these **servants?** And what is their relation to the
innumerable multitude of the succeeding vision? Since the one
4 group is said to be from **the tribes of Israel** and the other from
every nation, it might appear that these are the two great
divisions of the early church, Jewish Christians and Gentile
Christians. But closer consideration shows that this is impossible.
The **hundred and forty-four thousand** of the present vision
cannot be different from the hundred and forty-four thousand
of xiv. 1, who are the whole body of martyrs without distinction

of race. The number, like the twelve **tribes** which make it up, cannot have been intended literally, because in the first century A.D. the twelve tribes literally did not exist; and the hope of their eventual restoration, which is frequently found in Jewish literature, belonged to the ideal world, not to the real. On the other hand, the idea that the new Israel, like the old, has twelve **tribes,** occurs elsewhere in the New Testament, and is apparently derived from a saying of Jesus (Jas. i. 1; 1 Pet. i. 1; cf. Matt. xix. 28; Luke xxii. 30). In the Revelation John has already applied to the church so many descriptions of the old Israel that it would be perverse to treat the present case as an exception to the general rule. To make an exception here would in any case involve a most improbable sequence in John's thought: only the Jewish Christians receive the protective **seal,** yet it is only the Gentile Christians who, without **the seal,** survive the great ordeal to enter the presence of God. The **hundred and forty-four thousand,** then, are identical with the great throng from every nation. This conclusion is confirmed by the description of them as God's **servants.** In John's vocabulary servant is almost synonymous with prophet and prophet with martyr (see esp. x. 7; xi. 3, 18; xix. 10). Those who receive the seal are thus the prophet-martyrs who in the following vision are seen to emerge triumphantly from the great ordeal.

Farrer has put forward an interesting suggestion to explain the relation between the symbolic number and the countless reality. John, he believes, was using as a pattern the census of 1 Chronicles iv-vii, in which the twenty-four thousand from each of the twelve tribes are heads of families, with no account taken of their wives and children. A census might properly be taken 'by genealogy', whereas complete numeration, as David discovered to his cost (2 Sam. xxiv), was an encroachment on the omniscience of God. So here in Revelation we have the countless families symbolized by their heads of households. Attractive as it seems, this theory has two weaknesses: it assumes, wrongly as we shall see, that the martyrs are the whole church, and it overlooks the distinction between the literal warfare of Israel and the figurative warfare of Christian martyrdom. The census of the Chronicler is a military roll-call of warriors drawn up in battle array, and it is understandable that in such a company there should be no place for women and children. But when the Lamb appears on Mount Zion with his **hundred and forty-four thousand,** marshalled for the great battle from which they are to emerge as victors, these are not just heads of families but the whole army of martyrs with no distinction of age or sex. There is in fact no need to go outside the Revelation itself to find an explanation for the relation between the two visions. In John's vision of the heavenly council he heard a voice speak of the Lion of Judah, and when he looked to see this Lion he in fact saw a Lamb. The scriptural image had been transformed by the historic fact. So in the present passage what John *hears* is the scriptural image of the army of Israel, but what he *sees* is the Christian fact of the noble army of martyrs.

We now have to ask whether John believed that the whole church or only a part of it was destined to undergo martyrdom. If we are to be consistent in our interpretation of this vision, we are bound to say that he expected only partial martyrdom. For if **the tribes of Israel** represent the whole church, then **twelve thousand from** each **tribe** can mean only a proportion of the church marked out by God's seal for special service. This by itself would admittedly be tenuous evidence on which to base an important conclusion. But we have already had the evidence of the letters to the churches, and particularly the letter to Sardis, which shows that in John's estimation the Conquerors were not the only faithful Christians. Even more important is the vision of xi. 4 ff., where the martyrs are symbolized by two lampstands, in contrast with the seven lampstands which represent the church in its fulness.

In second-century Christianity baptism was regularly spoken of as a seal (Herm. *Sim.* ix. 16. 4; for other references see Charles, Vol. I, p. 197), and it is probable that this usage has its roots in the New Testament (2 Cor. i. 22; Eph. i. 13; iv. 30). But there is no thought of baptism in John's vision of the sealing. **The seal** is given only to prospective martyrs to protect them from a specific danger. There are two Old Testament passages which have contributed to the picture, even though they do not wholly determine its meaning. One is Ezekiel's vision of seven angels, one with a writing case who marks the foreheads of all loyal servants of God, and six with swords to kill all the citizens of Jerusalem who do not bear the protective mark (Ezek. ix. 1 ff.). Ezekiel himself may well have had in mind the second passage, the story of the Israelites in Egypt marking their doorposts and lintels with the blood of the paschal lamb to protect them from the angel of death (Exod. xii. 23). In each case the mark is a protection against the destructive agents of a divine judgment. Now John undoubtedly envisaged the great martyrdom as a new Exodus (xv. 2-4), so that the sealing can properly be regarded as part of the new Passover; if the martyrs are not actually marked with the blood of the Lamb, they are certainly marked with his name (xiv. 1). But from what danger does **the seal** protect them, since clearly it does not protect them from a martyr's death? This is one question to which John has supplied an unambiguous answer. The **angel rising out of the east**—where the Sun of Righteousness himself rises—tells **the four** restraining **angels** not to let loose the destructive **winds** until the sealing is effected. The sealing therefore must be a protection from the disasters which the **winds,** who are also the four horsemen, are permitted to inflict on the earth. Others may die in these disasters, but not the martyrs; not because their persons are inviolate (cf. *Ps. Sol.* xv. 8), but because God has another and more significant death in store for them. We are reminded of Jesus, confident in his immunity from any threat of Herod, because Jerusalem has first claim on the blood of God's prophets (Luke xiii. 33); or of Paul, assured that he cannot be allowed to die in a mere shipwreck, because God has determined that he shall stand before Caesar (Acts xxvii. 24). For the man who knows himself to be designated for martyrdom war, famine, pestilence, and earthquake have no terrors.

One further question remains. If the martyrs are thus protected by **the seal of God,** what of the rest of the church? Are they left unprotected against the ravages of the four horsemen? There is to be sure no reason why John should not have thought so. He must have faced the fact that Christians die by other deaths than martyrdom, and sometimes by violent causes; and, except in the case of the martyrs, the cause of a man's death has

singularly little to do with his eternal destiny. It is likely however that the solution lies elsewhere. Although, literally speaking, Christians live on the earth and in the cities of the Roman
Empire, in places where Satan has his throne, in John's figurative language they are not among those whom he calls inhabitants
of earth, nor do they have their home in the city which is
allegorically called Sodom and Egypt, where their Lord was
crucified (xi. 8). They have obeyed the call to come out from
her, so as not to participate in her sins (xviii. 4). They have gone
forth to Jesus outside the camp (Heb. xiii. 11). Their home is in
the wilderness, where they live under God's care (xii. 6, 14).
Only the martyrs need the special protection of the Passover
seal, because their vocation is to bear their prophetic witness in
the streets of the figurative Egypt (xi. 7-8).

5-8   John's list of twelve **tribes** has three peculiarities: the position
of **Judah,** the extraordinary placing of the 'concubine tribes',
and the omission of Dan. In Old Testament lists where **Judah**
comes first the reason is geographical—the tribes are being
enumerated from south to north; but here the reason is that
Judah is the Messiah's own tribe (Num. ii, vii, xxxiv; Jud.
i. 17 ff.; Josh. xxi. 4 ff.; 1 Chron. iv-vii). All tribal lists are
either genealogical or geographical in arrangement, and this list
clearly belongs to the first category. But the four 'concubine
tribes' (Manasseh being a substitute for Dan) for some reason
interrupt the sequence of the Leah tribes. The easiest way of
dealing with this anomaly is to assume with G. B. Gray,[1] that
verses 5 and 6 have been displaced and ought to be restored to
their proper position, either at the end of the list or after verse
8a. On the other hand, Gray himself pointed out that in the
Old Testament lists there are no less than eighteen different
arrangements of the tribes, so that it is unwise to assume that
any one order is more rational or more traditional than another.
Farrer proposes to account for the order by relating the list of
the tribes to the description of the holy city in xxi. 12-21.
Since the city has twelve gates, each bearing the name of one
of the tribes of Israel, and the length of each side is twelve
thousand furlongs, there is an undeniable connexion between
the passages. But this connexion can be used to explain the

[1] 'The Lists of the Twelve Tribes', *The Expositor* (1902), pp. 225-240.

anomalous order of the tribes only if we suppose that John laid the tribes out on a diagram according to one principle and then read them off according to a different one.

Irenaeus (*Haer.* v. 30. 2) tells us that John substituted Manasseh for Dan because Dan was the tribe from which the Antichrist was expected to come, and in support of this contention he quotes Jeremiah viii. 16. From the Rabbinic writings it would seem that this was a traditional interpretation of this text from Jeremiah, on the grounds that Dan was one of the places where Jeroboam set up his idolatrous calf-worship (*Sanh.* 96ª; *Beresh. R.* 43. 2; *Targ. Jer.* I on Ex. xvii. 8). In the *Testament of Dan* (v. 6) Satan is said to be the tribe's prince. And this attitude to Dan may be as old as the Chronicler, who also omits Dan from his list, making up the number by including both Ephraim and Manasseh.

vii. 9-17. THE SONG OF VICTORY

(9) After this I looked, and there I saw a vast throng, which no one could count, from every nation, tribe, people, and tongue, standing in front of the throne and the Lamb, robed in white and with palms in their hands. (10) They were shouting aloud, 'Victory to our God who sits on the throne and to the Lamb!' (11) All the angels were standing round the throne and the elders and the living creatures, and they fell on their faces before the throne and worshipped God. (12) 'Amen!' they said; 'praise, glory, and wisdom, thanksgiving and honour, power and might be to our God for ever and ever! Amen.'

(13) Then one of the elders spoke to me and said, 'These people in white robes—who are they and where have they come from?' (14) I answered, 'You know, my lord, not I.' He said to me, 'They are the people who are coming through the great ordeal; they have washed their robes and made them white in the life-blood of the Lamb. (15) That is why they stand before the throne of

God and serve as his ministers day and night in his
temple; and he who sits on the throne will dwell among
them. (16) They shall never be hungry or thirsty again;
never again shall the sun strike them nor any scorching
heat, (17) for the Lamb who is in the heart of the throne
will be their shepherd and will guide them to the springs
of the water of life; and God will wipe every tear from
their eyes.'

10   The word here translated **victory** (*soteria*) is used elsewhere
in the New Testament to mean 'salvation'. But this cannot be
the meaning here. It is not their salvation that the martyrs are
celebrating, but their triumphant passage through persecution.
Their salvation was achieved long since, first by the act of
Christ, who loved them and released them from their sins with
his own life-blood, then by the faith which accepted his redeeming love and the baptism which had sealed the faith and
made them members of the redeemed and priestly community
(i. 6). It is worth nothing, too, that, with one minor exception,
all the New Testament writers who use *soteria* to denote the
Christian's salvation from sin also use the corresponding verb
sozein, but John never does; in his vocabulary *soteria* means
something quite different. It would be possible to take the word
here in one of the senses it bears in classical Greek—'safety',
'escape', or 'preservation', so that the martyrs would simply
be thanking God and the Lamb for providing a way of escape
from the persecution to which they have fallen victim; but
John's thought is so thoroughly biblical that this explanation is
unlikely. In the Septuagint *sozein* and *soteria* are the regular
equivalents for the Hebrew verb *yasha'* and the cognate nouns
yesha', *y'shu'ah*, and *t'shu'ah*. *Yasha'*, besides meaning 'to
save', frequently means 'to give victory to' or 'to win a victory'. In some contexts either meaning makes good sense, since
to save a beleaguered nation is the same thing as giving them
victory (see, e.g., 1 Sam. xiv. 6, 45; Ps. cxviii. 14, 15, 21). God
may be said to have granted victory to Israel (1 Chron. xi. 14;
xviii. 6; Ps. xx. 6; xliv. 4), or to have won a victory for himself
(Ps. xcviii. 1; Isa. lix. 16; lxiii. 5; Hab. iii. 8). Both ideas are
present in the martyrs' shout of triumph. For these are the

Conquerors, to whom the promise was made that they should share both the conquest and the throne of Christ (iii. 21), and they are attributing their **victory to** the **God** who was fully revealed in the Cross. In them **the Lamb** has won again the **victory** of Calvary, using only the weapons of redemptive love. But this **victory** of Christ is also the **victory** of **God** over the powers of evil which compete with him for the possession of the world. The new song with which the heavenly choir greeted the appearance of the Lamb (v. 9) is now swelled by the voices of the Conquerors.

'Sing to the Lord a new song,
For he has done marvellous deeds;
His right hand and holy arm have won him victory . . .
All the ends of the earth have seen the victory of our God.'
(Ps. xcviii. 1, 3).

The Conquerors appear **in white robes,** the symbol both of victory and of purity. That John intends the double meaning is clear, on the one hand because those who are robed in white also carry **palms in their hands,** on the other hand because they are said to **have washed their robes.** By this symbolic identification of victory with purity John prepares the way for those later visions in which the persecuting power is represented as the great whore, the seducer of the whole world (xvii-xviii), and at the same time warns his readers against an over-literal reading of his vivid military imagery. In all that follows they are never to forget that the victory is a spiritual one, the victory of faith over all that can seduce and contaminate. For it is not the threat of physical death which constitutes **the great ordeal,** so much as the grim conflict of loyalties, in **14** which a Christian may well be in genuine doubt where his duty lies, unless he keeps tight hold on the central affirmation of his faith, that the whole truth of God is to be found in Christ and him crucified. The man who, amid all the pretentious claims of imperial Rome, clings to that conviction may be said to have **made** his robe **white in the life-blood of the Lamb.** In the promise to the church of Sardis and in the vision of the fifth seal (iii. 5; vi. 11) the **white robes** were the gift of God, and John would certainly maintain that purity, victory, and eternal bliss are in no sense man's achievement. But here he gives the other side of the picture, which he holds with equal firmness. God never bestows his gifts or wins his victories without the free consent and choice of his human agents; the martyrs must wash their robes and make them white by the means which God's grace has provided.

The elder who is John's interpreter assumes that he (and we) will know what is meant by **the great ordeal.** We do indeed know that it is the testing time for which the Conquerors were being prepared by the letters to the seven churches (iii. 10), and that it will involve the completion of the roll of martyrs (vi. 11). But for further details we must wait until John is ready to give them. It is a characteristic of John's artistic method that he will introduce an idea in an exploratory fashion, sometimes more than once, before he is ready to expound it in full.

The reward of the martyrs is compounded of elements from many Old Testament promises (Isa. xlix. 10; Ezek. xxxiv. 23; Jer. ii. 13; Ps. xxiii. 2; Isa. xxv. 8). It is also in almost every detail an anticipation of the joys of the celestial city. In what way then did John conceive the two visions of bliss to be related? Are we to suppose that the present vision is wholly proleptic, and that the martyrs do not actually enter into the enjoyment of their reward until after the millennium and the last judgment? The difficulty is that throughout this passage there is a notable ambiguity of tenses. John seems in two minds whether to speak of the martyrdom as past and the heavenly triumph as present **(Where have they come from? . . . they have washed . . . they stand . . .)** or to speak of the martyrdom as present and the eternal bliss as future **(They are the people who are coming through the great ordeal . . . he who sits on the throne will dwell among them).** At one moment the standpoint is that of heaven, where the whole process is complete; at the next it is the standpoint of earthly experience. The present participle **(are coming),** however, gives the impression not only that the great ordeal is a prolonged process, which from John's temporal standpoint was partly past and partly future (cf. vi. 9-11), but also that, for the martyrs at least, entry into heaven follows immediately on physical death. Nor is this the only evidence pointing in this direction. In the

THE SEVENTH SEAL

vision of the fifth seal the martyrs were given their white robes
and told that they must wait a while for the final vindication of
God's purposes (vi. 11). The next time we hear of the martyrs
they appear as the two witnesses who are taken up to heaven
three and a half days after death 'in full view of their enemies'
(xi. 12). The full problem will emerge only when we come to the
millennium and are told that at the first resurrection the martyrs
'came to life and reigned with Christ' (xx. 4). Either John is
culpably inconsistent, or he is fully aware of the temporal
ambiguity which besets all attempts to relate time and eternity,
and has taken his own highly Semitic way of ensuring against
any possible oversimplifications.

viii. 1-5. THE SEVENTH SEAL

**(1) When the Lamb broke the seventh seal, there was
silence in heaven for what seemed half an hour. (2) Then
I saw the seven angels who stand before God, and they
were given seven trumpets. (3) Then another angel came
and stood at the altar with a golden censer; he was
given a vast quantity of incense to offer on the golden
altar before the throne in token of the prayers of all God's
people, (4) and the smoke of the incense went up from
the angel's hand to bring before God the prayers of
his people. (5) Then the angel took the censer, filled it
with fire from the altar, and threw it on the earth, and
there came peals of thunder, flashes of lightning, and
an earthquake.**

With the breaking of **the seventh seal** we expect the End,
for now the book of destiny is fully open, and the plan of God
not only fully revealed but fully achieved; yet the End does not
come. Instead John pauses for a moment before launching on
a new series of visions introduced by the **seven trumpets,**
which in turn are followed by the unnumbered visions of
chapters xii-xiv, the pouring out of the seven bowls, the fall of
Babylon, the great banquet, and the last battle. Accordingly, we

103

must pause, too, and ask what we are to make of the structure of the book.

The simplest and most obvious hypothesis would be that John's arrangement is chronological: he is describing 'what is bound to happen soon', and has set forth his visions in the order in which he expected events to happen. According to this view all the events symbolized by the **trumpets** were to be later than those symbolized by the seals and earlier than those of chapters xii ff. John, that is to say, expected that the imminent Parousia of Christ would be heralded by successive waves of earthly disaster. Now it is beyond question that in his description of the seals, the trumpets, and the bowls John has deliberately presented a crescendo of divine judgment; for the horsemen ravage a quarter of the earth, the trumpeters a third, and the bowls usher in the last plagues which bring total destruction. Yet simple chronology does not explain the structure of John's work, and even Charles, the most ardent advocate of this theory, was compelled to resort to excisions and rearrangements which other editors have found quite unconvincing. Some of the events to which John's symbols refer are manifestly not intended to be later in earthly history than all the events which precede them in the book: the birth of the Messiah, for example (xii. 1-6), or the emergence of the monster from the sea, five of whose seven heads represent kings already dead (xiii. 1; xvii. 10). Other events just as clearly occur in more than one series. The persecution of xi. 7-10 is not different from that of xiii. 7-18, nor is the judgment of Babylon in xvi. 19 different from that more fully described in the following two chapters. Moreover, we have to reckon with the completeness and finality of the number seven. **The seventh seal** *is* the End. Nothing can happen after the sounding of the seventh trumpet. God's wrath against Babylon (xvii-xviii) cannot be later than the last plagues, in which 'the wrath of God is accomplished' (xv. 1). Nor can we evade this difficulty by claiming that, although the breaking of the seventh seal is the End, this End is not a point in time but a period which encompasses within it all the contents of chapters viii-xix. For then we should have to add that the contents of chapters xii-xix are also included within the last trumpet, and the contents of chapters xvii-xix within the

last bowl—a regress of Ends, each contained within a more
comprehensive End.

A rather more plausible suggestion about the structure of
John's book is that it consists of several weeks, perhaps even a
week of weeks, beginning as it does on the Lord's day (i. 10),
and ending in the endless sabbath of the holy city. The influence
of the week can be seen in many of the Jewish speculations
about the course of history. The *Slavonic Book of Enoch*, by an
ingenious combination of the seven days of creation with Psalm
xc. 4 ('a thousand years in your sight are as yesterday'),
arrives at the theory that world history consists of seven 'days'
of a thousand years each, of which the last is to be the millennial
sabbath (2 *Enoch* xxxii. 2-xxxiii. 2). Daniel ix. 24-27 takes the
seventy years of Jeremiah's prophecy (Jer. xxv. 11-12; xxix. 10)
to mean seventy weeks of years. In 1 *Enoch* (xci. 12-17; xciii)
the so-called Apocalypse of Weeks arranges past history in
seven weeks of years. And the *Book of Jubilees*, building on the
levitical law of sabbath and jubilee (Lev. xxv. 1-17), divides
history into cycles of forty-nine years. The week has also influenced John, for it is the source of his symbolic number seven,
and, after the same fashion as 2 *Enoch*, of his millennium. How
convenient and convincing it would be if we could plot out the
contents of John's book in seven groups of seven! But any
attempt to do so founders on a reef of difficulties. There is the
awkward fact that all the examples cited from Jewish literature
are concerned with chronological sequence, and we have just
seen that John's material cannot be forced into any such framework. Then again, John has provided numbers for four series
of seven, but has left the rest of his visions unnumbered. He
tells us that, at the end of the trumpet series, he heard seven
thunders, but was forbidden to write down what they said
(x. 4). The succession of sevens is thus deliberately broken,
and instead of a new septet we have the unnumbered visions of
chapters xii-xiv. If we attempt to do what John himself has
so explicitly refrained from doing and force these chapters into a
sevenfold scheme, we soon find that this can be done only at
the cost of extreme artificiality. It is hardly surprising therefore
that among advocates of such a scheme there is no agreement
about the division of the material into its seven constituent

visions.[1] But the most serious objection to imposing a septiform pattern on the Revelation is that it obliterates the important distinction between numbered and unnumbered visions. John is like an expert guide in an art gallery, lecturing to students about a vast mural. First he makes them stand back to absorb a general impression, then he takes them close to study the details. In John's symbolic language seven is the number of completeness, and the sevenfold visions—seals, trumpets, and bowls—are his general views of the totality of divine judgment. The unnumbered visions are his close-ups, his studies of detail. They are not meant to be a comprehensive view and therefore do not constitute a seven. This explains why the numbered visions are more stereotyped and appear at first sight to add little or nothing to the teaching of the Old Testament, from which John has derived his framework. It is in the unnumbered visions and those which interrupt the sequences of seven that John is able to bring his Christian insight most powerfully to bear, and so to transform the whole corpus of his traditional imagery.

The unity of John's book, then, is neither chronological nor arithmetical, but artistic, like that of a musical theme with variations, each variation adding something new to the significance of the whole composition. This is the only view which does adequate justice to the double fact that each new series of visions both recapitulates and develops the themes already stated in what has gone before.

1-5   When the Lamb breaks **the seventh seal,** instead of the denouement there is a dramatic **silence.** It is as though there is one bar's rest for the whole orchestra and choir of heaven before they launch on the second of John's symphonic variations. Yet the **silence** has a traditional and theological significance as well as an artistic one. According to the Talmud (*Ḥag.* 12[b]; *'Abodah Z.* 3[b]), the angels sing unceasingly throughout the night, but are silent by day to allow the praises of Israel to be

[1] Four totally different solutions are offered by E. Lohmeyer (*Handbuch zum Neuen Testament*), who is followed by M. Rist (*Interpreter's Bible*); M. Kiddle (*Moffatt Commentary*); A. M. Farrer (*A Rebirth of Images*); and Hanns Lilje (*The Last Book of the Bible*). Dr. Farrer has recently abandoned the attempt to detect sevens except where John has indicated them (*The Revelation of St. John the Divine*).

heard in heaven. In John's heaven the choir sings day and night
(iv. 8 f.), and therefore a special interval must be left when **the
prayers of all God's people** may be heard. **The prayers**
are presented to God by an **angel** in the form of **incense.**
John's somewhat erratic grammar leaves us, to be sure, in some
doubt what relationship he intended between **incense** and
prayers. The phrases **'in token of'** and **'to bring'** in the
translation render nothing more than a simple dative in the
Greek, and some scholars have taken the view that the **incense**
was to be offered with or mingled with **the prayers** (so RSV
and NEB). But in v. 8 John has already spoken of seeing 'bowls
full of incense, the prayers of God's people', and it is reasonable to infer that in this passage too the **incense** is the symbol
of **the prayers** and the means by which they are brought
before God (the datives being datives of reference). It is to
be noted that these prayers come not from the martyrs alone,
like the prayers of vi. 9, but from **all God's people.** Some
things God bestows on men whether they ask or not, whether
they acknowledge the gift or not (Matt. v. 45). But some gifts
he withholds until men pray. Just as the seals could not be
broken until the Lamb had won the right to break them by his
obedience on earth, so the **trumpets** cannot sound until the
prayers of men have reached **the altar** of heaven. God will
not win his victories through the devotion of the martyrs alone,
but only if that devotion is supported by the prayers of the
whole church. The holy **fire** of his purpose becomes effective
on earth only when mingled with **the incense** of prayer.

Like the **angel** with the **censer the seven angels** are 2
Angels of the Presence, 'the seven holy angels who present the
prayers of God's people and enter into the presence of the Holy
One' (Tobit xii. 15). But what is the significance of the **trumpets** they carry? We know from the New Testament that the
last trumpet had already in Christian usage become the conventional signal for the Parousia of Christ (Matt. xxiv. 31;
1 Cor. xv. 52; 1 Thess. iv. 16), and this is beyond question the
meaning of John's seventh trumpet. But it is not a sufficient
explanation of his complex imagery to say that, since in the
Revelation everything comes in sevens, the last trumpet must
be the last of seven, and then to treat all seven merely as

heralds of the final crisis of history. We have already seen more
than one example of John's ability to combine in a single symbol
ideas drawn from many different sources, and we must expect
to find that his **trumpets** have the wealth of association which
the trumpet bears in the Old Testament and the Jewish
liturgy.[1] These associations may be classified under four heads.

(*a*) There are three Old Testament passages which speak of
seven trumpeters who formed part of a ceremonial procession,
and two of these include a mention of the ark (Josh. vi; 1. Chron.
xv. 24; Neh. xii. 41). The earliest of them is the story of the fall
of Jericho. Joshua's army marched round the city once every
day for six days and seven times on the seventh, led by seven
priests with trumpets, who were the escort for the sacred ark;
and when the priests blew their final blast and the army shouted,
the walls of the city fell flat. John must have had this story in
mind when he wrote; for he tells us that with the blowing of the
seventh trumpet the ark appeared (xi. 19), and also that one of
the consequences of the trumpet blasts was that a tenth of the
great city fell (xi. 13). Like ancient Jericho, which blocked the
entry of Israel into the promised land, Babylon the Great must
fall before God's people can find their permanent home in the
new Jerusalem (cf. Jer. li. 27). The typological parallel is clear,
yet it is only a partial parallel; for only a tenth of the city is said
to fall. There is something provisional about this blowing of
trumpets, for which we need a further explanation. (*b*) A trumpet was blown to proclaim the accession of a king (1 Kings
i. 34, 39; 2 Kings ix. 13), and came in the Jewish worship to be
associated particularly with the kingship of God (Ps. xlvii. 5;
xcviii. 6; Num. xxiii. 21; Zech. ix. 14). John's seventh trumpet
is the signal for the heavenly choir to sing their coronation
anthem, praising God because he has assumed the sovereignty
and begun to reign (xi. 15). (*c*) There are passages in the Old
Testament where the trumpet is an alarm signal, summoning

---

[1] Hebrew has two words for trumpet, *shophar* (ram's horn) and *hᵉṣoṣᵉrah*,
the metal trumpet, such as Moses made for ceremonial use (Num. x. 2). But
both are translated in the LXX by the one Greek word *salpinx*, and there is no
reason to suppose that John would be thinking of one rather than the other.
At a later date the Rabbis insisted on the distinction between the two,
particularly at the New Year festival, but in Old Testament times they seem
to have been used indiscriminately for many of the same purposes.

Israel to national repentance in the face of imminent divine
judgment (Jer. iv. 5; vi. 1, 17; Ezek. xxxiii. 3 ff.; Isa. lviii. 1;
Joel ii. 1, 15). John too believed that the purpose of the trumpet
blasts and the disasters they heralded was to call men to repentance, even if that purpose was not achieved. 'The rest of
mankind who survived these plagues still did not renounce the
gods of their own making' (ix. 20; cf. Amos iv. 6-11). Like
Jeremiah he knew that men could be too far gone in idolatry and
immorality to heed the divine trumpet call.

> 'I will appoint watchmen over you;
> listen for the trumpet call.'
> But they said, 'We will not listen.'
> (Jer. vi. 17).

But the very obdurate refusal of men to listen serves to enhance
the one thing that Jeremiah did not know, the power of the
Cross to batter down the walls of men's complacency through
the witness of the martyrs.

(d) In the Jewish liturgy trumpets were blown at all feasts, on
the first day of each month, and at the daily sacrifice 'for remembrance before your God' (Num. x. 10; cf. Ecclus. l. 16).
That is to say, the trumpet blast was a ritual expression of
Israel's constant prayer that God would remember his nation
and by remembering them assure them of pardon, protection,
and vindication. But the Feast of Trumpets *par excellence* was
the autumn festival of Tishri 1, described in the levitical code
as 'a remembrance day of trumpet blowing' (Lev. xxiii. 24).
In Rabbinic times this day came to be known as New Year,
though even then it was in fact only the beginning of the civil
year; the ecclesiastical year still began, as it had always done,
six months earlier on Nisan 1 (Exod. xii. 2). In the levitical code
Tishri 1 is called the first day of the seventh month and has no
connexion with New Year. It is rather the first day of the great
penitential season which culminates ten days later in the Day
of Atonement (Ezek. xlv. 20).[1] It is in fact the Day of Judgment.
In the Talmud (*Rosh H.* 16ᵃ) the Mishnah declares that, while
God judges the world at Passover in respect of produce, at

[1] For the proof of this assertion see N. H. Snaith, *The Jewish New Year
Festival*, pp. 150 ff.

Pentecost in respect of fruit, and at Tabernacles in respect of
rain, Tishri 1 is the day when he judges all mankind. The
Gemara adds that, except in the cases of the totally good or
totally bad, judgment is held in suspense until the Day of
Atonement. Another statement in the Gemara on the same
passage is even more illuminating: 'If a calamity or misfortune
happens to a man before the Day of Atonement, it is in virtue
of a judgment passed on the last Day of Atonement; if after the
Day of Atonement, of a judgment passed on the one just gone'.
In a later chapter of the same tract (16ᵇ) it is said that the
trumpets of Tishri 1 are blown to confuse Satan, and this is
further proof that the Rabbis regarded this day as the Day of
Judgment; for to them as to John (xii. 10) Satan was the
prosecuting counsel in the heavenly lawcourt. All this means
that to the Rabbis the season from Tishri 1 to Tishri 10 was
an annual anticipation of the final Day of Judgment, at which
divine sentences were passed which took effect not at death nor
at the end of time but during the course of man's earthly life.
But if John was accustomed, as we may well suppose he was,
to this ritual anticipation of the last day, it must have profoundly affected his attitude to eschatology. He would find it
just as easy to see the Day of the Lord anticipated in the decisive
events of history, and it would never have occurred to him to
think that any account of eschatological events would ever be
taken with meticulous pedantry to refer only to the ultimate
future.

Here then is the full and rich background to John's trumpet
imagery. But can we really suppose that all this welter of ideas
actually passed through his mind, and that he supposed his
readers would be prompted into following his train of thought
by the mere mention of the word trumpet? These are questions
which we ought constantly to ask ourselves; for the history of
exegesis of the Revelation shows how fatally easy it is for commentators to read into John's symbols ideas of their own culled
from a variety of alien sources. In this case the answer is to be
found partly in the synagogue liturgy and partly in John's own
statements. In the ritual for Tishri 1 the trumpet blowing was
accompanied by the recital of three sets of scriptural verses
drawn from a wide range of contexts: *Malkiyyoth* (verses about

kingship), *Zikronoth* (remembrance verses), and *Shopharoth* (trumpet verses). Whether the anthologies of verses preserved in the Rabbinic writings go back to the first century, we have no means of knowing, but the practice is certainly an old one. John must have been accustomed to hearing, along with the synagogue or temple trumpets, verses which spoke of the kingship of God, of God's remembering his people, and of the blowing of trumpets, including many of the passages to which reference has been made above. As for his readers, some of them would be acquainted with Jewish practices. But in any case John himself has told them clearly enough that the trumpets were an escort for the ark, a proclamation of the divine sovereignty, and a summons to general repentance; and by placing them in the hands of the Angels of the Presence he has indicated their close association with worship.

V

THE SEVEN TRUMPETS

viii. 6-12. THE NATURAL PLAGUES

(6) Then the seven angels who held the seven trumpets prepared to blow them. (7) The first blew his trumpet; and there came hail and fire mixed with blood, falling upon the earth. A third of the earth was burnt, a third of the trees were burnt, and all the green grass was burnt. (8) Then the second angel blew his trumpet; and what seemed a huge mountain ablaze with fire fell into the sea. A third of the sea turned to blood, (9) a third of the living creatures in it died, and a third of the ships were sunk. (10) Then the third angel blew his trumpet; and a huge star blazing like a torch dropped from the sky, and fell on a third of the rivers and fresh-water springs. (11) The name of the star was Wormwood; and a third of the water turned to wormwood, and people died of the water in large numbers, because it was poisoned. (12) Then the fourth angel blew his trumpet; a plague fell on a third of the sun and a third of the moon and a third of the stars, so that the third part of them turned dark, and there was no light for a third of the day and also of the night.

7   The first four **trumpet** blasts usher in a series of natural disasters, affecting earth, salt water, fresh water, and sky. In each case the devastation is restricted to one **third**; these plagues are God's judgment on human sin, but not his final judgment. They are intended to lead men to repentance. When the seventh angel trumpeter proclaims that God has assumed his sovereign power and begun the reign from which all things unclean must be for ever excluded, then and only then will the door of repentance be closed. That will be the time for 'destroying the destroyers of the earth' (xi. 18), when it is too late for any further change of character: 'let the wrong-doer still do wrong and the filthy remain in his filth; let the upright man still

do right and the holy continue in his holiness' (xxii. 11). But until then the heavenly trumpets will not cease to sound the alarm.

Modern readers are apt to be shocked at the idea that God should be prepared to kill off **large numbers** of men in order 11 to provide an object lesson for those who survive. John is more realistic about the fact of death. All men must die, and the question mark which death sets over their existence is just as great whether they die late or soon, alone or in company, violently or in their beds. Their ultimate destiny is not determined either by the moment or by the manner of their death, as the untimely death of the martyrs should prove, but by the opening of the heavenly books and by the true and just judgments which proceed from the great white throne (xx. 11-15). The idea that life on earth is so infinitely precious that the death which robs us of it must be the ultimate tragedy is precisely the idolatry that John is trying here to combat. We have already seen (see note on vi. 10) that John calls the enemies of the church 'the inhabitants of earth', because they have made themselves utterly at home in this transient world order. If all men must die, and if at the end heaven and earth must vanish, along with those whose life is irremediably bounded by worldly horizons, then it is surely in accord with the mercy of God that he should send men from time to time forceful reminders of the insecurity of their tenure.

The details of the plagues are drawn for the most part from 7- the seventh, first, and ninth of the plagues of Egypt, the plagues 11 of hail, blood, and darkness. The addition of **blood** to the plague of **hail and fire** is probably due simply to a memory of the portents of Joel ii. 30. But John makes a number of other changes to adapt the Old Testament material to his own purpose. He divides the plague on the Nile into two, partly to make a group of four corresponding to the four horsemen of the seal visions, partly because the plagues must be transferred from their local setting in Egypt to cover the whole natural order. The turning of the Nile **to blood** not only killed the fish but made its **water** undrinkable. Rather than repeat the same plague twice John has looked for a new symbol for the pollution of drinking **water,** and has found it in the story of the bitter water of Marah (Exod. xv. 23) and in God's threat to idolatrous Israel: 'I will feed this people with wormwood and give them poisonous water to drink' (Jer. ix. 15; cf. xxiii. 15).

8   Two other changes are considerably more allusive. The turning of **the sea** to **blood** is effected by the fall of **what seemed a huge mountain ablaze with fire.** It is possible that John means us to understand by this phrase a falling star, like the star **Wormwood** in the third plague; for Enoch has a vision of 'seven stars like great burning mountains', which turn out to be fallen angels (1 *Enoch* xviii. 13), and in the *Sibylline Oracles* (v. 158) a star falling into the sea brings about the destruction of Babylon (Rome). It is, however, more probable that here as elsewhere the sources of John's imagery are to be sought within the Old Testament, and that he is echoing Jeremiah's dirge over the fall of Babylon. This chapter of Jeremiah was undoubtedly one of the main sources of John's own dirge over the fall of Babylon in chapter xviii, and possibly also the source of his mysterious name Armageddon (xvi. 16).

> 'I am against you, destroying mountain,
> Destroyer of the whole earth.
> I will stretch out my hand against you
> And topple you over your crags,
> And make you a blazing mountain . . .
> The sea has engulfed Babylon,
> She is covered by its turbulent waves.'
>
> (Jer. li. 25, 42).

If John is indeed alluding to this passage, then he is preparing the way by the most subtle of hints, not only for those later visions in which he treats Rome as the current embodiment of Babylon, but also for his theological exposition of the self-destroying power of evil. God uses the 'blazing mountain' of Babylon, the 'destroyer of the whole earth', to pollute **the sea** on which Babylon itself depends for the maintenance of its commercial empire (cf. xviii. 9-19).

10-   That John's mind worked in this allusive fashion is confirmed
11   by his immediately following vision of the falling **star Wormwood.** The name, as we have seen comes from Jeremiah, but the image of the falling **star** has another origin. An ancient

myth told how Heylel, the morning star (Venus), tried to climb
the walls of the northern city of the gods to make himself king
of heaven, only to be driven from the sky by the rising sun. In
Isaiah xiv. 12-20 this myth is given a historical application. The
part of Heylel is played by the king of Babylon who has tried
to rival God.

> 'How you have fallen from heaven, Heylel, star of the morn-
>   ing!
> How you are felled to the earth, prostrate over the nations,
> You who said to yourself, "I will climb the sky,
> High above God's stars I will set my throne
> I will take my seat on the mountain of assembly in the far
>   north,
> I will soar above the highest clouds and rival the Most High."'

It cannot be accidental that John has used in such quick succession echoes of two Old Testament prophecies which have
to do with the fall of ancient Babylon. We are justified therefore
in supposing that **Wormwood** is the **star** of the new Babylon,
which has **poisoned** by its idolatry the **springs** of its own life.
When Babylon's star drops from the zenith, Babylon's ruin is
at hand.

    None of these details, however, compares in importance with
the salient fact that John likens the disasters of his own time to
the plagues of Egypt. This is the first statement of a typological
theme which he will develop in great detail in subsequent
chapters. Like other New Testament writers he believes that the
church is the new Israel (i. 6) and its redemption the new
Exodus (xv. 2-3). He is about to designate Rome 'the great
city which is figuratively called . . . Egypt' (xi. 8). Thus it
seems natural to him that the new Exodus should be preceded
by plagues, and this parallel materially assists his pastoral
object. For we must never forget in our wrestling with John's
symbolism that his book is not a manifesto hurled at a pagan
civilization, but a pastoral letter designed to strengthen and
comfort his fellow-Christians on the eve of martyrdom. His
Egyptian typology is an emphatic way of saying that present
disasters are but a prelude to God's great deliverance. In each
of the heavenly trumpet blasts God is saying to the Pharoah

of the new Egypt, 'Let my people go!' And at the same time he is saying to the Christians, 'When all this begins to happen, breathe again and hold you heads high, because your rescue is at hand' (Luke xxi. 28).

viii. 13 - ix. 12. THE FIRST WOE

(13) Then I looked and I heard an eagle crying aloud as it flew in mid-heaven, 'Woe, woe, woe to the inhabitants of earth because of the trumpet blasts which the last three angels are about to blow!' (1) Then the fifth angel blew his trumpet; and I saw a star fallen from heaven to earth, and he was given the key to the shaft of the abyss. (2) He opened the shaft of the abyss; and out of the shaft rose smoke like smoke from a huge furnace, and the sun and the air were darkened by the smoke from the shaft. (3) Out of the smoke locusts spread over the earth, and they were given such powers as earthly scorpions have. (4) They were told to do no harm to the grass or to any plant or tree on the earth, but only to those men who did not have God's seal on their foreheads; (5) they were allowed to torment them for five months, but not to kill them, and their torment was like a scorpion's sting. (6) While that time lasts, men will seek death but will not find it; they will long to die, but death will elude them. (7) In appearance the locusts were like horses equipped for battle, and on their heads were what looked like golden crowns. Their faces were like human faces, (8) they had hair like women's hair and teeth like lions' teeth. (9) They had chests like iron breastplates, and the noise of their wings was like the rattling of many chariots as their horses charge into battle. (10) They had tails and stings like scorpions, and in their tails lay their power to hurt mankind for five months. (11) They had as their king the angel of the abyss, whose name in Hebrew is Abaddon and in Greek Apollyon. (12) The first woe is over; but there are still two woes to come.

The sequence of trumpets is interrupted by the portentous
screech of **an eagle,** designed to give solemn emphasis to the **13**
last three blasts. It does violence to John's use of symbols to
suggest that this **eagle** is identical with the fourth living
creature from the heavenly throne (iv. 7). The Lion of Judah
is not to be equated with the first of the creatures, nor is the
sinister rider of vi. 2 to be identified with the heavenly figure of
xix. 11. It may be that John intends to maintain the Exodus
typology which is so much in evidence throughout the trumpet
series. For in a later vision he makes an unmistakable reference
to the words spoken by God to Moses at Mount Sinai: 'You
have seen what I did to the Egyptians, and how I carried you on
eagles' wings and brought you here to me' (Exod. xix. 4). If
this is what John has in mind, then the **eagle** is yet another
reminder to the church that the plagues are but the birth-pangs
of God's new age (cf. Mark. xiii. 8). On the other hand, this
same Greek word *aetos* is regularly used in the Septuagint and
in the New Testament of the vulture as well as of the **eagle,**
and it is possible that we ought so to translate it here (cf. Luke
xvii. 37); for a vulture hovering over a dying beast is an obvious
symbol of doom, and in one Old Testament passage it is the
cause for the sounding of a trumpet alarm.

> 'Up to your lips with the trumpet!
> There is a vulture over the house of the Lord.'
> (Hos. viii. 1).

The **eagle** or vulture with its warning of intensified suffering
can hardly have been introduced merely for artistic effect. Such
a solemn declaration must mean that there is a theological
reason why the last plagues are to be worse than the first. As so
often happens in this book, John prompts us to ask the question
some time before he is ready to supply the answer, and we must
have the patience to let him expound his theme in his own way
(see notes on xi. 15-19).

At the blowing of **the fifth trumpet** John sees an angel, whom **1**
he describes as a **fallen star.** There is all the difference in the
world between this fallen angel, to whom **was given the key to
the shaft of the abyss,** and the angel of xx. 1, whom John sees
descending from heaven with the key of the abyss in his hand.

The difference is not just that the one releases the destroyers
and the other locks them up. The one is an evil agent acting
by divine permission—he was given (*edothe*) the key (see on
vi. 1-8), the other a good agent voluntarily carrying out the
beneficent purpose of God. It is not God's gracious purpose that
men or angels should disobey him, but he allows them to do so,
knowing that he can use even their disobedience to further his
own good designs. It is not God's gracious purpose that the
denizens of the abyss be let loose to ravage the earth, but he
allows evil to be evil's own destruction.

We must not imagine, however, that John intends us to take
either the **fallen star** or **the abyss** more literally than any of
his other symbols. There is no place in his thinking for any
precosmic fall of angels who can be blamed for subsequently
corrupting the earth. He believes as firmly as any other New
Testament writer that evil has its origin in human sin. We have
already seen (1. 20) that the angels of the churches are to be
understood as the heavenly counterparts of the earthly communities, and that their status before God is determined by the
record of the churches they represent. Having given us this
explicit clue at the outset, John expects us to be able to apply
it again without reminder. It was the generally accepted view
of his time, among Jews and Christians alike, that earthly institutions had their representative angels, as witness Paul's
frequent mention of the principalities and powers which presided over the political, social, and religious institutions of the
Roman empire. A fallen angel represents some aspect of the
corporate life of men which is in open revolt against the purpose
of God.

To understand **the abyss** we must revert to the creation
myth in which we have already found the origin of the heavenly
sea of glass (iv. 6). According to the mythical view of creation,
God subdued the ocean monster of chaos (Tiamat or Leviathan
or Rahab), and out of the two halves of its body made heaven
and earth. In Genesis 1 this myth survives in the division of the
waters above the firmament from the waters under the earth,
and in the word *Tehom* (the Deep), which in the Septuagint is
translated by the Greek word *abyssos*. No doubt the ancients
really believed in a three-storey universe, but this is not quite

the same thing as saying that they took it literally. They believed in it for theological rather than geographical reasons. They recognized that within God's ordered universe there were elements still recalcitrant to his will, and in their world view the heavenly sea above and the abyss beneath symbolized all that had so far escaped the control of the divine sovereignty, a reservoir of evil from which human wickedness received constant reinforcing supplies. This does not mean that they put the blame for moral evil on impersonal forces beyond the determining influence and responsibility of man. The infernal reservoir was fed from the springs of human vice. It was the collective bad conscience of the race, from which came the haunting and avenging furies. One theory about the origin of the demons who inhabited the abyss was that they were the offspring of the illicit union between angels and women (1 *Enoch* vi. ff.; cf. Gen. vi. 1-13); but this was itself only a symptom of the general moral corruption of mankind. Another theory was that demons were the product of human idolatry; by worshipping that which is not God men set loose into the world demonic forces which corrupted the whole of life (Wis. xiv. 12 ff.). In 1 *Enoch* xcviii. 4 f. evil is expressly attributed to human origins. Both sides of the problem of evil are put in Wisdom i. 13-16 and ii. 23-24; God did not make death, which entered the world through the spite of the devil, but only because ungodly men by word and deed summoned death to themselves. The abyss, then, represents the cumulative power and virulence of evil, to which all men contribute, and by which all men, whether they choose or not, are affected.

Out of the pit John sees emerge a swarm of **locusts,** a further **2-3** reminder of the plagues of Egypt. His description owes a great deal to the first two chapters of Joel, in which the prophet depicts a plague of **locusts** as if they were an invading army of the Lord, sent out to punish the sins of God's people and to summon them to repentance. There is an element of realism too in the picture: the first appearance of a locust swarm above the horizon does look like a billowing cloud of **smoke** and can be dense enough to darken **the sun;** at one stage in their development locusts have a remarkable resemblance to **horses** **7-9** **equipped for battle,** as Joel had already noticed; and their

antennae bear comparison with waving **hair.** Nevertheless, this is no natural plague like the first four. These are demonic **locusts;** instead of injuring **grass** and plants they are to injure
10 **men,** they are armed with **a scorpion's sting,** and, unlike the natural locusts, they have a **king** (cf. Prov. xxx. 27). It is the more noteworthy that they are said to have **human faces.** Evil may take many sinister forms and ramify far beyond the immediate implications of individual sin; but in the last analysis it has a human face, for it is caused by the rebellion of human wills against the will of God.

Human wrong-doing returns with demonic venom to torment either its perpetrator or his associates or descendants. But the main point that John wishes to make is that this process of retribution is controlled and limited by God. The angel may open **the shaft of the abyss** only because he is **given the key.** The **locusts torment** men **for five months** only, and then only because they are **allowed.** Just as the natural plagues were limited in scope to one third, so this plague is limited in time. Evil is in its nature self-destructive; but God in his mercy limits its effects in order that men may see in their suffering a trumpet blast of heaven calling them to repentance.

11 **The angel of the abyss,** who is said to be **king** over the demon locusts, is probably the same as the angel who was allowed to unlock the pit from which they came. He is called by two names, each meaning the Destroyer. **Abaddon** occurs six times in the Old Testament as a synonym for Sheol or Hades, the universal graveyard, the land of death, darkness, silence, and oblivion, the destroyer of life and hope. John has personified **Abaddon,** just as earlier he personified Death and Hades; and the three are all variations on a single theme. **Apollyon** occurs nowhere else as a proper name. A possible explanation is that John intended a sidelong attack on the god Apollo, and indirectly on the emperor Domitian, who liked to be regarded as Apollo incarnate (cf. Aeschylus, *Agam.* 1082, where the name Apollo is derived from the verb *apolluein,* to destroy). But whatever be the origin of its Greek form, the purpose of the double name is to ensure that the reader, whether he knows any Hebrew or not, will understand what John is talking about when he later speaks of 'the destroyers of the earth' (xi. 18).

(13) Then the sixth angel blew his trumpet; and I heard a voice coming from the horns of the golden altar before God. (14) It said to the sixth angel, who held the trumpet: 'Release the four angels held in bonds at the great river Euphrates'. (15) So the four angels, who had been held in readiness for this very hour, day, month, and year, were let loose to kill a third of mankind. (16) Their squadrons of cavalry numbered, as I was told, twice ten thousand times ten thousand. (17) This is how the horses and their riders looked in my vision: the riders wore breastplates, fiery red, dark blue, and sulphur yellow; and the horses had heads like lions' heads, and out of their mouths came fire, smoke, and sulphur. (18) By these three plagues, the fire, the smoke, and the sulphur that came from their mouths, a third of mankind was killed. (19) The power of the horses lay in their mouths, but also in their tails; for they had tails like snakes, with heads that could inflict injury. (20) The rest of mankind who survived these plagues still did not renounce the gods of their own making, nor give up worshipping demons and idols made of gold, silver, bronze, stone, and wood, which cannot see or hear or walk. (21) Nor did they repent of their murders, their sorcery, their fornication, or their robberies.

A voice coming from the altar of incense can be construed 13 only as an answer to prayer, the prayers of the whole church already offered as incense by the Angel of the Presence (viii. 3-4). But does this mean that John thinks it right for Christians to pray and for God to grant that the civilized world should be devastated by Satanic hordes from beyond the frontier? If this were common Christian practice, Roman officials might well feel justified in condemning them on a charge of *odium humani generis*, hatred of humanity (Tac. *Ann.* xv. 44). The voice from the altar thus accentuates the question already raised by the cry of the eagle: why must horror piled on horror precede the coming of the reign of God? John is determined that his readers shall face this question with the grimmest realism before he is prepared to give the answer.

14   The threat of invasion by armies from beyond the **Euphrates** was guaranteed to produce a grue of apprehension in both Roman and Jew. For beyond the great river lay the empire of Parthia, which superstitious imagination was always ready to people with inexhaustible hordes of barbarian warriors (cf. 1 *Enoch* lvi. 5; xc. 13, 16). The Roman neurosis about Parthia began in 53 B.C. with the defeat of Crassus at Carrhae and the loss of the eagle standards of his legions, was renewed by the disgraceful capitulation of Paetus to Vologeses in A.D. 62, and was not finally exorcized until Trajan earned the title Parthicus by his victories of A.D. 114–116. To the Roman the Euphrates was the eastern frontier, but to the Jew it was the northern frontier of Palestine, across which Assyrian, Babylonian, and Persian invaders had come to impose their pagan sovereignty on the people of God. All the scriptural warnings about a foe from the north, therefore, find their echo in John's blood-curdling vision (Isa. xiv. 31; Jer. i. 14 f.; vi. 1, 22; x. 22; xiii. 20; xxv. 9, 26; xlvi. 20, 24; xlvii. 2; Ezek. xxvi. 7; xxxviii. 6, 15; xxxix. 2).

The terror of the Parthian army was its corps of mounted archers, whose tactics were to shoot one volley as they charged and another over their horses' tails as they withdrew beyond the range of the enemy's weapons. There was therefore some factual basis for John's surrealist picture of horses able to

15-19   wound with **their mouths** and **their tails.** But John is not here concerned with the possibility of a literal Parthian invasion—he has already covered that under the symbol of the rider on the white horse. This is an army straight from the jaws of hell. The snake-like **tails** of the horses indicate their Satanic nature, as emissaries of 'that old serpent' (xii. 9), and so do the **fire, smoke,** and **sulphur** which they exhale. John is using a nightmare version of a familiar first-century fear to instil a sense of some more ultimate and quintessential evil. In so doing he is heir to an apocalyptic tradition which we can trace to its source in Ezekiel's prophecy of the invasion of Gog from the land of Magog (Ezek. xxxviii-xxxix). This prophet seems to have thought of Gog as the fulfilment of earlier

prophecies of the coming of a foe from the north. But it was to
be a fulfilment with a difference. Jeremiah and others had
predicted an invasion by Israel's historic enemies as the means
by which God had chosen to punish Israel for her sins. But Gog
was to come after Israel had been punished and restored, after
peace had been restored to all the earth, so that the nations were
living in unsuspecting security (Ezek. xxxviii. 7-16), and he was
to come from beyond the horizons of the familiar world. Whatever may have been the source of this mythical figure, he
represents a most important theological affirmation: that the
powers of evil have an immense reserve army, from which they
can be steadily reinforced, so that no earthly order can find
security from attacks from beyond the frontier, except in the
final victory of God. In a world in which evil is so virulent and
tenacious, the progress of the gospel must not be expected to
produce a steady whittling away of Satan's power, until he is
reduced to impotence, but rather a steady hardening of resistance, leading inexorably to a last great battle.

John will make fuller use of the Gog myth at two later points
in his drama (xix. 11-21; xx. 7-9). For the present the part of
Gog is played by the demonic armies from beyond the **Euphrates.** Their invasion is necessary precisely because the
Roman world has tried to find security in that which is not God.
All men must worship either the God who made them or **gods 20
of their own making** and John reluctantly records that, in
spite of all God's efforts to batter his way through the defences
of men's self-sufficiency and pride, they **did not renounce**
their man-made gods. These man-made gods include not only
idols made of gold, silver, bronze, stone, and wood, but
also the **demons;** for human sin, once committed, tends to
propagate itself as an evil spirit, becoming embedded in the
individual character and insinuating itself into the fabric of
society, expressing itself in false beliefs, corrupt morals, social
evils, and political injustice. Like Paul in Romans 1, John believes that moral evils, **murders, sorcery, fornication,
robberies,** are not the fundamental sin, but only the symptom
of man's idolatry, his refusal to accept his own creaturely status
and his dependence on his Creator.

It is these demonic consequences of human sin that God

allows his angels to release against an obdurate world. Yet even
at this point their destructive powers are strictly limited in order
21 that men may have every opportunity to **repent**. Though he
uses the mythology of Gog, John is not yet ready for the final
battle or the last trumpet. God has something more to say to the
world than even a heavenly trumpet can express. It is true that
at the end of the sixth plague John comments that the survivors
still did not renounce their idolatry **nor did they repent**.
Many commentators have unwarrantably assumed that this is
John's last and irrevocable verdict on a hopelessly unregenerate
world. 'By exhausting every attempt to bring them to a better
mind, God demonstrates His sovereignty, vindicates His
holiness, and justifies His final sentence of doom.'[1] But if this
were all that could be said, John would certainly not deserve his
place in the New Testament, for his trumpets have so far
brought no revelation which could not equally be found in the
prophecies of the Old Testament. John makes good his claim
to be a Christian prophet when upon the trumpet notes of Old
Testament prophecy there supervenes a new and more hopeful
voice, the voice of the faithful witness, whose way of dealing
with sin was not to denounce but to suffer. If that voice was to
be heard in John's own day, and to succeed where the angelic
trumpets had failed, it must be heard through the living (and
dying) witness of those who were heirs to the 'testimony of
Jesus'. John interrupts his sequence of trumpets, therefore, to
explain to the prospective martyrs how indispensable is their
witness to the consummation of the redemptive purpose of God.
For until their work is done, the seventh trumpet must be
delayed.

x. 1-11. THE LITTLE SCROLL

**(1) Then I saw another mighty angel coming down from
heaven, robed in cloud, with a rainbow round his head;
his face was like the sun and his legs like pillars of fire.
(2) He held a little scroll open in his hand. He set his**

[1] M. Kiddle, *ad loc.*

right foot on the sea and his left on the land. (3) Then he gave a loud shout like the roar of a lion; and when he shouted the seven thunders spoke. (4) When the seven thunders had spoken, I was about to write, but I heard a voice from heaven saying, 'Seal up what the seven thunders have said; do not write it down'. (5) Then the angel I saw standing on sea and land raised his right hand to heaven (6) and swore by him who lives for ever and ever, who created heaven, earth, and sea, and everything in them, 'There shall be no more delay. (7) When the time shall come for the seventh angel to blow his trumpet, the secret purpose of God will have been accomplished, as he has assured his servants the prophets.'

(8) Then the voice which I had heard from heaven was speaking to me again and saying, 'Go and take the open scroll in the hand of the angel who is standing on sea and land.' (9) So I went to the angel and asked him to give me the little scroll. He said to me, 'Take it and eat it. It will be bitter to swallow, although in your mouth it will taste as sweet as honey.' (10) So I took the little scroll from the angel's hand and ate it, and in my mouth it tasted as sweet as honey, but when I swallowed it I found it bitter. (11) Then I was told, 'Once again you must prophesy over many peoples and nations and tongues and kings.'

Of all the angels who inhabit the pages of John's book only three are called **mighty**. The first mighty angel was the herald 1 who proclaimed the challenge to all comers to try their strength at opening the scroll with seven seals, and who thus prepared the way for the advent of the Lamb (v. 2). Now, in what can only be a deliberate cross-reference, John speaks of **another mighty angel,** and we are encouraged to look for a new disclosure comparable in importance to the earlier one. The description of the **angel** gives us an inkling of what to expect. He is wrapped in the **cloud** of the divine presence, and over his head is the **rainbow** of the divine mercy (cf. iv. 3). He bears the delegated attributes of deity, but he is also the angel of

Jesus Christ, whose face John has seen shining **like the sun** (cf. i. 16). The **legs like pillars of fire** are reminiscent of Israel's journeys in the wilderness. This is the angel who is to guide the new Israel through the darkness of its Exodus pil-

2 grimage from Egypt to the promised land. The **scroll** he carries, then, will contain the gospel of God's mercy, but particularly as it affects the people of God in their earthly pil-grimage. The great scroll contained the purposes of God in so far as they were to be achieved by the Lamb. The **little scroll** contains a new version of those same purposes in so far as they are to be achieved through the agency of the church. The angel plants his feet on sea and land because his message, though directed in the first instance to the few, is of eventual signifi-cance to the whole world.

3   **When he shouted, the seven thunders spoke.** To John's ear they conveyed an articulate statement, which he could have written down, had he been allowed to do so. Some of the older commentators, including J. Weiss and W. Bousset, believed

4 that the command to **seal up what the seven thunders** said was a purely literary device: John had access to a number of different apocalyptic traditions, which were known also to his readers, and he thought it necessary to explain why he had omitted from his own work one of the familiar sequences of apocalyptic woes. Charles suggested instead that John was forbidden to write down the message of the thunders because, like Paul's vision in the third heaven, it belonged to the realm of the 'ineffable things which human lips may not utter' (2 Cor. xii. 4). He accordingly labelled these two verses 'an intermezzo', though if either of these two theories were correct they would be more accurately termed an intrusion. Treated as an integral part of its context, the sealing has a weighty theological meaning. If God's prophet is ordered not to write down what he has heard the seven thunders say, but to seal it away, this can only mean that God has cancelled the doom of which they were the symbol. Other seers may depict human history as seven weeks of weeks, but not John; for him there are to be no more sevens but the last one. He is told to break in upon the sordid cavalcade of human sin and its ineluctable nemesis, because this is precisely what God himself has done.

Humanity must be stopped forthwith from endlessly producing
the means of its own torment and destruction. 'If the Lord had
not cut short the time, not a living creature could have escaped'
(Mark xiii. 20).

The angel now takes a solemn oath that **there shall be no** 5-6
more delay. At this point John begins to adapt to his own
purposes an Old Testament passage which will figure promin-
ently in many of his subsequent visions. 'I asked the man
dressed in linen, who stood on the bank of the river, "How long
will it be before the end of these portents?" The man . . . raised
his right hand and his left hand to heaven, and I heard him
swear by him who lives for ever, "It shall be a time, two times,
and a half. When the power of the persecutor of the holy people
comes to an end, all these things too will end."' (Dan. xii. 6-7).
The persecutor was Antiochus Epiphanes, and the three and a
half times were years, whether literal or symbolic, during which
the author of Daniel expected the persecution to last. But this
prediction raises a most important question—one which must
be asked about all apocalyptic writing—concerning the temporal standpoint of the author. The book purports to be written
by Daniel, living in exile in Babylon in the sixth century B.C.
In a series of visions he sees the future history of Israel with
increasing accuracy of detail up to 166 B.C.: four beasts representing the empires of Babylon, Media, Persia, and Greece, ten
horns of the fourth beast representing the ten Seleucid successors of Alexander, and a little horn representing Antiochus. It is
generally agreed that these long range predictions are a literary
convention, that the author was actually living in the reign of
Antiochus, and that the line between past and future ought to be
drawn between the emergence of the little horn and its destruction (Dan. vii. 8-11), between the setting up of the desecrating
horror and its removal (Dan. viii. 13 f.; ix. 27; xi. 31-35), after
the cessation of the daily sacrifice in December 167 B.C. and
before its restoration by Judas Maccabaeus. But where in the
visions of John are we to draw the line between past and future?

John believed that the prophecy of Daniel, along with other
Old Testament prophecies, was about to have a new and richer
fulfilment. The three and a half years were about to start (xi.
2-3); and he interpreted the last sentence of the angel's words to

7 Daniel to mean that with the destruction of the persecutor **the secret purpose of God will have been accomplished.** The persecution of the church is thus the secret weapon by which God intends to win his victory over the church's persecutors and to achieve his purpose of redemption. It is also the content of the **little scroll.**

The promise that **there shall be no more delay** offers us a clearer answer than anything else in John's book to the question about his temporal standpoint and the dividing line between past and future. **Delay** there has been, that is implied—the delay which wrung from the lips of earlier martyrs the cry, 'How long?' (vi. 10). If the threats of the seven thunders had not been cancelled, there would have been further delay before the three and a half year period could begin. It seems to follow from this that the delay implied by the angel was that involved in the woes of the seals and trumpets. At any time during these series God would have been justified in foreclosing on the world's bankruptcy; but he held his hand, limiting the destructive effects of sin, in order that men should have every opportunity of repentance. 'The Lord is not as slow to keep his promise as some suppose. He is being patient with you, not intending any to be lost, but all to reach repentance' (2 Pet. iii. 9). We have already found reasons to be dissatisfied with the hypothesis that the whole content of chapters iv-xxii were future to John at the time of writing, and it can now be dismissed once and for all as absurd. For John wrote to warn his friends about 'what is bound to happen soon', and particularly about 'the great ordeal'. Even when we treat the seals and the trumpets as parallel series, if the three and a half years of Daniel's prophecy could begin only after delays as long as the divine patience and longer than the patience of men, they could hardly be said to happen soon. The only tolerable conclusion is that John, like Daniel, stood at the beginning of the great persecution, and that his urgency in writing to the churches had been stimulated by the promise of **no more delay.** The visions of the seals and trumpets were not future to him, any more than the emergence of the four beasts was future to the author of Daniel. His purpose has been, like that of Paul in Romans i-ii, to depict a world impenitent and inexcusable, surrendered by God's wrath to the

disastrous consequences of its own idolatry, with no hope except
the gospel of God's sovereign mercy.

John's angel makes one important addition to the words of
Daniel's angel. He swears, not simply by the eternal God, but
by him **who created heaven, earth, and sea, and everything in them. The secret purpose of God** which is to be
achieved through the martyrdom of the church is no after-
thought, but the original purpose of creation. John uses the
term 'earth' in two senses, much as the fourth evangelist uses
kosmos (world): it may mean the world as God created it, or the
world organized in rebellion against its Maker. He knows how
fatally easy it is for those who have been compelled by persecution to adopt a negative attitude to the world in the second
sense to transfer their negation to the first sense also. But it is a
travesty of Christian belief to suppose that God has no purpose
for creation as a whole, and is content to rescue the small
company of the elect like brands snatched from the everlastng
bonfire. John believes that the redemptive work of God,
achieved through the death of Christ and the martyrdom of his
followers, will bring the created universe to its proper goal; for
though the present heaven and earth must pass away, whatever
in them is worth saving will find a place in the new heaven and
earth that follow.

God will accomplish his purpose **as he has assured his
servants the prophets.** It might appear self-evident that this
refers to the prophecies of the Old Testament, and in particular
to Daniel. But nowhere else does John use the word prophet
except to denote the Christian martyr. Moreover, the Greek
word here translated **'assured'** is *euengelisen* (evangelized). John
would no doubt assent to the proposition that the fulfilment of
God's purpose was promised to the Old Testament prophets.
But what he is here saying is that it has been guaranteed to the
martyr church in the gospel. In the Cross there is all the
assurance God's servants need that 'through many hardships
we must enter the kingdom of God' (Acts xiv. 22).

The two scrolls of John's visions are variations on a theme
by Ezekiel. Ezekiel was handed a scroll 'written back and front
with elegies, dirges, and laments' (Ezek. ii. 9-10). He was made
to eat it, and found it **sweet** to the **taste,** no doubt because the 10

harshness of its contents was congenial to his austere spirit. John has adopted Ezekiel's image, but has given it a new, double significance: his great scroll contained the redemptive purpose of God as it was made effective by Christ; his **little scroll** contains the same purpose, to be made effective through the martyr witness of the church. If the redemptive work of Christ is to become operative in the present, it must be through the witness of his servants the prophets. Accordingly John is 11 told that he must prophesy **once again,** and this time not in words only. Ezekiel was bidden to eat his scroll so as to assimilate its contents and be able to reproduce them in speech, but John is to **eat** so as to make the scroll a part of his inmost furnishing. The word of grace, which not all the angel trumpeters of heaven can utter, must be spoken by the prophet-martyrs not only with their lips but with their lives. This is why the scroll **tasted as sweet as honey** but was **bitter** to **swallow.** The way of victory is the way of the Cross.

xi. 1-3. THE MEASURING OF THE TEMPLE

(1) Then I was given a cane to use as a measuring-rod, and was told: 'Go and measure the temple of God and the altar and those who worship there. (2) But leave the outer court of the temple exposed and do not measure it; for it has been given over to the heathen, and they will trample the holy city underfoot for forty-two months. (3) And all through those twelve hundred and sixty days I will give my two witnesses free scope to prophesy, dressed in sackcloth.'

1   Ezekiel had a vision of an angel with **a measuring rod** going to measure the temple, and Zechariah had a similar vision of an angel measuring Jerusalem. John borrows the image, but as usual adapts it to his own ends. For the Old Testament prophets were dealing with the restoration of the ruined Jerusalem after the Exile, and for them the measuring was part of the heavenly architect's survey. But John is told to **measure the temple**

in order to protect it; not to measure any part of it is to **leave 2
it exposed**. So we must ask what John means by **the temple**
and from what dangers it is to be thus protected.

**It has been given over to the heathen, and they will
trample the holy city underfoot.** These words are reminiscent of the prediction of Jesus: 'Jerusalem shall be trampled
down by the heathen, until their time has run its course'
(Luke xxi. 24). But John is not simply reiterating a dominical
saying, for the gospel apocalypse in all its three versions begins
with a prophecy that the temple is to be destroyed without one
stone left standing on another (Mark xiii. 2; Luke xxi. 6; Matt.
xxiv. 2); and this prophecy had come true within John's lifetime. At the time when he wrote there was no temple in the
once holy city. Accordingly there has been a remarkable
amount of scholarly support for the idea first put forward by
Wellhausen, that John has here incorporated an oracle of a
Jewish prophet, spoken during the siege of A.D. 70, when the
inner courts of the temple were the one remaining Zealot
stronghold in the city. In spite of the eminence of its advocates
this theory must be judged improbable, useless, and absurd:
improbable, because, once the outer court had fallen to the
army of Titus, not even the most rabid fanatic could have
supposed that he would be content to occupy it for three and a
half years and leave the sanctuary itself inviolate; useless,
because, whatever these words might have meant to a hypo-
thetical Zealot, they certainly meant something quite different
to John twenty-five years after the siege; and absurd, because
of the underlying assumption that John could not have intended
these words to be taken figuratively unless someone else had
previously used them in their literal sense. Indeed, it is hardly
too much to say that, in a book in which all things are expressed
in symbols, the very last things **the temple** and **the holy city**
could mean would be the physical temple and the earthly
Jerusalem. If John had wanted to speak about them, he would
have found some imagery to convey his meaning without
lapsing into the inconsistency of literalism. But in fact John
regarded the Jews as the synagogue of Satan, and was not
interested in the preservation of their religious institutions. As
we shall see in the next paragraph, he held that the earthly

Jerusalem had already in A.D. 30 joined Sodom and Egypt as one
of the typical samples of the great unholy city.

The temple, the outer court, and **the holy city** are symbols. **The temple** stands for the church, the house of God not
made with hands, but built of living stones (iii. 12; 1 Cor. iii. 16;
2 Cor. vi. 16; Eph. ii. 20; 1 Pet. ii. 5). But what of **the outer
court** which is to be left unprotected? We cannot say that **the
holy city** represents the world outside the church—holy
because it is still God's world—and that **the outer court**
means all members of the church who have compromised with
the world, the Nicolaitans, Balaamites, and followers of
Jezebel, the loveless folk at Ephesus, the lifeless at Sardis, and
the lukewarm at Laodicea. For when the heathen begin to
trample the holy city underfoot, it is not those who have come
to terms with heathendom who will find themselves exposed,
but the faithful Christians who refuse to bear the mark of the
monster (cf. xiii. 7, 17). The trampling of **the holy city** is
equivalent to the great martyrdom.

This conclusion is immediately confirmed by the **forty-two
months** and **twelve hundred and sixty days,** an emphatic
double rendering of Daniel's 'time, two times, and a half', on
which John is to ring the changes in the ensuing chapters. As
we saw in the previous paragraph, this was Daniel's cryptic
estimate of the duration of the persecution of Antiochus
Epiphanes. John uses this figure as a kind of cross-reference, so
that every time it occurs we know we are being shown a new
aspect of his one central theme.

From this it follows that **the outer court** and **the holy
city,** no less than **the temple,** symbolize the church in part of
its existence. Like the seal which was set on the foreheads of
God's servants, the measuring of the temple betokens an inner
security against spiritual dangers. But the angel's orders are to
leave the outer court exposed, because God does not offer
to the church security from bodily suffering or death. It is his
intention that they should remain outwardly vulnerable to the
full hostility of their enemies, secure only in their faith in the
crucified and risen Lord. The one thing he guarantees is that
3 his witnesses shall have **free scope to prophesy;** for to
prophesy is to die the death of a martyr.

(4) These are the two olive-trees and the two lamps which stand before the Lord of the earth. (5) If anyone tries to harm them, fire pours from their mouths and consumes their enemies; this is the death a man is bound to meet, if he should try to harm them. (6) They have power to shut up the sky, so that no rain may fall throughout the time of their prophesying, and they have power to turn water to blood and to smite the earth at will with every kind of plague. (7) When they have completed their testimony, the monster that rises from the abyss will wage war on them and conquer them and kill them. (8) Their bodies will lie in the streets of the great city, which is figuratively called Sodom and Egypt, where also their Lord was crucified. (9) For three days and a half men from every people, tribe, tongue, and nation stare at their bodies and refuse them burial. (10) The inhabitants of earth gloat over them and celebrate by exchanging presents; for these two prophets were a torment to the inhabitants of earth. (11) But after the three and a half days a breath of life from God came into them, and they stood up on their feet; and a great dread fell on those who were watching them. (12) Then they heard a loud voice calling to them from heaven, 'Come up here!' And they went up to heaven in a cloud in full view of their enemies. (13) At that very moment there came a great earthquake, and a tenth of the city fell. Seven thousand people were killed in the earthquake; the survivors in awe did homage to the God of heaven. (14) The second woe is over; but the third woe is coming soon.

The object of measuring the temple was to ensure that God's two witnesses should have free scope to complete their testimony without hindrance from inner doubts or outward coercion. John now proceeds to explain who these two witnesses are. His explanation has commonly been regarded as the most enigmatic part of his whole book; yet if we follow his guidance point by point, we shall find that it is free from any sort of ambiguity.

4   First the witnesses are **the two olive-trees.** John takes us back once again to Zechariah's seven-branched candelabra, which has already furnished so much of his imagery. Beside the candelabra Zechariah saw two olive-trees, which fed the lamps with oil; and he was told, 'These are the two anointed ones who stand beside the Lord of the whole earth' (Zech. iv. 14). They were Zerubbabel and Joshua, the anointed king and the anointed priest. But where at the end of the first century A.D. are we to look for a Christian king and a Christian priest? Not in any two individual members of the church, but rather in the whole people of God, on which had devolved the regal and priestly functions of Christ. For John has told us that Christ has made the whole community of the redeemed 'a royal house of priests to his God and Father' (i. 6), and the heavenly choir has echoed his words (v. 10). But it is to the martyrs above all that this rank belongs (iii. 12, 21; xx. 6). There is good Old Testament precedent for this democratic diffusion of royal and priestly privilege. Deutero-Isaiah declared that God would make with Israel 'an everlasting covenant, the enduring love which I promised to David' (Isa. lv. 3). The promise that David's royal line would never come to an end was to be made good, not by the restoration of the monarchy, but by the renewal of the covenant with the nation as a whole, which would thus inherit David's commission to be 'a prince and lawgiver for the peoples'.

Any lingering doubts we may have about this interpretation of **the two olive-trees** are dispersed when John adds that the witnesses are also **two lamps.** For we know that the seven lamps are the seven churches and therefore the universal church (i. 20). We might have concluded from this that John expected only two of the seven churches of Asia to suffer martyrdom (perhaps the blameless churches of Smyrna and Philadelphia), were it not that in each of the seven letters there was a promise to the Conqueror. **The two lamps,** then, are a proportion of the church in all parts of the world; and they provide the clearest possible evidence that John did not expect all loyal Christians to die in the great ordeal. We must not, of course, take the fraction two-sevenths any more literally than

John's other numbers. He has good reason for this use of the number **two**. The evidence of a single witness was not admissible in a Jewish court of law. 'Only on the evidence of two witnesses or of three witnesses shall a charge be sustained' (Deut. xix. 15; cf. xvii. 6; Num. xxxv. 30). The Christian martyrs will provide the dual evidence necessary to sustain their case and to thwart the accuser, whether he be a Roman *delator* or the arch-prosecutor Satan himself (cf. xii. 7 ff.). In the human lawcourt their evidence will not secure an acquittal, but in the heavenly court of appeal that same evidence will secure both their own vindication and the condemnation of the city which has rejected their testimony and put them to death.

Heirs to the crowns of Zerubbabel and Joshua, the witnesses are to succeed also to the rod of Moses and the mantle of Elijah. For it was Moses who had **power to turn water to blood, 6** and Elijah who had **power to shut up the sky, so that no rain** might **fall** (Exod. vii. 17; 1 Kings xvii. 1). According to the Elijah saga the drought he caused lasted less than three years, but the two witnesses were to have power to cause drought **throughout the time of their prophesying,** i.e. for the full three and a half years. This would attract no comment, if it were not for the curious fact that Luke (iv. 25) and James (v. 17) give the duration of Elijah's drought as three and a half years. They must have been relying on a Jewish tradition of interpretation, which had already made the link between Elijah and Daniel's symbolic number, on the ground that three and a half years was the proper period for any national calamity.

The Moses and Elijah typology of this passage is apt to cause qualms to the Christian conscience, since it seems that John is approving in the witnesses a vindictiveness which Jesus had censured in the sons of Zebedee (Luke ix. 54 f.). Yet it is sheer presumption to assume that his conscience was less tender than ours. In the roles of Moses and Elijah the Christian witnesses were to be prophets **(these two prophets),** and John has his own deeply Christian conception of what it means to be a prophet. 'The testimony of Jesus is the spirit that inspires prophets' (xix. 10). An Old Testament prophet was one to whom the word of the Lord came; but a Christian prophet was one to whom the Word had come in the flesh, who had taken the

testimony borne by Jesus in his life, teaching, and above all in
the Cross, and had made it his own. John must have felt that
such a definition of prophecy was in no way incompatible with the
typological details he derived from the stories of Moses and Elijah,
for all these activities must be included in the summarizing
conclusion: **when they have completed their testimony.**

The difficulty is to some extent alleviated when we recall the
part that Jewish tradition ascribed to Moses and Elijah in the
dénouement of history. God would send a new Moses (Deut.
xviii. 15; cf. John i. 21; vi. 14; vii. 40, 52) or he would send
Elijah (Mal. iv. 5-6; cf. Mark i. 2; ix. 11-13; Matt. xi. 14; Luke
i. 17) to prepare a penitent people before the day of judgment.

> 'It is written that you are to come with warnings at the ap-
>   pointed time,
> To allay the divine wrath before its final fury,
> To reconcile father to son
> And to restore the tribes of Jacob.'
>
>   (Ecclus. xlviii. 10).

The plagues inflicted by Moses and Elijah are thus an indication
of their utter determination to bring men to repentance at
whatever cost, before it is too late. But did John suppose that
the Christian witnesses would literally possess the miraculous
powers attributed to Moses and Elijah in the Old Testament?
On general principles we should be inclined to doubt this, and
John gives substance to our doubts by a characteristic alteration
of his traditional material. The new Elijah does not call down
5 fire from heaven like his Old Testament prototype: **fire pours
from their mouths.** As with Jeremiah (v. 14), God has made
the words in their mouths a fire, and the fire is the actual
testimony that they must bear in a Roman court of law. Jesus
had brought to men an offer of eternal life, but had said that
Sodom and Gomorrah would fare better at the judgment than
those towns which rejected the gospel (Matt. x. 15; xi. 24;
Luke x. 12); and the Christian witnesses must speak words of
fire which lay before the world a similar choice between life and
death. Jesus had warned his earthly judge that he must stand
before the judgment-seat of the Son of Man (Mark xiv. 62); and
the Christian witnesses must by any means in their power

persuade their accusers that they are on trial before a higher
tribunal, and on a capital charge sustained on the evidence of
two or three witnesses. They are to be a torment to the inhabitants of earth because their testimony is a searing indictment
of the world they live in.[1]

The Christian martyr will go to his death under sentence from
a Roman judge; and John has a high enough regard for Roman
administration to recognize how easily the humble believer
might be brought to think that after all Rome must be right
and he himself wrong. He is likely to be armed against such
doubts if he knows that the real author of his condemnation is
the monster that rises from the abyss. In two later chapters 7
John will have more to say about **the monster** (xiii and xvii).
Here he contents himself with one illuminating phrase. He does
not say that **the monster** is going to rise **from the abyss** at
some predictable moment of the future, or that it has risen at
some datable moment in the past. This monster has a long
history, and rising **from the abyss** is not a single episode in its
career, but the permanent cast of its character (cf. xvii. 8). The
four beasts of Daniel's first vision were seen to rise out of the
great sea, which is another name for the abyss (Dan. vii. 1 ff.);
and they symbolized the four empires to which Jerusalem had
been successively made subject. The biblical history of the
monster, then, begins in the original Babylon and ends in the
latter-day Babylon, which is Rome. For wherever men lay
claim to despotic power, refusing to acknowledge that they are
responsible to God for the use to which they put it, there **the
monster** rises **from the abyss. The monster** is a myth, but one
which expresses a perennial hazard in the political life of men.

Postponing for a time the full exploration of this potent symbol, John moves on to another: the **bodies** of the witnesses **will** 8
lie in the streets of the great city. Where on the map of the
ancient world are we to locate this city? Those who have voted
for a literal interpretation of the measuring of the temple will
here vote for Jerusalem, and in confirmation they can point to
John's statement that it is the place **where also their Lord was
crucified.** This last phrase is, however, more naturally taken as

---

[1] Cf. 2 Esdras xiii. 10, 38, where the fire from the mouth of the Son of
Man is said to mean the Torah.

part of the general description of the city, which John has expressly called figurative. The city is heir to the vice of **Sodom,** the tyranny of Pharaoh's **Egypt,** and the blind disobedience of Jerusalem, but it is not literally to be identified with any of them. John uses this same phrase, **the great city,** seven times more (xvi. 19; xvii. 18; xviii. 10, 16, 18, 19, 21), and in each case the context makes it clear that Rome is intended. If in spite of all this we still opt for Jerusalem, we find ourselves involved in a grotesque consequence. For the bodies of the witnesses were to be on view in the streets to sightseers of

9 **every people, tribe, tongue, and nation.** Jews from every part of the world were accustomed to travel to Jerusalem for the great festivals, but the gloating crowds are not restricted to

10 Jews; they are **the inhabitants of earth.** The ancient world had no Cook's Tours capable of assembling in Jerusalem the international audience John here envisages. This absurdity does not arise if we take the city to be Rome, for the city limits of Rome extended from the Euphrates to the Pillars of Hercules and from the North Sea to the Sahara Desert. **Bodies** left without **burial** in the streets of that city would lie in full view of the world. Our conclusion about the city incidentally confirms what we have said about the witnesses. If the witnesses were two individual Christians, the city in which they died would have to be a city in the narrow, literal sense; and this hypothesis leads, as we have seen, to a *reductio ad absurdum.*

The city is Rome. Yet even this cannot be said without qualification. For this city has a longer history than Rome. Like the monster the great city is a myth, which John intends to use to delineate the true nature of Roman imperial power. Rome is simply the latest embodiment of something that is a recurrent feature of human history. The great city is the spiritual home of those John dubs inhabitants of earth; it is the tower of Babel, the city of this world, Vanity Fair.

The martyrs die in the same city as **their Lord,** and like him they have their Easter Day. For them it comes, not on the third

11 day, but **after three and a half days,** because John's mind is still running on the mysterious half-week of Daniel's prophecy.

12 Like their prototypes, Moses and Elijah, they are carried **up to heaven in a cloud** (2 Kings ii. 11; Josephus, *Ant.* iv. 8. 48).

And the earthly sequel to all this is **a great earthquake.**   13

John has already used the symbol of the **earthquake** in the vision of the sixth seal, and now he repeats it in the vision of the sixth trumpet; but there are three variations in his handling of the theme. There the earthquake was the sixth woe, and the two visions of the sealing of the martyrs and their victorious entry into heaven were not directly related to it; here the sixth plague is the invasion of the demonic army, and the earthquake is a direct consequence of the measuring of the temple and the death of the witnesses. There the effect of the earthquake extended to the whole cosmos; here it is limited to one **tenth** of the city and a small number of its inhabitants. There the earthquake reduced all men to cowering panic, here to **awe** and **homage.** The question we must ask is: are these differences merely stylistic variations, or has John at this point reached a fresh theological disclosure?

The almost overwhelming consensus of scholarly opinion has been that John was another Jonah, who would have resented the idea that the inhabitants of the great city might repent and be forgiven. But it is at least worth while to consider the contrary opinion. We have seen (vi. 12-17) that the earthquake was a familiar Old Testament symbol, representing the overthrow of an idolatrous and ungodly political order, and that John did no more in his first use of it than follow Old Testament usage. But here he seems to have aimed at a rebirth of images, such as he achieved in the lion turned lamb: the death and vindication of the martyrs is itself the earthquake shock by which the great city is overthrown. What exactly this means we are to be told at a later stage. For the present John is content to hammer home the point of the whole trumpet series, that God limits the destructive effects of retribution in order that men may repent. Everything turns on the meaning of the words in which he describes the reactions of **the survivors** of the earthquake, who **in awe did homage to the God of heaven.** Did they in fact repent? Or did they recoil in impenitent and hopeless terror? Was the great dread that fell on them the fear of the Lord which is the beginning of wisdom or merely panic fear of an ineluctable doom? Was the homage they offered the first earnest of true worship or a reluctant submission to *force majeure*? Fortunately

there is a clear and decisive answer ready to hand, provided
we are prepared to be bound by Johannine usage. 'Fear God and
do him homage', cries the angel commissioned to proclaim the
eternal gospel (xiv. 7). 'Who shall not fear, Lord, and do
homage to your name?' sing the martyrs on the threshold of
heaven, 'For you alone are holy. All nations shall come and
worship before you' (xv. 4). And John himself comments that
the victims of the fourth bowl 'refused to repent or do him
homage' (xvi. 9). In John's vocabulary 'fear', 'do homage',
and 'repent' are almost synonymous terms.

It is possible, too, that John had in mind the law of malicious
witness (Deut. xix. 16-21). By this law a man found guilty of
perjury must suffer the penalty which his evidence would have
brought on the accused. 'You shall do to him as he meant to do
to his fellow. . . . And the rest shall hear and be afraid and never
again do any such wrong among you. You shall have no compunction; it shall be life for life.' The martyrs have been put to
death by malicious witness, and justice demands life for life.
But the martyrs are Elijah and his faithful followers, the seven
thousand who have not submitted to the seductions of Jezebel
and bowed the knee to Baal. This explains why in expiation for
their death **seven thousand people were killed,** and the rest
were afraid. But the implication is that the evil was thus purged
from the city, never to recur.

There seems then to be a good case for holding that John had
wider hopes for the conversion of the world than he is commonly given credit for, especially when we remember his
confidence that the church of Philadelphia would convert even
members of the synagogue of Satan (iii. 9). Where retributive
punishment had failed to bring men to repentance, the death of
the martyrs would succeed. Corporately they would discharge
the traditional function of Elijah so fully that only **seven
thousand** would be left obdurately worshipping Baal.

xi. 15-19. THE LAST TRUMPET

**(15) Then the seventh angel blew his trumpet; and loud
voices were heard in heaven, saying:**

'The sovereignty of the world has passed to our Lord
and to his Christ, and he shall reign for ever and ever!'

(16) The twenty-four elders, seated on their thrones
before God, fell on their faces and worshipped God:

(17) 'We thank you, Lord God Omnipotent, who are
and were, because you have assumed your full power
and entered on your reign. (18) The heathen rose in
their wrath, but now your wrath has come. Now is the
time for the dead to be judged, for rewarding your servants the prophets and your people great and small who
fear your name, for destroying the destroyers of the
earth.'

(19) Then God's temple in heaven opened, and inside
the temple appeared the ark of his covenant; and there
came flashes of lightning and peals of thunder, an earthquake and a great storm of hail.

The first six trumpets have sounded the alarm, calling men to
repentance in the face of imminent judgment. The last **trumpet** 15-
is a jubilant fanfare, proclaiming the enthronement of the King 17
of kings. In one sense God's sovereignty is eternal: he entered
on his reign when he established the rule of order in the midst
of primaeval chaos (Ps. xciii. 1-4); he has reigned throughout
human history, turning even men's misdeeds into instruments of
his mercy; and above all he reigned in the Cross of Christ
(xii. 10). But always up to this point he has reigned over a
rebellious world. A king may be king *de jure*, but he is not king
de facto until the trumpet which announces his accession is
answered by the acclamations of a loyal and obedient people.
Hitherto God has been the Omnipotent 'who is and was and is
coming' (i. 8), because the realization of his full power lay still
in the future. Now futurity is caught up in the eternal present,
and the choirs of heaven address him as **Lord God Omnipotent, who are and were.**

In this paragraph John begins an exposition of Psalm ii, to
which he will return more than once in the following chapters.
The psalm begins with a description of the rebellion of the
nations against **our Lord** and **his Christ,** continues with God's
decree that his son, the anointed king, is to reign on mount

Zion until the rebellion is broken and his sovereignty acknowledged, and ends with an appeal to the kings of the earth to
come to terms with him and not to expose themselves to the
retributive wrath of God. Already in the letter to Thyatira we
have been given a hint of John's intention to baptize this psalm
with the spirit of the gospel by reinterpreting its second stanza:
the iron rod with which the Messiah is to smash the rebellion
of the pagan world is his own death and that of his martyrs
(ii. 26-28). In the present context he deals only with the begin-

18 ning and end of the process. **The heathen rose in their
wrath, but now your wrath has come.** There is no need for
him to repeat what he has said in the previous paragraph, that
God's decree has taken its effect, that through the death and
resurrection of the two witnesses the Messiah has received the
nations as his inheritance, that the inhabitants of the earth have
accepted his invitation to 'serve the Lord with fear' (Ps. ii. 11).
Once the last trumpet has sounded, all that matters is that
rebellion is at an end and God's sovereignty complete.

Ever since the screech of the eagle John has been deliberately
creating an atmosphere of mounting terror. 'Woe, woe, woe to
the inhabitants of earth because of the trumpet blasts which the
last three angels are about to blow!' (viii. 13). 'The first woe
is over; but there are still two woes to come' (ix. 12). 'The
second woe is over; but the third is coming soon' (xi. 14). It is
plain that he has intended the seventh trumpet to be the third
woe: **your wrath has come.** Yet he never actually narrates the
coming of the third woe. The climax, when it comes, turns out
to be more of a *dies gaudii* than a *dies irae*. It is true that John
calls it 'your wrath', because he is using the terminology of his
Old Testament text, but he is careful to explain exactly what he
understands by it. It means **the time for the dead to be
judged.** He has no doubts about the reality of judgment: there
are heavenly books to be opened and a great white throne before
which all must stand (xx. 11-15). A man may find that his name
has been expunged from the book of life (iii. 5), that he bears
indelibly the mark of the monster (xix. 20). But John knows that
it is neither his business nor ours to decide whom the death cap
fits. Over the throne is the rainbow of mercy, and judgment is in
the hands of him who has spared neither his Son nor his saints

to bring about the world's redemption. Only two things are
certain: the judgment is the time **for rewarding your
servants the prophets and your people great and small
who fear your name,** and **for destroying the destroyers
of the earth.** Whatever judgment may mean, it holds no
terrors either for the martyrs or for any who **fear** the **name** of
God. This last phrase is part of the exegesis of the second psalm,
but it also follows far too closely on verse 13 to leave any real
doubt that John includes here those who, in awe at the death
and vindication of the witnesses, did their belated homage to
God. Their part in the wrath of the heathen, their worship of
the monster, their gloating over the bodies of the martyrs—all
this is blotted out by repentance. The martyrs, who have
worked all day in the scorching heat, will not be jealous if the
owner of the vineyard chooses to pay these late-comers the
same wage as he pays to them. For they know that their warfare
has not been 'against human enemies, but against cosmic
powers, the potentates and rulers of this present dark world'
(Eph. vi. 12)—**the destroyers of the earth.** It is the purpose
of the succeeding chapters to tell us in detail who and what are
these powers who destroy the earth, but already we have had
five clear pointers to their identity: the four horsemen, but
especially Death with his companion Hades (vi. 8); the blazing
mountain which recalled Jeremiah's dirge over Babylon,
'destroyer of the whole earth' (viii. 8); the fallen star Wormwood, the embittered rival of God (viii. 11); the angel of the
abyss whose name was Destroyer both in Hebrew and in Greek
(ix. 11); the monster that rises from the abyss (xi. 7). It is their
death throes that constitute the third woe, and it is for their
destruction that the weapons of **thunder** and lightning, earthquake and hail are summoned from the armouries of heaven.

> 'Have you visited the armouries where snow is stored
> Or seen the armouries of the hail,
> Which I have kept in reserve against the time of crisis,
> The day of battle and war?'
>> (Job. xxxviii. 22 f.; cf. Josh. x. 11;
>> Ps. xviii. 12; Isa. xxx. 30; Ezek.
>> xiii. 11, 13).

The **wrath** of God against **the destroyers** is an integral part
of John's doctrine of salvation. There can be no security for
mankind as long as **the destroyers** are at large to ravage the
earth. Babylon must be destroyed if her citizens are to be set
free from her seductions to enter the heavenly city, and the
monster must be destroyed if men are to be liberated from its
worship to do homage to the one true God. If Jesus, like his
namesake Joshua, is to lead God's people into the promised
land, every Jericho that stands in their way must be flattened;
19 and so **the ark of the covenant** appears, following its escort
of seven trumpets.

The earthly ark had stood in the Holy of holies of Solomon's
temple. If it had not previously been removed by Shishak
(1 Kings xiv. 26) or Manasseh (2 Chron. xxxiii. 7), it was certainly destroyed along with the temple in 586 B.C. A later legend
had it that Jeremiah removed the ark to safety in a cave on
Mount Sinai, where it would remain hidden until the final
restoration of Israel (2 Macc. ii. 4-8; cf. 2 *Bar.* vi. 5-10; lxxx. 2).
But John has no interest in the fate of the earthly ark. What he
sees is the heavenly archetype of which the earthly ark was but a
copy (Exod. xxv. 40; cf. Heb. viii. 5). But like its copy the
heavenly **ark** stands in the inner sanctuary of the temple. In
the earthly temple no one entered the Holy of holies except the
high priest, and he only on the Day of Atonement, the day for
which the trumpet-blowing of the Feast of Trumpets was a
preparation (see notes on viii. 2). On the heavenly Day of
Atonement no priest needs to enter the sanctuary, for the
curtain is drawn aside so that all the congregation may see for
themselves the symbol of God's presence in their midst,
assuring them that their sins are forgiven and that God's
covenant stands firm.

Now that we have come to the end of the sequence of trumpets, we are in a position to give a firmer answer to some of the
questions raised along the way. The **flashes of lightning,
peals of thunder,** and **earthquake** which accompany the
appearance of the ark are a cross-reference to the earlier passage
where the prayers of the church were offered by an angel in the
form of incense and produced similar manifestations (viii. 5;

cf. xvi. 18). What were these prayers? We might have thought that they were the prayers of the martyrs for vindication, which we had already heard in the vision of the fifth seal, but that they were said to be the prayers of all God's people. Now that the answer to the prayer has been given in the proclamation of the enthronement of God as King, we know that the prayer must have been the daily petition of all Christians, 'Let your king-dom come'. Before that prayer could be granted, Christians must have spelt out for them letter by letter what it is that they have been praying for. They have been praying that the de-stroyers of the earth should be allowed to burn themselves out in a last monstrous effort to frustrate the plans of God, and that men should be given repeated and agonizing warnings not to be involved in their destruction. They have been praying that all men's eyes should be opened to the lie they have been living and their consciences pricked by the martyr-witness of the servants of God.

Why does the Day of God have to be ushered in by a cre-scendo of disaster? Because nothing unclean can be admitted to the holy city, and therefore, before it can finally descend from heaven, evil must be allowed to run its course and work its own destruction. We have been repeatedly shown the self-destructive nature of evil. But God cannot allow this to act as an impersonal nemesis, a self-operating moral principle; for then the powers of evil would carry earth and its inhabitants down with them in their own ruin, leaving God with a hollow, Pyrrhic victory, scarcely distinguishable from defeat. If God's victory is to be man's victory also, it must be won through human agents. In his scroll of destiny the sins of men which produce wars, famines, and pestilences are transformed into messengers of his purpose. But he will not himself open the scroll. He waits until someone on earth has won the right to open it. It was only because of Christ's perfect submission to God's will that sin's instrument, the Cross, was transformed into sin's destruction. It is only when others are found to bear with the same obedience their witness to the power of the Cross that sin's destruction becomes complete. Sin must be allowed to gather all its forces against the servants of God and to fall back defeated by their loyalty and faith.

Finally, there is the question of what Farrer has called John's 'cancelled conclusions'. With the breaking of the seventh seal and the blowing of the seventh trumpet he has twice brought us to the End, and he will do it a third time with the pouring of the seventh bowl. There might, to be sure, be some doubt about the finality of the seventh seal, on which John makes no comment, but there can be none about the seventh trumpet. There can be no future once futurity has been removed from the very name of God. But in each case the conclusion is cancelled by a new beginning. Now it may be that John records three series of seven plagues because he saw three series. It may be, as we have already suggested, that he set down his visions with the skill of a consummate literary artist, composing symphonic variations on the theme of divine judgment. But he also had a theological reason. God himself has his cancelled conclusions. 'I said, "Lord God, forgive; how can Jacob survive, he is so small." Then the Lord relented and said, 'It shall not happen!' (Amos vii. 2-3). 'The whole land shall lie waste; yet I will not make its devastation complete' (Jer. iv. 27). 'Who knows, God may yet relent; he may turn from his fierce anger and not leave us to perish' (Jon. iii. 9; cf. Joel ii. 13). John knows that the victims of persecution may be tempted to think that God has forgotten both their undeserved plight and his own justice. The truth is, not that God cares the less for justice, but that he cares the more for mercy, not that he has ceased to care for the martyrs, but that he cares also for their persecutors. With justice alone as his guide he would long since have closed the books and called men to their final account. But he holds his hand, cancels his conclusions, to give men time to repent; and, because he holds his hand, the innocent suffer. Martyrdom, like the Cross, is the price of the divine forbearance.

VI

THE GREAT ORDEAL

xii. 1-6. THE BIRTH OF THE MESSIAH

(1) A great portent appeared in the sky, a woman robed with the sun, with the moon as her footstool, and a crown of twelve stars on her head. (2) She was soon to have a child, and in the agony of her labour cried out to be delivered. (3) Then another portent appeared in the sky, a great red dragon with seven heads and ten horns; on his heads were seven diadems, and his tail swept away a third of the stars in the sky and flung them to the earth. (4) The dragon stood before the woman who was about to give birth, to devour her child as soon as it was born. (5) She gave birth to a male child, who is destined to smash all the nations with an iron bar; but her child was snatched away to God and to his throne. (6) The woman escaped into the desert, where she had a place prepared for her by God, there to be sustained for twelve hundred and sixty days.

In the folklore of many nations there are found stories of the usurper who, doomed to be killed by a prince as yet unborn, attempts to cheat the fates by killing the prince at birth. The prince is miraculously snatched from his clutches and hidden away, until he is old enough to kill the usurper and claim his inheritance. The same theme is found in many forms in the mythology of the ancient world. In Greece it is the dragon Python who attempts to kill the new-born son of Zeus and is foiled by the escape of the mother, Leto, to the island of Delos; there Apollo is born, and he subsequently returns to Parnassus and kills the dragon in its Delphic cave. In Egypt it is Set, the red dragon, who pursues Isis and is later killed by her son Horus. These two stories were forms of the solar myth: the dragon of darkness tries to kill the sun god, only to be killed by him when the new day dawns. Now a folk tale is a story told for the sheer delight of story-telling, and it need have no significance other than its power to entertain. But a myth is an interpretation of life. As we have already seen in connexion with the glassy sea (iv. 6), a myth is a story told about the remote past, but told in order to explain the present. It must be capable of being re-enacted by those who have found in it a stimulus to the imagination and a spur to action. Indeed, it may well be argued that all genuine convictions require a mythology for their adequate expression and cannot influence the conduct of men until they have bodied forth in powerful imaginative symbols. We know that the myth of the sun god was a living myth in the first century, and not just an old familiar tale. For there are coins on which the emperor's head appears irradiate,[1] a proclamation to the world that in the drama of man's existence, where light and darkness are at constant warfare, the role of Apollo was now being played by imperial Caesar.

John rewrites the old pagan myth deliberately to contradict its current political application. The killing of the dragon *is* being re-enacted, but not by the emperor, who turns out instead to be one of the dragon's minions. It is not the emperor who is son to the Queen of Heaven. We have seen that the goddess Roma was worshipped in the cities of Asia and closely associated with the local cults of the Mother Goddess. On a coin of Pergamum there is the head of Augustus and a female figure with the legend, THEAN ROMEN (the goddess Roma). On another coin, from the reign of Tiberius, Augustus and Livia, the ideal embodiments of Roman imperial authority, are represented as sun and moon. The coinage was the one universal form of propaganda for the imperial ideology, which declared that Roma was the new queen of the gods and mother of the world's saviour. John is going to portray her as the new Jezebel, the seducer of the world, clad in all the finery of earth. She who claims to be queen of earth (xviii. 7) must be seen to be a travesty of the resplendent Queen of Heaven.

1-3   Who then in John's version of the story are the **woman robed with the sun** and the **great red dragon?** John calls

---

[1] H. St. J. Hart (*J.T.S.* 1952, pp. 66 ff.) has conjectured that Christ's crown of thorns was a deliberate caricature of the radiate crown which the Roman emperors copied from earlier oriental kings.

each of them a *semeion*, which can mean **portent,** but which commonly also means a constellation interpreted as a portent. It is likely then that he envisaged them both as constellations in the sky. But it is a waste of time to search for them on any map of the stars. The woman is certainly not Virgo, the sixth of the signs of the zodiac; for she wears the **twelve stars** of the zodiac as **a crown.** She belongs, like all John's other symbols, to the realm of vision. The **dragon** is not Draco, nor Serpens, nor the many-headed Hydra, but a combination of all three;[1] he is called the **dragon** and the serpent (xii. 9), and he has **seven heads.** The **third of the stars in the sky** which he sweeps with **his tail** leave no blank in the night sky; for this element in the picture is drawn from Daniel viii. 10, and the stars are angelic representatives of pagan powers. We must look beyond astronomy for an answer. The woman and the dragon are figures of the imagination, projected on to the starry heavens.

The woman is the mother of the Messiah, not Mary, but the messianic community. This John makes abundantly clear now by a verbal echo of a prophecy about mother Zion (Isa. lxvi. 7-9), and later by speaking of the members of the church as 'the rest of her children' (xii. 17). She is the Jerusalem above who is our mother (Gal. iv. 26). **The agony of her labour** is the suffering endured by the loyal people of God as they waited for their anointed king. John's modern critics make much of what they take to be a curious and lamentable anomaly, that in the present passage he can jump directly from the Nativity to the Ascension, without any mention of the intervening life of Jesus. But the jump exists entirely in their own fancy, for there is no reference here to the Nativity. By the birth of the Messiah John means not the Nativity but the Cross. The reason for this is that he is continuing his exposition of the second psalm, begun in the vision of the seventh trumpet. In the psalm it is not at his birth but at his enthronement on mount Zion that the anointed king is addressed by God, 'You are my son; today I have begotten you', and is given authority to smash all the nations with an iron bar (Ps. ii. 7-9). A king's birthday is the day of his accession. For the Christian exegesis of this psalm John had as guide the preaching tradition of the primitive

[1] See G. B. Gray (ICC) on Isa. xxvii. 1.

church that Jesus 'was appointed Son of God with power after
he rose from the dead' (Rom. i. 4). Sonship and enthronement
belong inseparably together, and therefore the male child is no
sooner born than he is snatched away to God and to his throne.
But for John as for the fourth evangelist, the Cross is the point
at which Jesus entered upon his kingly glory. 'I conquered and
sat down beside my Father on his throne' (iii. 21). Thus the
interests of scriptural exegesis and Christian theology have
dictated the way in which John has rewritten his myth. The
prince is snatched from the dragon's clutches not by magic but
by death; and his place of safety is not some secluded island but
the throne of God, whence he will return to kill the dragon.

The dragon is Satan, 'the old serpent', as we shall be told in
the next vision. But his seven heads identify him also with that
other mythical creature, Leviathan or Lotan, the ocean dragon
of the Canaanite creation story, whose aliases are Tiamat and
Rahab. Farrer has argued that John can have had no acquaintance with the seven-headed monster of a Canaanite myth
known to us only from the Ras Shamra tablets, and that he
must have arrived at the figure seven by adding together the
heads—three ones and a four—of the four beasts of Daniel's
vision. But we have found ample evidence from the Old Testament (see on iv. 6) to prove that the creation myth was still part
of the living language of theology down to the time of Daniel,
and the many heads of Leviathan are actually mentioned in
Psalm lxxiv. 14. This is not to deny that the dragon has an
affinity with the beasts of Daniel. His **ten horns** are the horns
of the fourth beast. They are also one of the marks of the
monster which he himself is to summon out of the primaeval
sea (xiii. 1). The characteristics of Satan, we are to understand,
are those of his earthly representatives. Nor is John the first
to make this point. Jeremiah had compared Nebuchadrezzar
to a dragon which had gulped Jerusalem down whole (Jer. li.
34); Ezekiel had pictured Pharaoh as 'the great dragon lying in
the midst of his streams' (Ezek. xxix. 3); and in the Psalms of
Solomon (ii. 29) the dragon seems to be Pompey. The dragon's
4 attempt **to devour** the child may include the temptations and
dangers of Jesus' earthly life, but its primary reference is certainly to the crucifixion. Satan thought that death was the means

by which Jesus would come permanently within his power, when in fact it was the means by which he was carried for ever beyond his power, **snatched away to God.** As long as he lived, there 5 was always a possibility that he might give way to temptation and so put himself in Satan's power, but death carried him beyond this possibility. He died 'out from under the power of the elemental spirits' (Col. ii. 20).

It was Paul's belief that Christ had died as the inclusive representative of the whole people of God, so that all who were 'in Christ' could be said to have died with him and so passed beyond the reach of the powers of darkness. Satan might do what he would with their outer man (2 Cor. iv. 16; xii. 7; 1 Thess. ii. 18), but their inner life was secure, 'hidden with Christ in God' (Col. iii. 3). This was the secret plan of God which 'the demonic rulers of this world did not know; for if they had, they would not have crucified the Lord of glory' (1 Cor. ii. 8). John expresses the same belief in different terms. The first consequence of the crucifixion and ascension of Christ is that **the woman escaped** to **a place prepared for her by** 6 **God.** To those whose eyes are fixed only on what is seen and temporal the church is a vulnerable human society, utterly exposed to the attacks of Caesar; but to those with eyes to see what is unseen and eternal the church is inviolate to the assaults of Satan himself.

The place of security is **the desert.** This is an excellent example of the ambivalence of symbols. (Ambivalence is not the same as ambiguity. Words too are symbols, and all words, in so far as they express ideas and not things, are capable of multiple meaning. Without multiple meaning language could hardly function as a means of communication, for there could be no comparative language—simile, metaphor, parable, allegory and the like; and without that there could be no comparison of the unknown with the known. What a word means in any given case ought to be clear from the context; meaning is dictionary definition plus context—what the user intends the word to mean. Ambiguity arises only if more than one meaning is equally appropriate to the context. Here the context leaves us in no doubt which of the two meanings of desert John intends.) In many parts of the Bible the desert is the very opposite of an

asylum; it is the part of creation where chaos still reigns, un-
subdued as yet by Adam the gardener, the haunt of unclean
animals and unholy spirits (Isa. xiii. 20-22; xxxiv. 13-15; Luke
xi. 24; Mark i. 13). On the Day of Atonement two goats were
used, the one to be sacrificed to God and so brought within the
sphere of the holy, the other to be loaded with the sins of the
nation and driven out into the desert, where sin belonged
(Lev. xvi. 7 ff.). John's **desert** comes from a different strain of
biblical imagery, the typological use of the Exodus story. To
the Israelites escaping from Pharoah, the Egyptian dragon in the
midst of his streams, the desert was the place of safety and
liberation; and it was to such a sanctuary that the woman was
taken **to be** protected and **sustained** by God. To John the
sphere of unholy spirits and unclean beasts was not the desert
but the great city, figuratively called Sodom and Egypt, where
also the Lord was crucified (xi. 8); and since that city was
coterminous with the civilized world, it follows that **the desert**
is anywhere outside the authority of the unholy city. There
throughout the **twelve hundred and sixty days** of Daniel's
prophecy, when the outward and visible church is being
trampled by the heathen (xi. 2), the church which is visible only
to the eyes of faith, whose life is hidden with Christ in God,
will be kept from ultimate harm.

xii. 7-12. WAR IN HEAVEN

**(7) Then war broke out in heaven. Michael and his
angels were to wage war on the dragon. (8) The dragon
and his angels fought, but they were overpowered, and
left not a trace to be found in heaven. (9) So the great
dragon was overthrown, that old serpent whose name is
the Devil, or Satan, the deceiver of the whole world, —
thrown down to the earth, and his angels with him.
(10) And I heard a loud voice in heaven say: 'Now is the
hour of victory for our God! Now his power and sovereignty have come, and the rightful reign of his Christ!**

For the accuser of our brothers is driven out, who accused
them day and night before our God. (11) They have
conquered him by the life-blood of the Lamb and the
testimony they bore; no love of life caused them to
shrink from death. (12) Rejoice for this, you heavens and
all who dwell in them! But woe to you, earth and sea,
for the Devil has come down to you in great fury, knowing that his time is short!'

If John's ancient story is to end in story book fashion, it is not
enough for the prince to escape with his life from the usurper,
for Apollo to be rescued from Python; he must return and kill
him. If the creation myth is to be re-enacted, the chaos dragon
Leviathan must be defeated. The story is indeed to have its
proper ending, but first it takes an unexpected twist: **war broke 7
out in heaven,** and a war in which apparently the Messiah
was not involved, since the task of overpowering the dragon
is assigned to **Michael and his angels.**

It need hardly be said that this is no premundane battle. As
we shall see below, the Bible knows nothing of the premundane
fall of Satan, familiar to readers of *Paradise Lost.* If John was
familiar with a Jewish tradition of a primordial conflict between
the angels of light and the angels of darkness (2 *Enoch* xxix.
4-5; *Vit. Ad. et Ev.* xvi. 1; cf. 1 *Enoch* ix-x; lxxxvi), he is certainly using it here, as he uses all his other inherited myths,
to draw out the significance of the gospel story. As often happens in the Revelation, what he sees is described largely in
traditional imagery, and what he hears gives the Christian reinterpretation. The theological comment is provided by **a loud 10
voice in heaven. The hour of victory for our God,** the
hour which establishes God's **sovereignty** and **the rightful
reign of his Christ,** can in the present context be nothing
other than the crucifixion. This is why it has to be Michael and
not Christ who is God's champion in the heavenly war. Everything that John sees in heaven is the counterpart of some
earthly reality. When the victory is being won in heaven, Christ
is on earth on the Cross. Because he is part of the earthly
reality, he cannot at the same time be part of the heavenly
symbolism. The heavenly chorus explains that the real victory

has been won **by the life-blood of the Lamb.** Michael's
victory is simply the heavenly and symbolic counterpart of the
earthly reality of the Cross. Michael, in fact, is not the field
officer who does the actual fighting, but the staff officer in the
heavenly control room, who is able to remove Satan's flag from
the heavenly map because the real victory has been won on
Calvary.

It has been assumed in the translation that these events took
place **in heaven,** though the Greek phrase could be translated
'in the sky', and has been so translated in the previous paragraph. The fact is that in the biblical tradition Satan regularly
appears in heaven and has every right to be there. The Hebrew
word *satan* mean 'adversary' and can be used of a man who
brings an accusation against another in a lawcourt (Ps. cix. 6).
In the Book of Job one of the angels in the heavenly court is
called the Satan (with the definite article), because he holds
an appointment as **accuser** or prosecutor in the lawcourt of
God. His task is to arraign men before the bar of the divine
justice. When not occupied with his official duties, he spends
his time going to and fro on the earth collecting evidence, even
to the point of putting temptation in men's way when the
necessary evidence for a conviction is lacking (Job i. 6 ff.).
Satan appears again as **accuser** in the visions of Zechariah,
where the high priest Joshua is on trial. Here he looks like win-
ning his case, for Joshua is the representative of Jerusalem, and
his filthy garments symbolize the moral and religious condition
of that city. But God intervenes on behalf of the accused and has
Joshua clothed in clean robes (Zech. iii. 1 ff.). Here Satan
actually comes into conflict with God because, martinet that he
is for the full rigour of the law, he is totally blind to the other
side of God's character. Retribution is not God's last word on
human sin.

In the New Testament and the Rabbinic writings Satan still
retains his legal duties as prosecutor, frequently with Michael
as the counsel for the defence (1 Pet. v. 8; Jud. 9; 1 Tim. iii. 6;
Ber. 46[a]; *Yom.* 20[a]). For Michael is the great prince who has
charge of the people of God (Dan. x. 21; xii. 1; *Yom.* 77[a];
Ḥul. 40[a]). To his antinomian opponents who treat with con-
tempt the moral law and its angelic guardians, whom he calls

'the glories', Jude commends the behaviour of Michael, who in a debate over the body of Moses paid Satan the respect due to a fellow barrister (Jud. 8-9). As long as there are human sinners to accuse, Satan's presence in heaven must be tolerated, for God himself recognizes the justice of the indictment. Thus, although John depicts the battle between Michael and Satan in military terms, it was essentially a legal battle between opposing counsel, which resulted in one of them being disbarred.

The earthly side of this legal battle is worked out fully in the Fourth Gospel, to which we may turn for further light. The turning-point comes when Satan, through his earthly minions, of whom Judas Iscariot is the chief (John xiii. 2), accuses Jesus and demands the death penalty. Jesus is innocent, as Pilate thrice declares, and Satan, though he wins his case in the earthly court, loses it in the court of final appeal: 'the prince of this world is approaching, but he has no rights over me' (John xiv. 30). But he loses more than this one case. For Jesus, like his namesake Joshua the high priest, is a representative figure, standing trial on behalf of those he represents. He is the Messiah, in whose person God intends 'to gather into one the scattered children of God' (John xi. 52). He has 'loved his own' with a love which amounts to total identification (John xiii. 1). His death is therefore not his judgment alone but the judgment of all men. 'Now is the judgment of this world; now shall the prince of this world be driven out. And when I am lifted up from the earth, I shall draw all men to myself' (John xii. 31-32). Because he has identified himself with all men where they are, under the judgment of God, he draws all men through his death into unity with himself where he is, in the bosom of the Father; and Satan, having lost his case, loses also his job. There is no room for him any more in heaven, and it remains only for Michael to drum him out. As Paul puts it, 'there is now no condemnation for those who are in Christ Jesus' (Rom. viii. 1). Or as John puts it, **they were overpowered, and left not a 8 trace to be found in heaven.**

Satan's legal functions account for his presence in heaven, but they also help us to understand some of his other activities. Because of his narrow, one-sided devotion to law he misunderstands and misrepresents God. It is primarily for this reason

9 that he is called **the deceiver of the whole world.** The arch-
enemy of God is a parody of God's own truth. He deceives by
telling lies about God. He is to be identified with **that old
serpent** of Eden, who, not knowing the truth of God, told lies
to Eve and so brought death to her and Adam (John viii.
44-47; cf. Wis. ii. 24). At the root of all the world's evil there
is a lie, which distorts man's proper relationship both to his
fellows and to his Creator (cf. Rom. i. 21).

So far the heavenly commentary has guided us to a consistent and theologically intelligible interpretation of the war in
heaven. It is not to be regarded as a sequel to the birth and
enthronement of the Messiah, but rather as a second view of the
same events in the light of a different myth. But now we have
to face a difficulty. The voice continues: **the accuser of
11 our brothers is driven out ... they have conquered him
by the life-blood of the Lamb and the testimony they bore.**
The interpreter is apparently treating not only the Cross but
the great martyrdom as a *fait accompli.* Can it be that we were
wrong in identifying the symbolic victory of Michael with the
real earthly victory of the Cross? Ought we to have identified
it instead with the victory of the Conquerors? Was it because
they had already borne their martyr testimony to the redeeming power of the Lamb that there was now no room left for
Satan in heaven? If we read this one verse in isolation, there
would indeed seem to be no other possible way of taking it.
Yet this cannot be what John intended. For Satan's expulsion
from heaven calls forth from the heavenly choir a song of
12 jubilation, but also a solemn warning to earth and sea: **the
Devil has come down to you in great fury, knowing that
his time is short;** and it is the ejected Satan who, thwarted in
his attack on the woman, goes 'to make war on the rest of her
children' (xii. 17). The great attack upon the church which is
described in the following two chapters is to be understood as
the death throes of the Devil. At this stage in the story, then,
the martyrdom is still ahead; but it can be treated as a *fait
accompli* because in one sense the work of salvation was fully
accomplished on the Cross. Christ died as the last Adam, and
his death and victory were all-inclusive. This is not a concept
peculiar to the theology of Paul, it is shared by John. He has

already spoken of 'the ordeal and sovereignty and endurance which are ours in Jesus' (i. 9), and he is about to pronounce a blessing on 'the dead who die in the Lord henceforth' (xiv. 13). But this union with Christ was effected by the Cross. In him the martyrs had already borne their testimony, with him they had already died, with him they had already conquered the accusing Satan and entered on their reign. **No love of life** had **caused** him **to shrink from death,** and in his story theirs was already written. Their task was but to ratify and appropriate what he had done once for all in their name.

It is to be noted, however, that Satan does not accept defeat without a struggle. The real victory of Michael may be a forensic one, the victory of an advocate whose case is wholly dependent on the record of his client; but it takes open war to clinch it. Satan is stripped of his rights, but not of his power to do appalling harm. He is thus made the symbol for two different aspects of the problem of evil. For sin has two different kinds of consequence: it estranges man both from God and from his fellows, but it also sets in motion a chain reaction of damage, which continues to operate independently of its original author. God's amnesty may end man's rebellion, but it does not automatically make good, or even halt, the damage that rebellion has caused. Satan as accuser is a reminder that there can be no amnesty which is a denial of the fundamental holiness and justice of God; it must be plain that God 'is both himself just and the justifier of men' (Rom. iii. 26). But because he is a parody and distortion of God's truth, Satan as the Devil continues to have an independent existence of his own, even after the claims of justice have been satisfied. The Cross is God's cure for sin, both for its guilt and for its power. It is his declarative act of acquittal, grounded in Christ's self-identification with sinful men, and needing for its completion only that they should accept in faith what he has offered in love. But it also shows how the power of evil may be absorbed by innocent suffering and neutralized by forgiving love. If the world is to hear and accept God's amnesty, there must be witnesses; and if evil is to burn itself out to the bitter end, their testimony must be the testimony of suffering.

(13) When the dragon found that he had been thrown down to the earth, he went in pursuit of the woman who had borne the male child. **(14)** But the woman was given two great eagle's wings, to fly away to her place in the desert, where she was to be sustained for a time, times, and half a time, out of the serpent's reach. **(15)** Then the serpent spewed out a river of water after the woman, to engulf her in its flood. **(16)** But the earth came to the woman's rescue, and opened its mouth and swallowed the river which the dragon had spewed from his mouth. **(17)** So the dragon stormed at the woman, and went off to wage war on the rest of her children, those who keep God's commandments and hold the testimony of Jesus; and he stood on the sea-shore.

Having failed in his attempt to prevent the birth, i.e. the enthronement of the Messiah, a failure which incidentally cost him his place in the heavenly court, Satan now turns to attack the church. This paragraph is clearly a detailed elaboration of xii. 6, and proves that we were fully justified in treating xii. 7-12 as an elaboration of xii. 4-5. John now reverts to his Exodus typology. As Pharoah pursued the escaping Israelites (Exod.
13 xiv. 8), so **the dragon** now **went in pursuit of the woman.**
14 Like Israel, she was borne on **eagle's wings** to the safety of the desert (Exod. xix. 4). Just as Pharaoh had given orders to drown
15 the Israelite children in the Nile, so the dragon **spewed out a river of water** to engulf the woman. **Water,** we recall, is his natural weapon, for his home is the primaeval abyss. As the earth opened to swallow the rebels in the desert and so to protect the sanctity of the people of God (Num. xvi. 33), so now
16 the earth **opened its mouth and swallowed the river.**
   The sources of John's imagery are clear enough. But to what earthly realities do they correspond? What was happening in
15 Sardis or Pergamum, Ephesus or Thyatira, when **the serpent spewed out** his **river,** only to see it sink ineffectually, like the Syrian Abana, into the sands of the desert? What was this rush

of great waters, this torrent of destruction, this flood which would have swept God's people away (Ps. xxxii. 6; xviii. 4; cxxiv. 4), if God had not kept his promise to dry up the rivers through which they must pass (Isa. xlii. 15; xliii. 2; l. 2)? John clearly distinguishes this Satanic weapon from those Satan uses **to wage war on the rest of her children.** It was the failure of the river that sent the dragon off in a storm of temper to summon the monster from the infernal sea. The river then cannot represent either persecutions which had taken place before the time of John's vision or the destruction of Jerusalem by the armies of Titus; for both of these were works of the monster, whose seven heads were the seven hills of Rome. The river must be some more direct activity of Satan and we recall that John has told us in his letters what tricks Satan has been up to in the churches of Asia. In Smyrna and Philadelphia there has been trouble from 'Satan's synagogue', 'liars who claim to be Jews when they are not'. Slanderous attacks from without, false teaching designed to corrupt the church's faith and to destroy it from within—this is the river of lies which the serpent **spewed from his mouth.** To give the lie to the slanders, to hold fast to the true gospel and hate the works of the Nicolaitans, is to escape to the safe **place in the desert.** For the desert is that vantage point outside the great city from which its seductive falsity can be seen in its true colours (xvii. 3).

In the desert the woman is **to be sustained for a time, times, and half a time.** This is the original form of Daniel's mysterious crisis period (Dan. xii. 7), which John has previously paraphrased as forty-two months (xi. 2) or twelve hundred and sixty days (xi. 3; xii. 6). This three and a half year period is not to be reckoned from the enthronement of the Messiah and the consequent ejection of Satan; it is not the whole of world history from the Ascension to the Parousia. It begins when Satan goes **off to wage war on the rest of** the woman's 17 **children,** and to that end calls forth the monster from the abyss. For forty-two months is also the period during which the monster is allowed to wage war against God's people (xiii. 5).

Satan is powerless to destroy the church, but he can at least vent his thwarted fury through state persecution on individual Christians—**the rest of her children.** The word John uses for

children is *sperma* (seed). This is a conscious echo of the words of God to the serpent in Eden:

'I will put enmity between you and the woman,
  Between your seed and her seed;
  They shall wound your head,
  And you shall wound their heels'

(Gen. iii. 15).

It is an echo inevitably roused by the fact that **the serpent** is the same serpent. But it is scarcely more than an echo. It would be quite misleading to suggest that the woman is Eve, the mother of all the living. She is a symbol who has some of the attributes of Eve, but her children are **those who keep God's commandments and hold the testimony of Jesus.**

The scene closes with Satan taking his stand **on the seashore.** The dragon has returned for reinforcements to the same cosmic ocean which is his native element. (The AV here followed an inferior text, which read: 'I stood on the seashore'. The words were therefore taken to be the opening of the next chapter. But there is no doubt that the correct reading is that given in the translation above.)

xiii. 1-10. THE MONSTER FROM THE ABYSS

(1) Then out of the sea I saw a monster rising, with ten horns and seven heads. On its horns were ten diadems, and on each head a blasphemous name. (2) The monster I saw was like a leopard, its feet were like a bear's, and its mouth like a lion's mouth. The dragon conferred on it his own power and throne and great authority. (3) One of its heads bore the deadly marks of slaughter; but its deadly wound was healed. The whole world gaped after the monster; (4) they worshipped the dragon because he had conferred his authority on the monster, and they worshipped the monster, saying, 'Who is like the monster? Who can fight against it?' (5) It was allowed to utter boasts and blasphemy, and was given free scope for

forty-two months. (6) It opened its mouth in blasphemy against God, blaspheming his name and his dwelling, that is, those who dwell in heaven. (7) It was allowed to wage war on God's people and to conquer them; and it was given authority over every tribe, people, tongue, and nation. (8) All the inhabitants of earth will worship it, all whose names have not been written in the book of life of the Lamb slaughtered from the foundation of the world. (9) Hear, if you have ears to hear! (10) Whoever is for prison, to prison he goes. Whoever kills with the sword must with the sword be killed. This calls for the endurance and faith of God's people.

The **monster** which John now sees emerging **out of the sea** 1 is the same as the one he has already described as rising from the abyss (xi. 7). In the Greek Old Testament *abyssos* is used as a rendering for the Great Deep, the primaeval ocean of the creation story (Gen. i. 2; vii. 11), and for the sea in general (Job xxviii. 14; xxxviii. 16). It is said of Wisdom that she guided Israel through the Red Sea, but engulfed their enemies 'and cast them up again out of the depths of the abyss' (Wis. x. 19). In Romans x. 7 Paul quotes a Greek version of Deuteronomy xxx. 13, in which the question, 'Who will cross the sea for us?' has become 'Who will descend into the abyss?'; and he takes the abyss to be synonymous with the underworld. The sea, then is the nether reservoir of evil, which has its upper counterpart in the heavenly sea of glass. But this does not exhaust its significance. For John contrasts the monster from the sea with another monster rising out of the land (xiii. 11). This is certainly an allusion to a Jewish tradition that God had created on the fifth day two mythical creatures, Leviathan and Behemoth, the one to inhabit the sea and the other the land (1 *Enoch* lx. 7 ff.; 2 Esdras vi. 49 ff.; 2 *Bar.* xxix. 4; *Baba B.* 74ᵃ). So the first monster is Leviathan; and it is hardly surprising that, like the dragon which summons it from the deep, it has **seven heads** (see notes on iv. 6). But John does not employ mythological detail merely to adorn his narrative, and it is therefore likely that the contrast between sea and land had a geographical significance as well as a mythical one. As Ramsay pointed out (*op. cit.* pp. 103 f.), whatever comes from the sea is a foreign import, and whatever comes from the land is a native product. The first monster represents the Roman imperial power which, for the province of Asia, annually came up **out of the sea,** with the arrival of the proconsul at Ephesus. The second monster represents an indigenous authority. There is a good parallel in the Apocalypse of Ezra, where an eagle, representing Rome, appears from the sea (2 Esdras xi. 1); for the eagle has none of Leviathan's mythical associations with the cosmic deep, and its coming from the sea must be a simple geographical fact.

Out of the same cosmic depths Daniel had seen four beasts rise: a lion with eagle's wings, representing Babylon; a bear, representing Media; a winged leopard with four heads, representing Persia; and a grim nameless horror of a beast with ten horns, representing the Greek kingdom of the Seleucid successors of Alexander (Dan. vii. 2-7). In an earlier chapter Daniel had told how Nebuchadnezzar had for idolatry been turned into a beast with eagle's feathers and talons, very like the symbolic creature of the subsequent vision. He recovered his human shape only when he had learnt the lesson that 'the Most High controls the sovereignty of the world and gives it to whom he wills' (Dan. iv. 17, 25, 32). All political power is the gift of God; but when men deify the state, either directly by a religious cult or indirectly by demanding for it the total loyalty and obedience that are due to God alone, it ceases to be human and becomes bestial. Some Jewish expositors had identified Daniel's fourth kingdom with Rome (2 Esdras xii. 10; cf. '*Abodah Z.* 2ᵇ; *Shebu.* 6ᵇ). John, using a greater artistic freedom, depicts a monster with some of the characteristics of all four of Daniel's beasts, which he lists in reverse order: it had **ten horns,**
2 it **was like a leopard, its feet were like a bear's, and its mouth was like a lion's mouth.** It was thus the very epitome of worldly and tyrannical empire.

In Daniel's vision the **ten horns** were the ten kings of the Seleucid dynasty who preceded the little horn, Antiochus Epiphanes. John uses this symbol because it was the only identifiable characteristic of the fourth beast, and he needs it to complete his composite picture. But he has the **seven heads** to symbolize the Roman emperors, and does not require the

horns for this purpose. They are therefore demoted, and represent either the puppet kings of client kingdoms or men
potentially of imperial rank who never actually occupied the
throne (see xvii. 12). They wear diadems, because the monster is
making a blasphemous claim to be King of kings, a title which
by right belongs to Christ (xix. 16). Of the seven heads we shall
hear more in chapter xvii. For the moment all we are told is
that each bore **a blasphemous name.** Every one of John's
readers must have seen the heads of the emperors with their
blasphemous names on the imperial coinage. Julius Caesar,
Augustus, Claudius, Vespasian, and Titus had been officially
declared divine at death by the Roman Senate, and the three
last had anticipated the action of the Senate by using the title
Divus on coins in their own lifetime. In the eastern provinces,
where Greek was the official language, the coins bore the title
Theos, which constituted a rather more sharply defined claim
to deity. Augustus from his accession had called himself 'Son
of the Divine Julius', and all his successors except Claudius and
Vespasian had followed his example. All emperors inherited the
name Augustus, in Latin a title of majesty with somewhat vague
religious overtones, but in its Greek form Sebastos a positive
invitation to emperor-worship. Nero had appeared on coins as
Apollo or Helios. The province of Asia had been more assiduous
than other provinces in developing the imperial cult, and temples
to Rome and Augustus had been erected in many cities. To
crown all this Domitian had recently declared his wish to be
addressed as *Dominus et Deus*—Lord and God (Suet. *Dom.* 13).

When John says that **the dragon conferred on** the monster
his own power and throne, we must first note that, in spite of
his ejection from heaven, he still has a throne to confer. He has
lost his rights but not his power. He is still 'the prince of this
world' (John xii. 31; xiv. 20; xvi. 11), and the world is still
enemy-occupied territory, a house held by the 'strong man fully
armed' until a stronger than he shall come to dispossess him
(Mark iii. 27; Matt. xii. 29; Luke xi. 21 f.). Satan can still say
to the monster, as he once said to Jesus: 'To you I will give
authority over all this and the glory that belongs with it, for it
has been made over to me, and I give it to whom I will' (Luke
iv. 6). But it must not be thought that John is writing off all

civil government as an invention of the Devil. Whatever Satan
may claim, the truth is that 'the Most High controls the
sovereignty of the world and gives it to whom he wills' (Dan.
iv. 17). In the war between God and Satan, between good and
evil, the state is one of the defences established by God to
contain the powers of evil within bounds, part of the order
which God the Creator has established in the midst of chaos (cf.
Rom. xiii. 1-7). But when men worship the state, according to it
the absolute loyalty and obedience that are due not to Caesar
but to God, then the state goes over to the Enemy. What Satan
calls from the abyss is not government but that abuse of
government, the omnicompetent state. It is thus misleading to
say that the monster *is* Rome, for it is both more and less: more,
because Rome is only its latest embodiment; and less, because
Rome is also, even among all the corruptions of idolatry, 'God's
agent of punishment, for retribution on the offender' (Rom.
xiii. 4).

The monster is a parody of Christ. Previously John had seen
the Lamb 'bearing the marks of slaughter'; now he sees one of
3 the monster's heads bearing **the deadly marks of slaughter,**
and its death had been followed by something that could pass
for a resurrection. Now the head must be one of the emperors,
but John cannot mean simply that he had died; for 'five have
already fallen' (xvii. 10). He was an emperor who, more than
any other, typified the monster's character, for John goes on to
talk about the monster itself as though it had died and come to
life again (xiii. 12; xvii. 11). Since the main trait of the monster's
character is that it wages **war on God's people,** the emperor
who best fits the specifications is Nero. His suicide in A.D. 68
could have been regarded as a deadly wound, not merely to one
head of the monster, but to the monster as a whole; for it was
followed by a year of civil war in which the whole future of the
empire was in jeopardy. The Julio-Claudian line was at an end,
and there were those in Rome, particularly among the Stoics,
who would have welcomed a restoration of the Republic. Only
with the accession of Vespasian did the monster come to life
again. But in the meanwhile rumours had been circulating. Nero
was not really dead; he had gone into hiding in Parthia, and
would return at the head of a vast Parthian army to take revenge

on Rome. Three impostors came forward, claiming to be Nero, and two of them were well received in Parthia (Tac. *Hist.* i. 2; ii. 8; Suet. *Nero* 57). Among the Jews there were some who comforted themselves for the fall of Jerusalem with the hope that Rome would suffer a worse plight when Nero returned; for to them his matricide as well as his claims to divinity and his attack on the Jewish nation made him so abhorrent as to be well-nigh demonic (*Sib. Or.* iv. 119 ff.; 137 f.; v. 28 ff., 137 ff., 215 ff., 386). They even called him a serpent (*Sib. Or.* v. 29), perhaps with some memory of the legend that a snake had been found in his cradle when he was a baby (Tac. *Ann.* xi. 11). John must have been aware of all this, but he does not take it literally: Nero will indeed return, but reincarnated in a new persecuting emperor, an eighth who is one of the seven (xvii. 11).

John does not actually use the title Antichrist for the monster, though he might well have done. Jesus had prophesied the coming of 'false Christs and false prophets' (Mark xiii. 22); and, since John calls the second of his two monsters 'the false prophet' (xvi. 13; xix. 20; xx. 10), it is a reasonable inference that he thought of the first as a false Christ. The name Antichrist occurs in the New Testament only in the Johannine epistles (1 John ii. 18, 22; iv. 3; 2 John 7), where the Antichrist is said to be present in a strong heretical movement which has split the church; but the author assumes that his readers will recognize this as a radically new interpretation of a familiar tradition. Other traces of the same tradition may be found in two other New Testament books. In Mark xiii. 14 there is a reference to a new 'desecrating horror', which was to pollute the temple. This phrase had originally been applied by Daniel to the pagan altar erected in the temple by Antiochus Epiphanes (Dan. ix. 27; xi. 31; xii. 11), but Mark personifies it by using a masculine participle where a neuter one might have been expected. In 2 Thessalonians ii. 3-8 Paul warns his converts that the End cannot come until the rebellion has broken out, when the 'man of lawlessness' will make his appearance, as the full expression of a 'mystery of lawlessness', which is already operative in the world, though held in restraint for the present. His definition of the 'man of lawlessness' is that 'he elevates himself above every god, so called, that men worship, even to

the point of taking his seat in the temple of God, claiming to
be a god himself'. This passage was written less than ten years
after Caligula's mad attempt to have his own statue erected in
the Holy of holies in Jerusalem, so that, though we cannot
say that Caligula is the Antichrist, he undoubtedly sat for the
portrait. The interesting point is that in each of these four New
Testament contexts Antichrist is associated with different
historical situations. The myth of Antichrist is thus a true
myth, capable of re-enactment in varying circumstances.

The whole world gaped after the monster. Emperor-
worship was never, before Domitian, forced by an arrogant
imperialism on a reluctant populace. It was from the first the
spontaneous gratitude of a war-weary world for the Roman law
and the Roman peace. Year after year men had prayed to the
old gods for security and plenty, and their prayers had gone un-
answered. Now that Rome had given what the old gods were
powerless to give, ought not Rome to receive the worship the
old gods had never earned? John is not insensitive to the
achievement of Rome; without genuine appreciation he could
never have had the insight to know how seductive her appeal
could be. All the more important then for Christians to be aware
that to worship the emperor is to worship the monster from the
abyss, and to worship the monster is to worship the dragon
4 whose demonic authority it wields. **They worshipped the
dragon . . . and they worshipped the monster.**

In verse 6 we have one of the very few instances in the
Revelation where the text is in doubt. A few inferior MSS.,
including those on which the AV was based, read: 'blaspheming
his name and his dwelling *and* those who dwell in heaven'. The
best MSS. omit the 'and'; this is the reading followed in the
translation. The Chester Beatty papyrus reads: 'his dwelling in
heaven'. The best attested reading is also the hardest, so that
we have a double reason for adopting it; the other two are
scribal attempts to eliminate a difficulty of interpretation. What
6 then can John mean by identifying **God's dwelling** with
those who dwell in heaven? It is possible that by **those who
dwell in heaven** John simply means the angels, though it is
very hard to imagine what would be involved in blaspheming
angels. But there is a more attractive answer open to us. The

Greek word for dwelling is *skênê*, and in the two other places where John speaks of God's dwelling, using either the noun or the corresponding verb, it is God's dwelling *with men* that he means (vii. 15; xxi. 3). In xxi. 3 *skênê* is used almost as the equivalent of the Hebrew Shekinah, to denote God's tabernacling presence, and we are told that with the descent of the new Jerusalem this presence is at last among men. Yet the word *skênê* has a long history—it is the word used in the Septuagint for the tabernacle in the desert—which implies that this final settling of the divine presence among men has been anticipated over and over again in the past. We have also suggested that the descent of the new Jerusalem is not only a single final event, but one of which Christians have had a foretaste throughout the history of the church. Wherever there has been anyone found worthy to be a pillar in the temple of God, there has been the new Jerusalem, coming down out of heaven from God (iii. 12). If this is so, then **those who dwell in heaven** are men whose 'citizenship is in heaven' (Phil. iii. 20). In the streets of Philadelphia the dwellers in heaven rub shoulders with the 'inhabitants of earth'. The monster's attack on the church is a blaspheming of that divine presence which is to be found wherever two or three are gathered together in the name of Christ.

For the **forty-two months** of Daniel's prophecy the monster **5-7** **was given free scope . . . was allowed to wage war . . . was given authority over every tribe, people, tongue, and nation.** We are not to be permitted to forget that the monster acts only by divine permission, and that all he does is foreseen and provided for in the grand strategy of God. The list, which John uses here for the fourth time, reminds us that every place where the writ of the monster runs will provide its quota to the noble army of martyrs, whose death will be the means of bringing others to penitential fear and homage (v. 9; vii. 9; xi. 9). Only **the inhabitants of earth,** those earthbound sons of the old Adam whose spiritual home is the great city of Vanity Fair, prove to be real worshippers of the monster; for the great persecution will prove that many who appeared to be doomed to perish with their earthly master have their names after all **written in the book of life.**

167

8   **The book of life** belongs to **the Lamb slaughtered
from the foundation of the world.** The phrase **from the
foundation of the world** is naturally taken with the participle
slaughtered, which in Greek immediately precedes it. Many
commentators have insisted that, although the phrase is sepa-
rated from the main verb of the clause by twelve words, the sense
requires that they should be taken together: 'all whose names
have not been written from the foundation of the world in the
slaughtered Lamb's book of life'. Now John certainly says in
xvii. 8 that the names of the elect were 'written from the
foundation of the world in the book of life'. But that is no
reason why he should not be allowed here to say something
complementary. For the elect are those who have been predestined by God to be ransomed out of all nations by the life-
blood of the sacrified Lamb. If the names of the redeemed are
included in the predestining purpose of God, why not also the
means of their redemption? If the Cross is indeed the full
revelation of God's love and purpose, then must it not belong
to the eternal order? Other New Testament writers did not
think it strange that Jesus should have been 'Handed over by
the deliberate will and plan of God' (Acts ii. 23), 'a lamb
without mark of blemish . . . predestined before the foundation
of the world' (1 Pet. i. 19 f.).

We must not read more into John's doctrine of predestination
than he intends. He is not saying that **the inhabitants of earth
will worship** the monster because they have no choice, because this is the fate to which they have been destined from all
eternity. His doctrine springs from the thoroughly biblical
idea that salvation is from start to finish the unmerited act of
God. But he constantly qualifies it with an equally strong statement of human responsibility. A man's name may be removed
from the book of life (iii. 5); and when the last judgment comes,
there are record books to be opened as well as the book of life
(xx. 12). Having a Semitic mind, John has no interest in carefully qualified statements, which would show how predestination and free will are related to one another; be simply sets the
two beliefs side by side without qualification and allows the one
to qualify the other.

The last two verses of the passage present some interesting

critical problems. Long ago Jeremiah had proclaimed God's
doom on sinful Jerusalem:

'Those who are for pestilence, to pestilence,
And those who are for the sword, to the sword;
Those who are for famine, to famine,
And those who are for captivity, to captivity'.

(Jer. xv. 2; cf. xliii. 11)

John is obviously using Jeremiah's words, but is he also adopting Jeremiah's meaning? **Whoever is for prison, to prison he 10
goes. Whoever kills with the sword must with the sword
be killed.** Is this, as in Jeremiah, a threat against the rebellious
world, or has John turned Jeremiah's threat into a warning to the
loyal Christian and an invitation to co-operate with the redemptive purpose of God? The question is somewhat complicated
by a textual variant. Most MSS. have the reading which is given
in the translation, but two important MSS. read: 'Whoever
is to be killed with the sword must with the sword be killed'.
We have also to take account of the relation between this saying
and the saying of Jesus in Gethsemane: 'All who take the sword
die by the sword' (Matt. xxvi. 52). If the reading in our text
is the correct one, then the other reading is a scribal assimilation
to the sense of Jeremiah. If the other reading is the correct
one, the reading in our text is a scribal assimilation to the saying
of Jesus. There are four reasons for believing that the reading in
our text is the right one, and that John has transformed Jeremiah's threat into a challenge to the Conqueror. (*a*) **Hear, if 9
you have ears to hear!** In each of the seven letters to the
churches these words accompanied the promise to the Conqueror. By their solemn repetition here at the heart of his book
John indicates that he is turning once again to give the church
its marching orders. If God allows the monster to wage war
on his people and to conquer them, what must God's people
do? They must allow themselves to be conquered as their Lord
had done, so that like their Lord they may win a victory not of
this world. (*b*) The threat of **prison** or captivity is meaningful
for the prospective martyr (cf. ii. 10), but not for the worshippers of the monster. When Jeremiah was prophesying,
transportation into captivity in Babylon was precisely what

Jerusalem could expect; but there is not the slightest suggestion that this is one of the punishments in store for the inhabitants of earth. (c) John frequently echoes the teaching of Jesus, and he does so here. Like Jesus in Gethsemane, the church must abjure the use of **the sword.** God has given to Rome the *ius gladii* (cf. ii. 12) for the suppression of crime and disorder, and even when that authority has become corrupt it must still be obeyed. There must be no resistance to the civil authority which God has ordained, like the insensate rebellion that ended in the destruction of Jerusalem. (d) The clinching argu-
10 ment is in the final sentence. **This calls for the endurance and faith of God's people.** For the prospect of retribution on an ungodly world calls for no such endurance and faith. What calls for loyal endurance is that the church must submit without resistance to the conquering attack of the monster, since only in this way can the monster be halted in its track. Evil is self-propagating. Like the Hydra, the many-headed monster can grow another head when one has been cut off. When one man wrongs another, the other may retaliate, bear a grudge, or take his injury out on a third person. Whichever he does, there are now two evils where before there was one; and a chain reaction is started, like the spreading of a contagion. Only if the victim absorbs the wrong and so puts it out of currency, can it be prevented from going any further. And this is why the great ordeal is also the great victory.

xiii. 11-18. THE MONSTER FROM THE LAND

(11) Then I saw another monster rising out of the land; it had two horns like a lamb's but spoke like a dragon. (12) It wielded all the authority of the first monster in its presence, and made the earth and its inhabitants worship the first monster, whose deadly wound had been healed. (13) It worked great miracles, even making fire come down from heaven to earth before men's eyes. (14) By the miracles it was allowed to perform in the presence of the monster it deceived the inhabitants of earth, telling

them to make a statue to the monster which had received the sword-wound and had come to life. (15) It was allowed to give breath to the statue of the monster to make it speak, and to have everyone killed who did not worship the statue. (16) It caused everyone, great or small, rich or poor, slave or free, to have a mark branded on the right hand or on the forehead, (17) and no one was allowed to buy or sell unless he had the mark, the name of the monster or the number of its name. (18) This calls for wisdom: anyone with intelligence may calculate the number of the monster, for it is a man's number, and the number is six hundred and sixty-six.

In the province of Asia the imperial cult was in the hands of a body known in Greek as the *koinon* and in Latin as the *commune*. The *commune Asiae*, a provincial council consisting of representatives from the major towns, was at least as old as Mark Antony, who found it already in existence. Augustus, who made a practice of using existing political institutions wherever possible, built it into his system of provincial administration, and used it as a model for similar councils elsewhere. The Asiarchs (Acts xix. 31) were members of the commune and probably local priests of the imperial cult as well. This indigenous body with its delegated power is John's **monster 11 rising out of the land.** In all matters of local government it could be said to wield the authority of the first monster. The presence of the monster from the sea was represented by the proconsul; but, since his was only an annual appointment, he would normally be only too pleased to leave the routine administration to the local authority. It was historically true that the commune had made the earth and its inhabitants worship the first monster; for it would never have occurred to Augustus to claim divinity, if the eastern provinces, accustomed as they were to the worship of their previous oriental rulers, had not taken the initiative in elevating him to a place among the immortals, city vying with city for the right to erect a temple to Rome and Augustus. It was the commune that had given orders to make a statue to the emperor. If other emperors had subsequently gone further in their demands for worship, it was because Augustus had first accepted in the east a spontaneous tribute of loyalty and gratitude which he discouraged to the end of his life in the less demonstrative west.

It had two horns like a lamb's but spoke like a dragon. Like its master, the first monster, the monster from the land is a parody of Christ, its lamblike appearance belied by its Satanic voice. It seems to have been part of the Antichrist

13 tradition that the false Christ should work **miracles** (2 Thess. ii. 9; cf. *Asc. Isa.* iv. 10; 2 Esdras v. 4; *Sib. Or.* iii. 63 ff.). John, perhaps with a memory of the warning against false prophets in Deuteronomy xiii. 1-2, transfers this function to the false prophet. He is to be the false Elijah, **making fire come down from heaven to earth,** and so preparing the way for the false

14- Messiah. It is not clear whether the word **deceived** means that
15 John regarded the miracles as fraudulent, the stock tricks of the magician and the ventriloquist in the service of a fake religion, or as genuine manifestations of demonic power, derived from Satan 'the deceiver of the whole world'. We have only John's word for it that such methods were used in the imperial cult to impress a superstitious populace, but there is no need to question his accuracy. The widespread influence of sorcery and ventriloquism attested in Acts (xiii. 6 ff.; xvi. 16; xix. 13 ff.) reached even into court circles; for Tiberius had surrounded himself with astrologers in his retreat on the island of Capri, Apelles the miracle-monger of Ascalon had been welcomed at the court of Caligula, and Apollonius of Tyana had been the friend of Nero, Vespasian, and Titus. There may be little solid history in Philostratus' life of Apollonius, whom he credits with a miraculous birth, sudden appearances and disappearances, and the power to cast out demons, to heal the sick, and to raise the dead. There may be still less history in the Christian stories which gathered around the name of Simon Magus, who was reputed to have brought statues to life (*Clem. Recog.* iii. 47; cf. Just. *Apol.* I. 26; Iren. *Haer.* i. 23; Eus. *H.E.* ii. 13. 1-8). But both cycles of legend accurately reflect the spirit of the age. Even the Pythagorean philosophy, which had a new wave of popularity at this time, was a strange amalgam of magic, mysticism, and mathematics.

Many ancient practices have been suggested as the back-

ground for **the mark of the monster.** *Charagma* was a tech- 16-
nical term for the imperial stamp on commercial documents,[1] 17
and also for the impress of the emperor's head on the coinage.
Either of these usages would explain the mark on the hand and
the inability **to buy or sell** without the mark, but not the
setting of the mark **on the forehead.** Slaves were branded on
the forehead, but this was regarded as a sign of disgrace, not of
loyalty. In the fifth century B.C. defeated soldiers were branded
on the forehead if they took service under their victors (Herod.
vii. 233; Plut. *Nic.* 29; Curt. v. 5)—the Athenians branded the
men of Samos with an owl (Plut. *Per.* 26);[2] but there is no
reason to think that this practice still prevailed in the first
century A.D. The Jews wore the *tephillin* or phylacteries
(leather pouches containing verses of scripture) on the forehead
and the left forearm. Stauffer has conjectured that the high
priest of the imperial cult 'wore the imperial image on the
golden circlet on his brow and on his signet ring'.[3] Probably
John's symbol was compounded of many remembered elements;
for he did not expect the mark to be visible to the eye, any more
than the seal of the living God, of which it is a travesty. But a
parody of the seal of God required only a mark on the forehead,
and this suggests that John was prompted to add the mark on
the hand because he was thinking of the emperor's head and
superscription on the coinage. It is unlikely that he expected
Christians to be starved to death or to submission by a boycott
officially imposed by the commune. No doubt Christians were
accustomed to the unofficial social pressures of pagan commercial life. But John knew from experience that, when Rome took
official cognisance of an illegal religion, it was always by criminal
charges in the lawcourt, and not by economic sanction. The one
way in which the commune could make it impossible to buy or
sell without the mark of the monster was by the coinage, for
which it held responsibility in the province of Asia.

[1] A. Deissmann, *Bible Studies*, pp. 240 ff.; *Light from the Ancient East*,
p. 345.
[2] Plutarch says that the Samians branded their Athenian prisoners with an
owl, because the Athenians had branded Samian prisoners with a *samaena*
or galley. But he must have got the story back to front: the owl was the
emblem of Athens, and the *samaena* appears on Samian coins.
[3] E. Stauffer, *Christ and the Caesars*, p. 179.

18 **The number of the monster** is explicitly said to be **the number of its name** and **a man's number**. Whatever else may remain obscure, there can be no doubt about the method by which John invites his intelligent readers to calculate the number. He is using the device known to the Jews as gematria, but practised by Greeks as well as Jews. In both Hebrew and Greek the letters of the alphabet were used as numerals (the Greek alphabet for this purpose including the obsolete letters digamma and koppa), and this double function of the alphabet was a standing invitation to convert a name into a number or a number into a name. The Jewish Rabbis used gematria as an esoteric method of expounding the meaning of scripture, sometimes thereby sucking an elevating sense from an otherwise unintelligible or immoral passage (*Yoma* 20ᵃ; *Nazir* 5ᵃ; *Sanh.* 22ᵃ; *Uzkin* 12). Among the Greeks it seems to have been more of a parlour game. Deissman cites two examples from the *graffiti* at Pompeii, one of which reads: 'I love the girl whose name is phi mu epsilon (545)'.[1] But a very important example in Greek occurs in the *Sibylline Oracles* (i. 324 ff.), where the numerical value of the name Jesus is given as 888 (I = 10, H = 8, Σ = 200, O = 70, U = 400, Σ = 200). Later in the same work there is a list of emperors, beginning with Julius Caesar, given under the numerical value of their initial letters (*Sib. Or.* v. 12-42).

Since anyone with intelligence may calculate the number, John must have thought that the identity of the man was self-evident. Unfortunately for the modern reader, though it is easy enough to turn a name into a number, it is not so simple to proceed in the opposite direction. A sum has only one correct answer, but an answer may be the answer to many sums. The first writer to make a serious attempt to solve the conundrum was Irenaeus, who, proceeding on the assumption that the units, tens, and hundreds must add up separately without any carrying, produced three solutions: Euanthas, Lateinos, and Teitan, of which only the first and least probable is a man's name (*Haer.* v. 30.3). Most modern scholars have preferred to start from the obvious hypothesis that the man who has given his identity and number to the monster is Nero, and to try to

[1] *Light from the Ancient East*, p. 276.

equate the number with his name. This cannot be done in
Greek, for the Greek Neron yields a total of 1,005; but the
Greek Neron Kaisar, transliterated into Hebrew script, pro-
duces the required 666 (nun = 50, resh = 200, waw = 6, nun =
50, qoph = 100, samech = 60, resh = 200). One advantage of
this solution is that it explains the western tradition, known to
Irenaeus, that the number was 616; since a Hebraized version
of the Latin form Nero Caesar would lack the second nun.
The only objection to it, and it is rather a serious one, is
that John was writing in Greek and could not count on a knowledge even of the Hebrew alphabet among his readers (but see
also xvi. 16). The difficulty with a Greek solution is that Greek
names tend to give far higher totals than Hebrew ones, because
of the absence of vowels from the Hebrew alphabet. Titos adds
up to 880, and Sebastos to 978. Gaios Kaisar and Kaisar Theos
each give 616; but the manuscript evidence is heavily in favour
of 666 as the original reading. An ingenious solution has been
put forward by Stanislas Giet,[1] on the basis of the passage in
the *Sibylline Oracles*, mentioned above, where the emperors are
listed by the number of their initial letters. The initials of the
emperors' names in Greek from Julius Caesar to Vespasian,
add up to 666 (K = 20, Σ = 200, T = 300, Γ = 3, K = 20,
N = 50, Γ = 3, O = 70). This result, however, is attained by
the curious and not obviously justifiable means of including
Galba, but omitting Otho and Vitellius. But a more serious
objection is that it cannot be said to be the number of a man's
name. An even more ingenious solution is that of Stauffer,[2]
who suggests that John was calculating the numerical value of
the legend on the current coins of Domitian. Domitian's full
title was Imperator Caesar Domitianus Augustus Germanicus,
or in Greek Autokrator Kaisar Dometianos Sebastos Germani-
kos. The Greek title abbreviated to Α.ΚΑΙ.ΔΟΜΕΤ.ΣΕΒ.ΓΕ.
duly yields the required total. This theory fits well with what
we have said about the mark of the monster. Apart from its
complexity it has only one flaw: although each of these ab-
breviations by itself is well attested, there is no single coin on
which all five occur together.

[1] *L'Apocalypse et l'histoire, étude historique sur l'Apocalypse johannique.*
[2] *Coniectanea Neotestamentica*, XI, pp. 237 ff.

Lohmeyer and Farrer have argued that, whatever irre-
coverable name may lie behind John's cryptogram, he would
not have used gematria at all unless the number 666 had
appealed to him for other symbolic reasons. For 666 is a remarkable number in many ways. It is the number which per-
sistently falls short of the perfect number seven. It is the
parody of the number of Jesus, 888; six being the number of
Good Friday and eight the number of Easter Day. It is two-
thirds of a thousand, one third of the monster's kingdom having
been destroyed by the trumpet plagues. Above all it is a
triangular number, in sinister contrast with the square numbers
of the martyrs and the heavenly city (vii. 4; xxi. 16). The Greeks,
lacking a mathematically manageable system of numerals, used
to solve arithmetical problems by geometrical arrangements of
dots. The product of two numbers was a plane number, or, if
the two numbers were the same, a square number. The product
of three numbers was a solid number, or, if they were the same,
a cube. The sum of a series of consecutive numbers beginning
with unity$\frac{n(n+1)}{2}$was a triangular number; and 666 is
the triangular number of 36, which is itself the triangular
number of 8—and the monster is an eighth (xvii. 11). How
much of all this, if any, passed through John's mind, it is hard to
say. The trouble with this sort of computation is that it always
proves too much. The sinister character of the triangular
number 153 was apparently lost on the author of John xxi. 11.
If 666 is all that is left out of a thousand after the destruction of a
third by the trumpet plagues, what has happened to the quarter
destroyed by the four horsemen, or the tenth of the city that
fell in the great earthquake? And how can 8 be at one and the
same time the symbol of the monster and the symbol of Easter
Day?

The enigma of the monster's mark and number can easily
distract our attention from the much more important question
raised by the passage as a whole. What did John expect to
happen to the church? Did he think that through the machinations of the second monster the whole world would be divided
without remainder into two classes, those who earned eternal
condemnation for worshipping the monster and those who lost

their lives for refusing to do so? A little reflection will show that
this is more than his words imply. When he says that the commune **was allowed . . . to have everyone killed who did** 15
not worship the statue, he is talking about the legal status of
the Christians, not about their actual fate. It would be within
the legal competence of the local authorities to bring a capital
charge against anyone who did not join in the worship of the
emperor; how systematically they did this would be another
matter. We have already seen that John expected only some at
Smyrna to be imprisoned (ii. 10), and only two lampstands to
be called to martyrdom (xi. 4). His words here are a quotation
from the story of the fiery furnace (Dan. iii. 5-6); and no one
would suppose that, because only Shadrach, Meshach, and
Abednego were thrown into the furnace, all other Jews in
Babylon must have been apostates who obeyed the command
to worship Nebuchadnezzar's statue. Like Nebuchadnezzar's
decree, the threat of the second monster expresses the demand
of the state for total submission, but it does not necessarily
imply total martyrdom. Nor does the worship of the monster
necessarily imply inescapable reprobation. All oracles of doom,
whether prophetic or apocalyptic, are expressed in uncondi-
tional terms, but carrying an unarticulated condition: unless they
repent.

xiv. 1-5. THE SOLDIERS OF THE CROSS

**(1) Then I looked, and there on mount Zion stood the
Lamb, and with him a hundred and forty-four thousand
who had his name and the name of his Father written on
their foreheads. (2) I heard a sound from heaven like the
roar of many waters and the peal of mighty thunder.
The sound I heard was like the music of harpers playing
their harps (3) and singing a new song before the throne
and the four living creatures and the elders. No one
could learn that song except the hundred and forty-four
thousand who had been ransomed from the earth.
(4) These are men who did not defile themselves with**

**women, but kept themselves chaste; and they follow the
Lamb wherever he goes. They have been ransomed from
all mankind to be firstfruits for God and the Lamb.
(5) No lie has been found on their lips; they are without
blemish.**

1   The mention of **mount Zion** recalls to our attention, in case
we have forgotten, that John is engaged in an exposition of
Psalm ii as Christian scripture (cf. xi. 18; xii. 5). The psalm
depicts a world-wide rebellion of the nations against God, and
tells of God's plan to entrust the suppression of the revolt to
his son, the anointed king—'I have set my king on Zion, my
holy hill'; and it ends with an appeal to the rulers of the earth
to do homage before they are overtaken by God's final day of
reckoning. Like other New Testament writers, John believed
that this psalm was in the first instance Christological: it was
Jesus against whom 'Herod and Pontius Pilate conspired with
the heathen and the peoples of Israel' (Acts iv. 27), Jesus who
'was appointed Son of God with power after he rose from the
dead' (Rom. i. 4). But the point that he has been hammering
home in chapter after chapter is that the initial victory of Jesus
needed to be repeated in the victory of the Conquerors (iii. 21),
who were to share with Christ the task of reducing the rebellious
world to submission (ii. 26-27). In the last chapter he has shown
in some detail the form which Christians could expect heathen
hostility to take. Now he is ready to describe the decisive battle,
and, with a characteristic twist for which we should by now be
prepared, he sees **on mount Zion,** not the terrible warrior king
of the psalmist's hope, but **the Lamb.**

With him come the Conquerors, readily identifiable by their
number (vii. 4), the names **written on their foreheads**
according to the promise given to the church of Philadelphia
2   (iii. 12), and the accompaniment of **harpers playing their
harps** (xv. 2). We can now see why the **hundred and forty-
four thousand** were enumerated by tribes (vii. 4-8). It was a
military roll-call, like the census of 1 Chronicles iv-vii. This is
the army of the Lord, and, while it is taking its action stations,
John seems to hear already from heaven the mighty cadences of
the paean of victory. We do not need to be told the meaning of

the **new song,** for we have heard it twice before, once sung by 3
the heavenly choir to celebrate the victory of the Lamb, and
once sung by the Conquerors themselves in the proleptic
vision in which they appeared with the palms of victory in their
hands (v. 9; vii. 10; cf. Ps. xcviii. 1-3). But John hastens to add
that the real song of victory was still to be heard in the future,
since **no one could learn that song except** the martyrs whom
he now saw facing their ordeal. For this song would be compounded of agony and groans, transmuted by the mysterious
power of the Cross into the harmonies of heaven.

The military setting helps us to understand what would
otherwise be John's most puzzling sentence: **these are men** 4
who did not defile themselves with women, but kept
themselves chaste (lit. virgins). John is not asking his
readers to believe that all the victims of persecution would be
male, still less that they would all be celibate. He is not disclosing in an unguarded moment his personal predilection for
asceticism. Like everything else in his book this is a symbol,
and the source of his symbolism is the Deuteronomic regulations
for holy war (Deut. xx; xxiii. 9-10; cf. 1 Sam. xxi. 5; 2 Sam.
xi. 11). In ancient Israel war was initiated with religious ceremony, the technical term being to 'consecrate war' (Jer. vi. 4;
Mic. iii. 5; Joel iii. 9). Soldiers were therefore required to preserve ceremonial purity. 'When you go to war against your
enemies, you shall protect your camp against all contamination.
If there is a man among you who is unclean because of what
happens at night, he shall go outside the camp and not come
back into it; but when evening comes, he shall bathe himself
with water, and then after sundown he may come back into the
camp' (Deut. xxiii. 9-10; cf. Lev. xv. 16). To John this ceremonial purity was a natural symbol for moral purity from the
seductions of the great whore of Babylon and from that fornication which is idolatry (cf. ii. 14-20). The true virginity is that
which belongs to the pure of heart.

Like good soldiers the martyrs **follow the Lamb wherever**
he goes. The best commentary on this verse is the saying of
Jesus to Peter in the Fourth Gospel: 'Where I am going you
cannot follow me now, but later you shall follow' (John xiii. 36).
Peter could not follow because Jesus was going to that death

which was the salvation of the world and the glorification of the Son of Man. He was the grain of wheat which remained alone, until it should die and bear fruit; for even the disciples were to desert him and leave him alone (John xii. 24; xvi. 32). Only when on the Cross he had drawn all men, Peter included, into unity with himself, could Peter follow him on the road of self-sacrificing love (John xii. 32; xxi. 18 f.). Along that road the martyrs are now ready to travel, and we shall find that it leads them where it led Jesus—outside the city. They have been ransomed from the earth, and that means, as we have been told more than once, that they have been called to share Christ's royal and priestly office, so that through them he may complete his redeeming work (i. 6; v. 10; xi. 4). They are the blessed ones who die henceforth in the Lord (xiv. 13).

The ceremonial purity of the warrior enables John to make an easy transit from the language of battle to the language of sacrifice. The idea behind the offering of **firstfruits** was that all living things belong to God and must not be put to secular purposes without a recognition of his rights. The dedication of the firstfruits 'redeemed' the harvest, and so released it for common use, God's rights in the whole being guaranteed by his special possession of the part (Exod. xxxiv. 22; Lev. xxiii. 15-22; Num. xxviii. 26; Deut. xvi. 9-12). In the same way the first-born sons of men properly belong to God; but provision was made for their redemption, because God had accepted the Levites in their place (Num. viii. 14-18), to be a symbol of the holiness to which the whole nation was called. In the New Testament Jesus is called firstfruits because his resurrection was the token and guarantee of a greater ingathering (1 Cor. xv. 20, 23), and the Spirit is called firstfruits because it is the pledge of the full inheritance to come (Rom. viii. 23; 2 Cor. i. 22; v. 5; Eph. i. 14). Thus when John says that the martyrs **have been ransomed from all mankind to be firstfruits,** he cannot conceivably mean that they 'alone from the whole world have been ransomed' (NEB). He must mean that the offering of their lives to God in sacrifice is to be the opening ceremony of a great harvest-home. This conclusion is confirmed by the quotation which follows from Isaiah liii. 9. Like Jesus (1 Pet. ii. 22-24), the martyrs are to fulfil the Old Testament

prophecy of the innocent sufferer, numbered with the trans-
gressors although **no lie has been found on their lips;** for 5
it is God's will that their death should bring salvation to the
heathen. As Jesus had been the lamb without blemish or spot,
offered for the redemption of the world (1 Pet. i. 19; cf. Heb.
ix. 14), so **they are without blemish;** they are to prove by
their unwavering loyalty their fitness to be offered on the altar
of sacrifice.

xiv. 6-13. THE ETERNAL GOSPEL

**(6) Then I saw an angel flying in mid-heaven, with an
eternal gospel to proclaim to the inhabitants of earth, to
every nation, tribe, tongue, and people. (7) He cried
aloud, 'Fear God and do him homage; for the hour of his
judgment has come! Worship him who made heaven and
earth, the sea and the fresh-water springs!' (8) Another
angel, a second, followed, saying, 'Fallen, fallen is
Babylon the great, she who made all nations drink the
wine of the wrath of her fornication!' (9) And another
angel, a third, followed them, crying aloud, 'Whoever
worships the monster and its statue, and receives a mark
on his forehead or hand, (10) he shall also drink the wine of
the wrath of God, mixed undiluted in the cup of his anger.
He shall be tormented in fire and brimstone before the
holy angels and before the Lamb. (11) The smoke of their
torment will rise for ever and ever; there will be no
respite day or night for those who worship the monster
and its statue and receive the mark of its name. (12) This
calls for endurance from God's people, those who keep
God's commandments and their faith in Jesus.' (13) Then
I heard a voice from heaven say, 'Write this: "Blessed
are the dead who die in the Lord henceforth!" "Yes,"
answers the Spirit, "let them rest from their labours;
for what they have done goes with them."'**

To those who are convinced that John had nothing to offer
to an idolatrous and immoral world except relentless doom the

6 **angel flying in mid-heaven** presents some difficulty. His
gospel, they assure us, cannot be *the* gospel, for there is no
trace of gospel in the grim sequel. It may be good news to the
beleaguered church that their persecutors are to receive their
deserts, but to the pagan world it is only a last and *ex hypothesi*
unavailing appeal for repentance. One might have thought that
the obvious absurdity of such an argument would have led its
learned exponents to question their hypothesis. For whether
it has an article or not, the word *euangelion* can only mean
'good news', and it is improbable that John should have
thought of using it in a cynical sense. Moreover, he says nothing
about the gospel being good news for Christians; this is a gospel
to proclaim to the inhabitants of earth, the members of the
worldly and persecuting society. Nor is it any casual or ephe-
meral news; it is **an eternal gospel,** a gospel rooted and
grounded in the changeless character and purpose of God. If
the angel carried a **gospel** which was **eternal** good news **to
every nation, tribe, tongue, and people,** it is hard to see
how this could differ from *the* gospel. For John really believed
in the gospel: he believed that Christ had ransomed for God
men from every tribe, tongue, people, and nation' (v. 9). This
gospel had to be proclaimed if men were to have a chance of
accepting it; 'how can they believe in one they never heard of?
How can they hear without someone to proclaim the news?'
(Rom. x. 14). The distinctive fact about John's gospel is not
that it is a different gospel, but that he believes proclamation to
mean martyrdom. The gospel was first proclaimed by Christ
himself, 'the faithful witness'; and the function of the martyr-
witnesses is to preserve and repeat the testimony of Jesus. The
great martyrdom, then, is the earthly reality which corresponds
to the flight of the angel.

But where is the gospel in the words the angel utters? The
7 command to **fear God and do him homage** and to **worship**
the Creator is not in itself a gospel. The gospel does not require
men to achieve their own salvation by an act of repentance. The
gospel is a declaration that 'Christ Jesus came into the world to
save sinners' (1 Tim. i. 15), that 'God loved the world so much
that he gave his only Son' (John. iii. 16), that 'Christ died for us
while we were yet sinners' (Rom. v. 8); and John's gospel is the

same: 'to him who loves us and has released us from our sins with his own life-blood . . . be glory and dominion for ever and ever' (i. 5-6). One possibility is that John never intended the angel's words to be an exposition of the gospel, because he thought that unnecessary. Having written the word gospel, he expected his readers to fill it with the full rich content of the apostolic preaching. As Dodd has shown,[1] the preaching of the primitive church was a statement of the facts of the gospel story, interpreted by means of Old Testament citations as God's promised act of deliverance, and followed by the great 'therefore': because God has done this, therefore repent. When Luke makes Paul say at Lystra, 'We . . . bring you good news to make you turn from these vanities to the living God who made heaven and earth and sea and all that is in them' (Acts xiv. 15), no one would suppose that this was the whole of Paul's gospel or that Luke thought it to be so; the content of the good news is simply being taken for granted, because it has been amply stated in earlier chapters. So here the angel's message could be simply the great 'therefore' following his proclamation. The other possibility is that the gospel is contained within the announcement that **the hour of his judgment has come.** Whether or not we accept this view will depend on how closely we are prepared to relate John's theology to that of the Fourth Gospel. For in the Gospel Jesus first proclaims a judgment by light, whereby men are divided into those who come to the light and those who shun it because their deeds are evil (John iii. 19); and then, with the shadow of death across his path, when even the disciples are on the point of deserting him who is the Light, leaving the whole world in darkness and in the power of the Evil One, he announces another judgment of the world, which is to liberate all men from Satan's accusations and draw them into unity with himself (John xii. 31-32). The words of the angel are so reminiscent of this passage in the Gospel, and of those other passages where the phrase 'the hour has come' recurs like the strokes of a great bell (John xii. 23; xiii. 1; xvi. 21, 32; xvii. 1), that it would be surprising if there were no relation between them. But if we allow this much common ground between the Revelation and the Gospel, then the angel's

[1] C. H. Dodd, *The Apostolic Preaching and its Developments.*

meaning must be that the **judgment** is present in the death of
the martyrs in the same way as it was present in the Cross.

In the same allusive fashion the angel speaks of the Creator
in terms which recall the first four trumpets, with their plagues
on **heaven and earth, the sea and the fresh-water springs**
(viii. 7-12). God is the Creator, not the destroyer, of his universe. There is a judgment of God which consists in his giving
men up to the consequences of their own lawless truancy
(Rom i. 24, 26, 28), so that the products of man's corporate
guilt—the four horsemen, the destroying mountain of Babylon,
the star Wormwood, the angel Apollyon, the monster—are
allowed to be destroyers of the earth (vi. 1-8; viii. 8-11; ix. 11;
xi, 7, 18). But the judgment which is at the same time the
eternal gospel is the removal of the destroyers, in order that the
purpose of the Creator for his world may stand firm. This is
8 why the angel of the gospel is followed by **another angel,** who
proclaims the fall of **Babylon the great.** There is no hope for
the rehabilitation of the alcoholic until the source of his supply
is cut off. As long as men are being made drunk with the heady
wine of Babylon's seductions, they are not free to accept the
cup of salvation. Only the fall of Babylon can liberate her
fuddled dupes. This connexion between redemption and the
fall of Babylon was as old as the Exile, when Israel was waiting
for the end of her captivity. One prophet conceived himself
to be a sentry on a watchtower, eagerly awaiting the couriers
who would bring the news of Babylon's fall and Israel's release
(Isa. xxi. 8-9). Another had depicted Babylon as 'a golden cup
in the Lord's hand, making all the earth drunken', a cup which
must be dashed to the ground if her victims were to go free
(Jer. li. 6-10). Yet another had spoken God's promise to those
'who are drunk, but not with wine . . . "See, I am taking from
your hand the cup of staggering; never again shall you drink the
bowl of my wrath; I will put it into the hands of your oppressors"' (Isa. li. 21-23). John is weaving his own patterns out
of these Old Testament themes, but there is no reason to
suppose that he has departed from the original intention of his
scriptural texts, in which the fall of Babylon brought the salvation, not the doom, of those who had been made drunk with her
wine.

None of these passages, however, gives an entirely satisfactory explanation of John's extremely difficult phrase: **the wine of the wrath of her fornication** (cf. xviii. 3). If he had written simply 'the wine of her fornication', as he did in xvii. 2, we should understand that he meant Rome's ability to deprave and to seduce the world from the worship of the true God. It is the extra word *thymos*, here translated **wrath,** that makes the difficulty. *Thymos* can also mean 'passion'. Some scholars, therefore, take thymos closely with wine and render: 'the raging wine of her fornication'. Others take it closely with fornication and render: 'the wine of her impure passion'. Both these renderings give excellent sense, but they miss the parallel between this verse and verse 10, where John speaks of the wine of the wrath of God. Others again, insisting on the parallel, translate: 'the wine of God's wrath on her fornication'. But this cannot be right; for John distinguishes between the cup which Babylon has forced upon the nations and the cup which God will force upon Babylon and her obdurate supporters. Probably A. T. Hanson (*op. cit.* pp. 161 ff.) is right in the distinction he draws between wrath and God's wrath, the one being the process of nemesis which God allows to work itself out in history, the other the final irrevocable judgment of God. **All nations** have been involved in Babylon's idolatry and its grim train of historical consequences, but they need not be implicated in her final débâcle.

But supposing that a man remains impenitent to the end, his conscience untouched by the death of the martyrs and by the redemptive love of Christ, of which that death is an acted preaching—what then? This is the question the **third angel** 9 is sent to answer. Without convicting John of grotesque inconsistency we cannot interpret this third message in any other light. **Whoever worships the monster and its statue, and receives a mark on his forehead or hand, he shall also drink the wine of the wrath of God, mixed undiluted in the cup of his anger.** He is not saying that a single pinch of incense offered in a Roman shrine is the unforgivable sin, or that the whole Roman world, because it has participated in emperor worship, is destined to eternal punishment (cf. xiii. 8). The church was full of people who before their conversion had been

'by nature children of wrath, like the rest of mankind' (Eph.
ii. 3), 'in bondage to beings that by nature are no gods' (Gal.
iv. 8). Even to be a persecutor of the church, though it might
make a man the chief of sinners, did not put him beyond the
reach of God's grace (1 Cor. xv. 10; Gal. i. 13, 23). John's
position is no different from Paul's. He knows that Christians
have been ransomed out of every race, and therefore from every
form of idolatrous worship. The Nicolaitans and that woman
Jezebel are in mortal danger for having come to terms with the
enemy, but only if they do not repent (ii. 16, 21). The Jews who
have enlisted in Satan's service may yet learn the truth of the
gospel (iii. 9). Even those who gloat over the bodies of the two
witnesses may come to give glory to God (xi. 13). Later, when
John sees the fall of Babylon in greater detail, he hears a voice
say, 'Come out of her, my people, or you will be partners in her
sins and receive a share of her plagues' (xviii. 4). Even at that
late stage, it appears, when the martyrs have gone to death and
glory, God can say of Babylon, as he said of Corinth, 'There are
many in this city who are my people' (Acts xviii. 10). It is those
who refuse even this last appeal who prove themselves inveterate worshippers of **the monster and its statue,** though
others may need the sternest warning of the peril of their course.

10   The **fire and brimstone** are not to be taken literally, any
more than John's other symbols. Literally they were the
traditional fate of Sodom and Gomorrah (Gen. xix. 24; Luke
xvii. 29), and metaphorically they are a suitably scriptural fate
for the great city which is figuratively called Sodom (xi. 8). The
almost repellent horror of this paragraph is a little mitigated
when we recognize that, although the angel purports to be
speaking of individual destiny, he does so in terms proper to the
11 destruction of a city. It is the doomed city from which **smoke
. . . will rise for ever,** leaving no prospect of restoration
(xix. 3; cf. Isa. xxxiv. 8-17). Only by transference can such
language be used of those men and women who through their
worship of the monster have fully identified themselves with
the great city. Because she was all they loved and lived for,
her fall is bound to be **their torment.** If we protest that we
cannot accommodate our minds to the idea of eternal torment,
the answer is that neither could John. He believed that, if at

the end there should be any who remained impervious to the grace and love of God, they would be thrown, with Death and Hades, into the lake of fire which is the second death, i.e. extinction and total oblivion (xx. 14 ff.).

What then does John mean when he says that they will **be 10 tormented . . . before the holy angels and before the Lamb.** Note first that he does not add: 'and before God's people'. He does not believe, as did some Jewish apocalyptists, that a view of the torments of the damned would be one of the entertainments provided to ensure the bliss of the redeemed (1 *Enoch* xxvii. 3; xlviii. 9; 2 Esdras vii. 36).[1] The simple fact is that John really believed in heaven, the eternal bliss which he endeavours to describe, even beyond the breaking point of language, in his final chapters. If words fail in describing the possession of eternity, must they not also fail in describing the privation of it? To John heaven meant living eternally in the presence of God; and, if even he could face that presence only in fear and trembling, what must it mean for those who had flouted it all their lives? Jesus had spoken of the Son of Man repudiating before the angels those who repudiated him (Luke xii. 8); and what could such repudiation be but torment **in fire and brimstone.** In a grim parody of the worship of the heavenly choir (iv. 8) we are told that they have **no respite 11 day or night;** even their self-imposed torment is a caricature of what they might have been.

Yet even this is not the angel's last word, for he adds, **'This 12 calls for endurance from God's people.'** Most commentators have felt the connexion of thought to be obscure. Kiddle calls the angel's closing words and the speech from heaven which follows it a 'parenthetic reference' and a 'welcome excursus'. Charles, consistent in his ruthless surgery, transplants both verses to another context. Others take the words to mean, 'This (i.e. the punishment of their persecutors) is what God's people have been patiently waiting for throughout their long suffering'; or, 'This (i.e. persecution) is what displays the endurance of God's people'. But Johannine usage is decisively

---

[1] This gruesome idea apparently arose out of a mistranslation of Isa. lxvi. 24. The words 'they shall be repulsive to all mankind' were read (e.g. in the LXX) as if they were 'they shall be a spectacle to all mankind'.

against either of these translations and in favour of the one we
have adopted above. A literal rendering would be, 'Hither the
endurance of God's people'; and this construction with *hôde*
(hither) is one which John uses on three other occasions (xiii.
10, 18; xvii. 9). When he says, 'Hither is wisdom', he is inviting anyone with intelligence to calculate the number of
the monster which he has just set forth (xiii. 18). When he says,
'Hither the mind with wisdom', he is again inviting the reader
to bring his wits to bear on a cryptogram (xvii. 9). So here the
angel is inviting the people of God to summon up all their
endurance to meet the crisis he has been describing. But why
should Christian endurance be called forth by a sentence of
doom on the unrepentant world? Surely because it was for
a doomed world that Jesus went to the Cross to bear his witness
to the redeeming love of God, and it is for a doomed world that
the martyrs must bear their derivative witness. Once again we
must remember that John is writing a pastoral book for his
friends, not a manifesto against the pagan world. The speech
of the third angel is addressed to the seven churches, not in
order that they may gloat over the retribution in store for the
ungodly, but in order that they may prevent it from happening.
If they **keep God's commandments and their faith in
Jesus,** they will face death in confidence that Jesus, crucified
and risen, is still the Lamb that takes away the sin of the world.
That is why John is told to inscribe for them a special beatitude.
All who die in the Lord go to eternal bliss and eternal rest. But
13 **blessed are the dead who die in the Lord henceforth.
Henceforth** reminds us that John is still on the eve of the great
martyrdom and is thinking of the achievement of those who are
to be witnesses to Christ. **What they have done goes with
them,** not as merit, nor as personal satisfaction, but in a more
solid fashion; for they are to win an innumerable host of
converts.

xiv. 14-20. THE REAPING OF THE SON OF MAN

**(14) Then I looked, and there before my eyes was a
white cloud, and sitting on the cloud one like a son of**

man, with a gold crown upon his head and a sharp
sickle in his hand. (15) Another angel came out of the
temple and called in a loud voice to him who sat on the
cloud: 'Ply your sickle and reap; for the hour has come
to harvest, and the earth's harvest is ripe'. (16) So he
who sat on the cloud swung his sickle over the earth,
and the earth was harvested. (17) Then another angel
came out of the heavenly temple, and he too had a sharp
sickle. (18) Then from the altar came another, the angel
who has authority over fire, and he shouted to the one
who had the sharp sickle: 'Ply your sharp sickle and
gather the grapes from the earth's vine, for its clusters
are ripe'. (19) So the angel swung his sickle over the
earth and gathered the earth's vintage, and threw it into
the great winepress of God's wrath. (20) The winepress
was trodden outside the city, and from the winepress
flowed blood which reached to the bridles of horses at a
distance of sixteen hundred furlongs.

In the Old Testament **harvest** and **vintage** are regularly
used as symbols of divine judgment, either on God's own
people (Hos. vi. 11; Lam. i. 15) or, more frequently, on their
enemies. In the dirge over Babylon, from which John has
already derived his picture of the destroying mountain (viii. 8),
the tyrant city is warned that harvest time is near (Jer. li. 33).
Joel's vision of all nations gathered for judgment in the Valley
of Decision involves, as here, a double harvest of grain and
grapes (Joel iii. 9-14). And the Third Isaiah sees the heavenly
vintager returning from the winepress of his wrath with his
garments dyed with the blood of the heathen (Isa. lxiii. 1-6).
Since John clearly has these passages in mind, and since he
actually says that he saw the grapes thrown into the great
winepress of God's wrath, it is natural to suppose that he has
given us a vision of the judgment to be meted out to the new
Babylon and its inhabitants, in accordance with the proclamation of the third angel (xiv. 9-11). Some commentators have
insisted that John's imagery must be interpreted in the light of
his Old Testament models. Kiddle, for example, describes the
scene as the mowing down of the nations: 'it is obvious enough

that the sharp sickle of the reaper is no less an instrument of
punishment than that of the vintager' (p. 289). John's pastoral
concern was to reveal 'the true focus of self-interest' (p. 288)
to waverers tempted to choose security rather than martyrdom.
There is nothing in this interpretation which is at variance with
John's theology; for he certainly believed in an inexorable
divine judgment, and wrote to disclose the true and eternal
nature of the choice which confronted his fellow Christians.
He was a realist, and we must be ready to share his realism.
'We may be horrified at the picture of blood up to the horses'
bridles, but, after the experience of two world wars in one
generation, many thinking people are much more ready to
admit that the root cause behind this terrible effusion of blood
is not ignorance, or social conditions, but sin, the breaking of
God's fundamental laws. They have seen in the history of the
last twenty-five years the wine-press of the wrath of God.'[1]

14 There are, however, better reasons than squeamishness for
questioning this interpretation and looking a little further below
the surface. The figure **sitting on the cloud** is said to be **like a
son of man,** and in the apocalyptic tradition of the Gospels
the coming of the Son of Man with the clouds of heaven is the
occasion when 'he will send out his angels and gather his elect
from the four winds, from one end of earth and heaven to the
other' (Mark xiii. 27; cf. Matt. xxiv. 31; 1 Thess. iv. 15-17).
The noun *therismos* (**harvest**) and the verb *therizo*, though they
could perfectly well have been used of the mowing down of
enemies, are never so used in the Septuagint, even in the
passages where judgment is likened to a reaping; and in the
New Testament they are used of the ingathering of men into
the kingdom of God (Matt. ix. 37 f.; Mark iv. 29; Luke x. 2;
John iv. 35-38). (Matt. xiii. 24-43 might seem to be a partial
exception, since the weeds are reaped along with the wheat,
and the reaping is a prelude to their destruction. But even here
the object of the reaping is the storing of the crop, not the
bonfire.) These two facts remind us that John has prepared us
for a scene of ingathering by his earlier use of the word 'firstfruits' (xiv. 4). Where the firstfruits have been offered to God,
the full ingathering may be expected to follow. The firstfruits

[1] R. H. Preston and R. T. Hanson, *Torch Commentary*, pp. 104 f.

here bear something of the same relation to the full harvest as in chapter vii the hundred and forty-four thousand did to the vast throng which no one could count. The offering of the 'omer or first sheaf by the priest in the temple set free the rest of the crop for general use, and was therefore the signal for reaping to begin; and this no doubt is why the command, **'Ply 15 your sickle and reap'**, is given by an **angel** who **came out of the temple.** For such reasons as these many scholars have wanted to distinguish the harvest from the vintage: the harvest is the ingathering of the elect, the vintage the gruesome fate of their enemies and persecutors; and the reaping of grace is carried out by the Son of Man himself, whereas the reaping of wrath is delegated to an angel.

Kiddle is surely right to protest that any such dichotomy is artificial and false. Harvest and vintage are described in too close a parallelism to be regarded as symbols for contrary realities: both are inaugurated with the same angelic command, **the earth's harvest** is balanced by **the earth's vine,** both are declared to be **ripe,** and the reaping of both is described in almost identical terms. It may be an angel who reaps the grapes, but it is the Son of Man who treads the winepress and returns with his garments dyed with blood, as we know from xix. 13-15. Nor can the element of judgment be eliminated from the harvest scene. The phrase, **the hour has come,** whether or not we connect it with the passion narrative of the Fourth Gospel, is undoubtedly an echo of xiv. 7: 'the hour of his judgment has come'. In one way or another both harvest and vintage are connected with judgment, though Kiddle's own theory that both simply represent the judgment of God on the heathen has been shown to be inadequate.

Harvest and **vintage** are variations on a single theme; and, since the Son of Man sends out his harvester angels to gather the elect, it follows that the vintager angels must have the same function. This is precisely what we should conclude if we began by giving due weight to the word 'firstfruits'. For Israel was required to offer firstfruits of wine as well as of grain (Exod. xxii. 29), and the harvest season which opened with the offering of the 'omer ended not with the grain harvest at Pentecost, but with the grape harvest at Tabernacles. But there are four other indications that John intends the vintage to be interpreted, like the harvest, as the ingathering of God's servants.

18   (a) He uses the word **vine,** which was never mentioned in any of the Old Testament pictures of vintage judgment on the heathen, because the vine was a traditional symbol for Israel (Hos. x. 1; Isa. v. 1-7; Jer. ii. 21; Ezek. xvii. 1-8; Ps. lxxx. 8-13). Like the fourth evangelist, John has applied this symbol of the old Israel to the new Israel (John xv. 1-8), and therefore we must infer that by the gory vintage he meant to portray the
20 death of the martyrs. (b) He tells us that **the winepress was trodden outside the city.** By the city he must mean 'the great city, which is figuratively called Sodom and Egypt, where also their Lord was crucified' (xi. 8; cf. xi. 13), the city to which he has just given the name of 'Babylon the great' (xiv. 8). But it makes no sense at all to say that the inhabitants of this city were subjected to a final divine judgment **outside the city.** In a later chapter it is those who impenitently remain within the city who share its sins and its doom. To come outside the city is to escape to that place of security where the church leads its protected life (xviii. 4; cf. xii. 6). A vintage of judgment ought to be celebrated in the very heart of the city. **Outside the city** was the place of the crucifixion, and so the proper place for the martyrdom of those who held to the testimony of Jesus. The author of Hebrews reminds his readers that Jesus 'suffered outside the gate, to consecrate the people by his own blood', and calls on them to 'go out to him outside the camp, bearing the disgrace he bore' (Heb. xiii. 12-13). So deeply had this idea impressed itself on the minds of the first century Christians that Matthew and Luke, in rewriting Mark's parable of the wicked tenants, have the landlord's son killed *outside* the vineyard (Matt. xxi. 39; Luke xx. 15; cf. Mark xii. 8). Whatever element of judgment there is in the vintage, it is analogous to the judgment of the world achieved once for all on the Cross.
19 (c) The grapes were trodden in **the great winepress of God's wrath.** At first sight this appears to be the one sure indication that the whole harvest and vintage scene represents the judgment of God on the heathen. But on closer scrutiny we find, as we might by now have expected, that John has used his Old

Testament models with creative freedom. For he has made a logical connexion between three metaphors which in the Old Testament were used independently: the vintage, the cup of wrath which God forces on the oppressor nation (Isa. li. 17 ff.; cf. Jer. li. 39, 57), and the land saturated, and therefore drunk, with blood (Isa. xxxiv. 7). A winepress may be a symbol for punishment, but it is also the place where grapes are made into wine. John has heard one herald angel announce the fall of Babylon, and another add that the worshippers of the monster will be compelled to share 'the wine of the wrath of God, mixed undiluted in the cup of his anger' (xiv. 10). The punishment of Babylon comes when she is forced to drink the cup of God's anger, and the winepress is not itself the punishment, but the place where the wine of God's wrath was being prepared. Before long John is to see Babylon 'drunk on the blood of God's people and on the blood of the witnesses of Jesus' (xvii. 6), and he is to hear a voice from heaven, 'In the cup she mixed for others mix her a double draught!' (xviii. 6). Babylon's atrocities and God's retribution together go to make the double draught. From an earthly point of view it is Babylon that sheds the great river of blood by which the soil of her own territory is saturated and made drunk, but to the eyes of faith what is happening is that the cup which will send Babylon reeling to her doom is being prepared in **the great winepress of God's wrath.**

(d) The fourth point is one of literary form. Chapter xiii ended with a threat of death to anyone who did not worship the statue of the monster or bear the number of its name. Chapter xv begins with a vision of the victorious martyrs who 'had won their freedom from the monster and from its statue and from the number of its name' (xv. 2). It is natural to think that the intervening chapter has described the battle in which that freedom was won, and that it has been concerned with nothing else.

John's object in this paragraph, then, has been to persuade the prospective martyrs that the world-wide carnage, in which their lives are to be forfeit, will not be simply the vindictive work of Babylon; it will also be the gracious work of the Son of Man, sending out his angels to reap a great harvest of souls, and incidentally to prepare the intoxicating cup that will prove the ruin of the mother of harlots. This explains why the one earthly event had to be symbolized by a double reaping. Any Christian at the end of the first century would without a moment's hesitation recognize that the coming of the Son of Man with his angel reapers meant the gathering of God's people into the kingdom, but he would not naturally associate this traditional symbol with martyrdom. On the other hand, the vintage by itself would readily call to mind the picture of a people crushed in a vast blood-bath, but without any suggestion that their death was other than defeat and loss. By his juxtaposition of the two symbols, and by the parallelism of language which so clearly converts them into a unit of imagery, John has achieved yet another rebirth of images, and has found a way of telling his friends that Christ, who turned the Cross to victory and the four horsemen into angels of grace, can transform even the shambles of martyrdom into a glorious harvest-home.

Once the main picture is established, the details begin to fit in. The **golden crown** worn by the Son of Man is a reminder of the nature and source of the sovereignty which he is to share with his servants. 'To the Conqueror I will grant a seat beside me on my throne, as I myself conquered and sat down beside my Father on his throne' (iii. 21). 'You are worthy . . . because you were slain and with your life-blood have ransomed for God men from every tribe, tongue, people, and nation; you have made them a royal house of priests in God's service, and they shall reign on earth' (v. 9-10). 'They have conquered him by the life-blood of the Lamb and the testimony they bore; no love of life caused them to shrink from death' (xii. 11). We can see, too, why the three angels who accompany the Son of Man are said to come **out of the temple** and **from the altar;** for the great martyrdom is the sacrifice offered to God by the royal house of priests. The mention of temple and altar as the places from which the vintage was inaugurated may have a secondary significance also. For reasons already explained John wanted the treading of the winepress to take place **outside the city,** but his river of blood bears some relation to the river of life which Ezekiel saw issue from the threshold of the temple, south of the altar (Ezek. xlvii. 1-12). That river was ankle-deep at a thousand cubits, knee-deep at two thousand, and at three

20 thousand deep enough to swim in. John's river **reached to the**

**bridles of horses at a distance of sixteen hundred fur-
longs.** No convincing explanation has been offered either for the
bridles or for the distance. The only Old Testament passage
which speaks of the bridles of horses is the Septuagint version
of Zechariah xiv. 20: 'on that day the inscription on the horses'
bridles shall be, "Holy to the Lord Omnipotent"'. Since this
comes at the end of a series of chapters often alluded to by John
and other New Testament writers, it is just possible that, by a
trick of the mind, he drew this detail from there.[1] **Sixteen
hundred** is a square number, but one which has no obvious
prototype in the Old Testament. If we set any store by numerology, it provides some slight confirmation for the interpretation
of the vintage as the great martyrdom, for the only other square
numbers in the book are the hundred and forty-four thousand
of the army of the Lord (which is basically twelve times twelve)
and the dimensions of the holy city (vii. 4; xiv. 1; xxi. 16).

[1] The Hebrew has 'on the jingles (*meṢilloth*) of the horses'; but the word
is a *hapax legomenon*, and obviously gave trouble to translators, as can be
seen from the nonsense produced by the literalist Aquila, who read it as
meṢuloth and rendered it by the Greek *bythos* (abyss). John normally makes
his own translation directly from the Hebrew, and it is by no means clear
what Greek version, if any, he was accustomed to using. But some Greek
text of the Old Testament must have been in current use in Asia.

VII

THE SEVEN BOWLS

xv. 1-8. THE EXODUS

(1) Then I saw another portent in heaven, great and marvellous, seven angels with seven plagues—the last, because with them the wrath of God is accomplished. (2) I saw what seemed a sea of glass mingled with fire, and beside the sea of glass, holding the harps which God had given them, stood the Conquerors, who had won their freedom from the monster and from its statue and from the number of its name. (3) They were singing the song of God's servant Moses and the song of the Lamb:

> 'Great and marvellous are your deeds, Lord God
>   Omnipotent!
> Just and true are your ways, King of the nations!
> (4) Who shall not fear, Lord, and do homage to your
>   name?
> For you alone are holy.
> All nations shall come and worship before you,
> For the justice of your decrees stands revealed.'

(5) After this I looked, and the shrine of the heavenly Tent of Testimony opened, (6) and out of it came the seven angels with the seven plagues. They were robed in linen pure and shining, and had gold girdles round their breasts. (7) Then one of the four living creatures gave the seven angels seven golden bowls full of the wrath of God who lives for ever and ever; (8) and the shrine was filled with smoke from the glory of God and his power, so that no one could enter the shrine until the seven plagues of the seven angels were accomplished.

By a slight shift of the kaleidoscope the ocean of blood through which the martyrs have passed in the great vintage now

becomes a heavenly Red Sea, poised after the passage of the
true Israel to engulf Israel's persecutors. Another Mosaic series
of **seven plagues** is to be poured out on the city which is 1
figuratively called Egypt, and these, unlike the call to repentance from the seven trumpeters, are to be **the last. With them**
—and not with any of the previous visions, not even the harvest
and vintage—**the wrath of God is accomplished.** Accordingly we have here a more complete and systematic use of
Exodus typology than in any other part of John's book: the
plagues, the crossing of the **sea,** the engulfing of the pursuers,
the song of Moses, the giving of the law amid the **smoke** of
Sinai, and the erection of the **Tent of Testimony**—all these
have their place in the vision; and, because the great city is
figuratively Sodom as well as Egypt, the **fire** that fell on Sodom
is added to the picture.

The **sea of glass** is the cosmic sea of John's opening vision 2
of heaven, the chaos over which God established his authority
at creation, without eliminating its power to resist him. We have
seen in the commentary on iv. 6 that many of the Old Testament
writers used this myth as a symbol for the continuing conflict
within the created order, but also as a description of the
Exodus. The myth was not an old wives' tale, for it had become
history in Israel's escape from Egypt. There God had cut the
sea in two and bruised the head of the primaeval dragon, and
this was the solid guarantee of his ultimate victory over evil.
John had therefore ample precedent for his interweaving of
cosmic myth and Exodus typology. The sea that was to overwhelm the figurative Egypt was none other than the seven-
headed ocean monster, which was that Egypt's *alter ego* (cf.
xiii. 1). But before it could be poured from the bowls of God's
wrath, it must be **mingled with fire,** the fire of God's holiness
and justice (cf. viii. 5). The proof of God's ultimate sovereignty
is that he can use even the powers of evil to be the means of
their own destruction (cf. viii. 8-11; ix. 11; xvii. 16).

The members of this new Israel which has come through the
sea are described in some detail. Because they are **holding the
harps which God had given them,** we know that they are
identical with the hundred and forty-four thousand who appeared to the accompaniment of harp music with the Lamb on

mount Zion (xiv. 1-5), and therefore with those who were
sealed from the twelve tribes (vii. 1-8). But they are also called
the Conquerors, and this tells us that they are those members
of the seven churches who have responded to the call to faithful
endurance and to the promises contained in the letters. They
are **the Conquerors, who had won their freedom from the
monster and from its statue and from the number of its
name.** This translation is an attempt to do justice to one of
John's characteristically compressed phrases, for which a
literal rendering would be: 'the Conquerors from the monster
and from etc.'. This is closely parallel to the use of the same
verb in v. 5, where we were told that the Lion of the tribe of
Judah 'has conquered to open the book'; and, unless we are
trying to make an exact reproduction of John's idiosyncratic
style, the sense can be given in English only by a double translation of the verb. The Exodus, which was the Conquerors'
victory, had brought them safely through the Red Sea of
martyrdom, and so had put them for ever beyond the power of
the monster and its idolatrous worship. Thus in one sentence
John has neatly tied together the symbols of his previous
visions.

3 Like the Israelites after the crossing of the Red Sea (Exod.
xv. 1), the Conquerors sing **the song of God's servant
Moses,** celebrating the triumph of God over the enemies of his
people; but because that triumph has been won by no other
weapons than the Cross of Christ and the martyr testimony of
his followers, this song is also **the song of the Lamb.** The song
is a cento of quotations from many parts of the Old Testament,
but John has so put them together as to make them a jubilant
anthem of Christian optimism. The angel who carried the
eternal gospel called on men to fear God and do him homage
(xiv. 6), and the martyrs are convinced that, through the **great
and marvellous** act whereby God has turned their death into
victory, the whole world will respond to the call of the gospel:
4 **all nations shall come and worship before you.** Those
scholars who think that John held out no hope of repentance
for the heathen world are embarrassed by the martyrs' confidence, and have to argue that in this context **fear** and **do
homage** indicate not a true conversion but only an awed

submission to superior power. We have already seen that this interpretation will not do for the two earlier passages in which John has used these expressions (xi. 13; xiv. 7). When the angel of the gospel calls on men to fear God, do him homage, and worship him, we cannot seriously believe that he is inviting them to do something which will make not an iota of difference to their eternal destiny. The song of the martyrs clearly states that God is **King of the nations** (and the idea is there even if we accept the variant reading, 'King of the ages'), and will be recognized by the nations as their King; and it implies that this world-wide turning to God will be the outcome of the world-wide martyrdom. Since John cannot be supposed cynical enough to put into the mouths of the martyrs sentiments which he himself did not share, we must accept this optimism as an essential part of John's theology. There are a few passages like this in his book where he speaks unequivocally and without the cloak of symbol, and, instead of ignoring them or treating them as erratic and inconsistent intrusions, we ought to allow them to control our interpretation of his symbolism.

The only clause in the song which is of doubtful interpretation is the last one: **the justice of your decrees stands revealed.** What is this revelation of God's justice which the martyrs are applauding? It can hardly be the sentence of doom which the seven angels are about to execute, because it is given as the reason for the confidence of the singers that all nations will be brought to the worship of God. The best way to discover what John meant by God's just decrees is to ask by what means he thought the nations would be drawn to God, for to that question there can be only one answer: it was God's decree that the death of the innocent should bear eloquent and persuasive witness to the redeeming love of the Lamb. By implementing this decree God has proved to the world that he is 'both just and the justifier of anyone who puts his faith in Jesus' (Rom. iii. 26).

After leaving the Red Sea, the Israelites came to Sinai, and in front of the smoking mountain placed the two tables of the law in the ark inside the **Tent of Testimony.** John now sees **the 5 shrine of the heavenly Tent of Testimony,** of which the earthly tent was but a copy (Exod. xxv. 9, 40; Acts vii. 44;

Heb. viii. 5). Once before, in the vision of the last trumpet (xi. 19), he has seen this same heavenly shrine open and the ark appear. This time it is not the ark but the **Testimony** it contains which occupies his attention. The time for mercy is over, and God's law must now take its course. The sanctity of the law is emphasized first by the appearance of the angels in the

6 vestments of priesthood, **robed in linen** and with **gold girdles round their breasts,** then by a complex allusion to a number of Old Testament passages about **the glory** of the Lord. Moses at the dedication of the Tent in the wilderness and the priests at the dedication of Solomon's temple had been unable to enter the shrine, because it was filled with the cloud of the divine presence (Exod. xl. 34; 1 Kings viii. 10). Isaiah had seen the temple filled with smoke, while the hymn of the seraphim rang in his ears (Isa. vi. 4). Ezekiel had fallen on his face in awe at the vision of the glory of God returning to the restored temple

8 (Ezek. xliv. 4). So now John sees the shrine **filled with smoke from the glory of God and his power.** There had been a time when all heaven was silent while an Angel of the Presence brought before God the prayers of his people (viii. 1); now **no one could enter the shrine until the seven plagues . . . were accomplished.**

xvi. 1-9. THE NATURAL PLAGUES

(1) Then I heard a loud voice from the shrine say to the seven angels: 'Go and empty over the earth the seven bowls of God's wrath. (2) So the first went and emptied his bowl on the earth; and a foul sore broke out on the men who had the mark of the monster and worshipped its statue. (3) The second emptied his bowl on the sea, and it turned to blood like the blood of a corpse; and every living thing in the sea died. (4) The third emptied his bowl on the rivers and fresh-water springs, and they turned to blood. (5) Then I heard the angel of water say, 'You are just in pronouncing this sentence, Holy One, who are and were; (6) for they shed the blood of saints

and prophets, and you have given them blood to drink. They have their deserts!' (7) And I heard the altar cry, 'Yes, Lord God Omnipotent, true and just are your judgments!' (8) Then the fourth emptied his bowl on the sun, and it was allowed to scorch men with its flames. (9) They were fearfully scorched; but they only blasphemed the name of God who had power to inflict such plagues, and refused to repent or do him homage.

The first four plagues in this final round bear a strong resemblance to the first four of the trumpet series. They too are based on the plagues of Egypt (Exod. ix. 10 ff.; vii. 17 ff.), and they are an attack on the same four elements of the physical world, and through them on the world of men. But there is a difference. The trumpet plagues, like the Egyptian ones, preceded the Exodus, and were a call to repentance in the face of imminent doom. These plagues follow the Exodus and are part of the doom, corresponding to the submersion of the Egyptians in the sea. For literary reasons John has chosen to divide each of his sevens into groups of four, two, and one; but this must not blind us to the fact that each series, and this one in particular, is a unit. The seals and the trumpets were interrupted after the sixth vision by lengthy visions of the martyrs and their fate, because John believed that, where all else had failed, martyrdom would succeed in bringing men to repentance. But with the coming of the last plagues the hour for repentance has passed, and the series hurries uninterrupted to its climax. It is important, therefore, that we interpret the parts of the series in the light of the whole. The three final plagues are the dethronement of the monster, the invasion of his empire by demonic hordes from beyond, and the destruction of his capital city, Babylon. In other words, the theme of the whole series is neither the collapse of the physical universe nor the punishment of individual men for their personal contribution to the world's iniquity, both of which come later when the record books are opened in front of the great white throne (xx. 11-12), but the ending of persecution through the removal of the persecutor. The first four plagues must be regarded as panels in the one great sevenfold picture of the last days of Babylon; for they

affect precisely those who are too deeply involved in Babylon's
2 sins to be dissociated from her fall, those **who had the mark
of the monster and worshipped its statue,** who **shed the
blood of saints and prophets,** who **blasphemed the name
of God.** The last phrase is of peculiar importance, because,
outside the present chapter, John in the apocalyptic part of his
book attributes blasphemy only to the monster (xiii. 1, 5, 6;
xvii. 3). The thrice repeated statement that men **blasphemed**
(xvi. 9, 11, 21) can only mean that they have wholly taken on
the character of the false god they serve. There can be no
question about John's belief that in some men **the mark of the
monster** might become indelible and earn for them final
reprobation and annihilation (xiv. 10-11; xx. 15; xxi. 8; xxii. 15).
But in this he is doing no more than faithfully representing the
teaching of Jesus. It is a serious misrepresentation of his
theology to magnify the passages in which he faces this possibility, and to neglect the many other passages in which he confidently speaks of the repentance and conversion of those who
have been enemies of God and God's people (ii. 16, 21; iii. 9;
xi. 13; xiv. 6; xv. 3-4; xviii. 4).

In this one passage John has combined the three principles of
God's providential ordering of history enunciated in the Book
of Wisdom: that God 'makes the whole creation a weapon to
repel his enemies' (Wis. v. 17); that 'the medium of men's sin
is also the medium of their punishment' (Wis. xi. 16); and that
'the very means by which their enemies were punished were
used to benefit God's people in their need' (Wis. xi. 5). Though
the bowls of wrath are poured on earth, salt water, fresh water,
and sun, the purpose of the pouring is not to destroy the natural
order, but to enlist it in the service of a divine retribution.
John shares the contemporary belief that all the elements and
forces of nature had their guardian angels (cf. vii. 1; xiv. 18;
5 cf. also 1 *Enoch* lx. 17, 19, 21; lxi. 10). **The angel of water,**
who approves the justice of the **sentence,** is spokesman for the
rest. Not only the stars in their courses but all nature is fighting
against Babylon. The second principle is seen at work when **the
mark of the monster,** the symbol of man's inveterate idolatry,
becomes a suppurating **sore,** the symbol of his punishment;
and when the ocean of **blood** which the worshippers of the

monster have shed contaminates their own water supply, so
that Babylon staggers to her appointed doom, drunk with **the 6
blood of saints and prophets** (cf. xiv. 19-20; xvii. 6). The
fourth plague has not a counterpart in the plagues of Egypt, but
has been added in order to bring out an important characteristic of the whole series, the contrast between the fate of the
idolaters and the reward of the redeemed, while the worshippers of the monster suffer pain and thirst and are **fearfully 9
scorched** by the sun, the martyrs have gone where 'they shall
never be hungry or thirsty again; never again shall the sun strike
them nor any scorching heat' (vii. 16), where 'pain shall be
no more' (xxi. 4).

xvi. 10-21. THE POLITICAL PLAGUES

**(10) The fifth emptied his bowl over the throne of the
monster, and its kingdom was plunged in darkness. Men
gnawed their tongues in pain, (11) and blasphemed the
God of heaven for their pains and sores, and did not
repent of what they had done. (12) The sixth emptied his
bowl over the great river Euphrates, and its waters dried
up, to prepare the way for the kings from the sunrise.
(13) Then I saw coming from the mouth of the dragon,
from the mouth of the monster, and from the mouth of
the false prophet three foul spirits like frogs. (14) They
were demon spirits, able to work miracles, and they went
out to the kings of the whole world to muster them for
battle on the great day of God Omnipotent. (15) (See how
I come like a thief! Blessed is the man who stays awake
and keeps his clothes by him, so as not to be seen walking
naked and ashamed!) (16) So they mustered the kings to
the place called in Hebrew Armageddon.**

**(17) The seventh emptied his bowl over the air, and
out of the temple there came from the throne a loud
voice, which said: 'It is over!' (18) Then came flashes of
lightning and peals of thunder and a violent earthquake,
so violent that its like had never been since men appeared**

on earth. (19) The great city split in three, and the cities
of the heathen fell, and Babylon the great was remembered before God and made to drink the wine cup of the
fury of his anger. (20) Every island vanished; there was
not a mountain to be found. (21) Huge hailstones, weigh-
ing about a hundredweight, fell on men from the sky;
and men blasphemed God for the plague of hail, so
severe was that plague.

    Three more Egyptian plagues supply John's imagery for the
last three bowls, but each is accentuated to give a sense of
10 finality. The **darkness** was not the three days' visitation of
Exodus x. 21 ff., nor even the paralysing terror so vividly described in Wisdom xvii, but the total eclipse of the monster's
imperial power. The **frogs** were no domestic nuisance from the
Nile, but **demon spirits,** pervading the whole world with their
deluding and seductive influences. The thunder and hail were
the accompaniment of **an earthquake** like none before it in the
history of man. Together the three plagues are a triad of
political disaster: internal anarchy and invasion from without,
leading to irreparable collapse. There is also a close parallel
between these three plagues and the three woes ushered in by
the eagle's screech and the three last trumpets: for the first let
loose smoke from the abyss which darkened the sun, the second
released a demon army from beyond the Euphrates, and the
third was accompanied by earthquake, thunder, and hail. Apart
from the completeness and finality of the present series, the
chief difference between it and the earlier one is that it is less
demonic and more obviously historical and political.

    The emptying of the fifth **bowl over the throne of the
monster** was for John no mere apocalyptic vision, for he had
lived through a crisis of Roman history which enabled him to
give the vision real content from his own experience. He has
told us that the monster had at one time received a deadly
wound (xiii. 3, 12), which had subsequently been healed; and
we have seen that this is almost certainly a reference to the
suicide of Nero and the year of chaos that followed it. During
that year it might well have seemed to a loyal Roman that
Rome's **kingdom** had been **plunged in darkness.** The doubts,

suspicions, terrors, and hysteria which had ended with the accession of Vespasian had given a foretaste of what might happen if ever the lights went out all over the empire. The pain, in which men gnawed their tongues, may be that caused by the first four plagues, since the effect of the whole series is cumulative. But we probably ought to take John's pictures of physical pain as symbols of a deeper spiritual anguish. He had a good precedent in the Wisdom of Solomon (xvii. 21), which said of the victims of the Egyptian plague of darkness: 'harder to bear than the darkness was the burden of their own selves'. For John tells us for the second time that men **blasphemed,** 11 and we have already seen that blasphemy is the typical activity of the monster; even when it is deprived of its throne, it lives on in each of its worshippers, whose deepest agony is to know that they are wholly identified with it in its fall. The title God of heaven is drawn from a passage in Daniel (ii. 19), which deals with God's ability to make and unmake kingdoms, and John has used it before in a context to which he intends a cross-reference (xi. 13). The survivors of the earthquake which followed the death and resurrection of the witnesses 'in awe did homage to the God of heaven', i.e. were brought to repentance; but those who remained the faithful servants of the monster till the bitter end had by then lost the capacity to **repent of what they had done.**

The sixth bowl is emptied **over the great river Euphrates,** 12 and there follows a massive invasion. Though John does not tell us in so many words, there can be no doubt that the objective of the attack is Rome, **the throne of the monster.** According to Jeremiah l. 38, the drying up of Babylon's **waters** was to be the prelude to Babylon's doom. From the point of view of the figurative Babylon, the Euphrates was the eastern frontier, beyond which lay the Parthian menace, constantly magnified by rumour (cf. vi. 2; ix. 14). In the parallel plague of the sixth trumpet a demonic army was released across the Euphrates to attack the demon-worshippers of the Roman world; and, though in this case the army is a human one, stirred up by demonic prompting, it may be presumed to come for the same purpose. But the simple and decisive evidence is the appearance of the **frogs.** In all the Old Testament prophecies about an enemy from beyond, who is to gather for a last decisive battle, there is no mention of frogs. They are introduced here for one reason alone, to maintain the sequence of Egyptian plagues. This plague, therefore, like the others of the bowl series, is directed against the latter-day Egypt.

13   The **frogs** are said to come **from the mouth of the dragon, from the mouth of the monster, and from the mouth of the false prophet.** This is the first we have heard of **the false prophet,** but it is not hard to identify him with the monster from the land which made all men worship the first monster (xiii. 11-18). It is a title which recalls Jesus' prophecy of the coming of false messiahs and false prophets (Mark xiii. 22), and it strongly suggests that the first monster is to be regarded as the false messiah or Antichrist. It also helps us to recognize the nature of the demon spirits which emerge from the mouths of each of these creatures. **From the mouth of the false prophet** came the seductive propaganda of the imperial cult (xiii. 12-15). **From the mouth of the monster** came blasphemous pretensions to deity (xiii. 6). **From the mouth of the dragon** came the river of lies with which he had tried to overwhelm the church (xii. 15). The foul spirits, then, represent the stream of court flattery and lying propaganda which John believed would ultimately spread beyond the confines of the

14   empire and stir up **the kings of the whole world** into an alliance against Rome. It is likely that John is here alluding for the second time to the legend of Nero *redivivus*; for Nero had been popularly supposed to be in Parthia, plotting a return at the head of a vast Parthian army to win back his throne (cf. xiii. 3). John does not believe in any literal return of Nero in person, but he does believe that Nero's spirit lives on, capable of deluding, infecting, and inspiring the enemies of Rome.

16   The battlefield is **called in Hebrew Armageddon,** which means Mount Megiddo. No simple explanation of this word can be given, and it is best understood as a composite image, compounded of many elements. Megiddo was indeed a famous battlefield, the scene of Sisera's defeat, when 'the very stars fought from heaven' against him (Jud. v. 19-20), and the scene also of Josiah's untimely death (2 Kings xxiii. 29). It is also mentioned in a somewhat obscure passage of Zechariah, from

which John has already quoted (Zech. xii. 10-11), and it is possible that this is the immediate source from which the word came to his mind. The difficulty is that the oracle from Zechariah correctly speaks of 'the plain of Megiddo', for Megiddo was no mountain, but a town on the edge of the Plain of Esdraelon. Lohmeyer has suggested that Mount Megiddo must be a name for the nearest real mountain, Mount Carmel, the site of Elijah's victory over the false prophets of Jezebel. This suggestion would have been more plausible if the contest at Armageddon had been between Rome, the new Jezebel, and the martyr-witnesses who had inherited the mantle of Elijah (xi. 4 ff.), and not between Rome and a horde of invaders from the east; but we should in any case have had to ask why, if John was thinking of Carmel, he should choose a pseudonym for it which the citizens of Ephesus could hardly have had the geographical knowledge to construe. On the other hand, we do know that John expected some of his readers to have at least an elementary knowledge of Hebrew; for he has already used the Hebrew name Abaddon (xi. 11), his cryptogram for the monster's name probably employs the Hebrew alphabet (xiii. 18), and in the present instance he draws attention to the Hebrew origin of the name, which presumably means that a knowledge of Hebrew is needed to decipher it. It is reasonable, therefore, to conjecture that the name is to be explained, in part at any rate, by Hebrew etymology. Now the name Megiddo could plausibly be derived from a root meaning to cut, attack, or maraud; and Mount Megiddo would then mean 'the marauding mountain', and would supply John with a variant on Jeremiah's destroying mountain, to which he has made an earlier allusion (viii. 8; cf. Jer. li. 25). But, whatever may have been the source or sources of the word **Armageddon**, this much at least is clear, that, like John's other names, it is a symbol. He was not expecting a battle in northern Palestine, but at Rome.

Into the prophecy of invasion there has been interjected a warning to Christians, which is reminiscent of the letters to the churches and of the teaching of Jesus (Matt. xxiv. 43; Luke xii. 39). **See how I come like a thief! Blessed is the man** 15 **who stays awake and keeps his clothes by him, so as not to be seen walking naked and ashamed!** This comes with a

suddenness which some commentators have found too abrupt
to be credible. Charles, never reluctant to rewrite the Apocalypse
if he thinks it capable of improvement, has spoken of the 'utter
inappropriateness of 15 in its present context', because the
elaborate preparations of the kings of the world could hardly
have caught anyone unawares, and because by now all Christians,
as he supposes, have died in the martyrdom; and he might have
added that the verse upsets his theory of a radical distinction
between the eschatological expectations of the letters and those
of the apocalyptic visions. Lohmeyer declares the verse to be
impossible where it stands, because it interrupts the strophic
arrangement which he discovers throughout the book, and
because Christ never speaks *propria persona* in the apocalyptic
section. Both scholars agree that it belongs at iii. 3. Both are in
fact admitting that the evidence does not fit their theories and
insisting that it shall be forced to do so. But before we resort to
surgery, it is worth while trying to frame a theory which will fit
the evidence. For, *pace* Lohmeyer, this is not the first time
that the voice of Christ has broken in upon John's visions with a
blessing which is at the same time a call to loyalty (cf. xiv. 13),
and *pace* Charles, the verse has a remarkable appropriateness to
its present context. Jesus had warned his disciples that the last
days of Jerusalem would come with an urgency which would
allow for not a moment's delay: the man who was taking his
siesta on the housetop must make for the mountains without
even going indoors to collect his belongings, and the man working in the fields must make his escape without returning home
for his cloak (Mark xiii. 15-16). In similar terms the heavenly
Christ warns his followers to be prepared for the last days of
Babylon: **blessed is the man who stays awake and keeps
his clothes by him.** It is, of course, a spiritual preparedness
that is required, like that demanded of Sardis and Laodicea
(iii. 2, 18); for the danger is, not that Christians should be
caught unawares by the invasion from the east, but that they
should fail to recognize in it the coming of the Lord. Here, as
in the letters (ii. 5, 16; iii. 3), John is reinterpreting the traditional belief in the coming of Christ, encouraging his friends to
look for it in the crises of history. He comes **like a thief** and
takes men by surprise, because the manner of his coming as well

as the hour is hidden from them. Charles is right in thinking that this warning is incompatible with the idea that all Christians have died in the great persecution; but we have found ample evidence that John expected only a proportion of the church to be called to martyrdom (ii. 7, 10; iii. 4, 10, 20; xi. 4 ff.; cf. xxi. 27).

Like the seventh seal and the seventh trumpet, the seventh bowl is the End, only this time there is no cancelled conclusion: **It is over!** The splitting of **the great city,** the fall of **the 17 cities of the heathen,** and the punishment of **Babylon the great** are not three separate consequences of the **earthquake,** but three aspects of the comprehensive disruption of imperial power. John describes the earthquake in geophysical terms: **every island vanished; there was not a mountain to be 20 found.** Yet it is a political catastrophe that he is depicting, not a natural one (cf. vi. 12-17); for after it has happened, its victims are still there to blaspheme and the onlookers to lament (xviii. 9-18), and world history has still a long way to run before the final folding up of the physical universe (xx. 6, 11). It is easy to see why John should single out mountains for special mention, for Rome was famous as the city of seven hills (xvii. 9), and in the Old Testament the mountain-tops had been notorious as the scene of idolatrous worship. His animosity against islands is less easy to understand, unless perhaps it is a reference to his own plight and to the Roman practice of using the Cyclades and Sporades as places of detention for political prisoners (cf. i. 9). The **huge hailstones** complete the series of 21 Egyptian plagues, as a final reminder that this plague, like the rest, has been directed against the heirs of Pharaoh's persecuting tyranny.

It must now be apparent how impossible it is to maintain that, when John set out to give warning about 'what is bound to happen soon' (i. 1), he included in these immediate expectations the end of the world. The utmost limit of his prophetic vision was the end of Rome's world, which he believed to be inherent in her forthcoming persecution of the church. In her attack on the church Rome would let loose into the world powers which would compass her own downfall. To describe this conviction he uses eschatological language, and in this limited use of eschatological language he was true to his calling as a prophet. Amos had a vision of the End, but it was the end of Israel's world: 'the end has come upon my people Israel' (Amos viii. 2). Daniel had visions of the End, but for him the only end that mattered was 'when the power of the persecutor of the holy people comes to an end' (Dan. xii. 7). Ezra had visions of the End, and his end was the end of the Roman eagle, brought about by its own three heads: 'they are called the eagle's heads because they will bring its wickedness to a head and so compass its end' (2 Esdras xii. 24-25; cf. xi. 44). Broadly speaking, it is true to say that no prophet ever used eschatological language except to give theological depth and urgency to the historical crisis which he and his people were facing at the moment. John, too, has had his visions of the End, but, because he had learnt his theology at the foot of the Cross, he knew that an end could also be a beginning.

VIII

THE LAST DAYS OF BABYLON

xvii. 1-6. THE GREAT WHORE

(1) Then one of the seven angels who held the seven bowls came and spoke to me: 'Come', he said, 'and I will show you the passing of sentence on the great whore, enthroned on many waters. (2) The kings of earth have committed fornication with her, and the inhabitants of earth have made themselves drunk on the wine of her fornication. (3) He carried me away in a trance into the desert, and there I saw a woman enthroned on a scarlet monster which was covered with blasphemous names and had seven heads and ten horns. (4) The woman was robed in purple and scarlet and bejewelled with gold and precious stones and pearls. In her hand she held a golden cup full of obscenities and the filth of her fornication; (5) and on her forehead was written a symbolic name: 'Babylon the great, mother of whores and of all the obscenity on earth'. (6) I saw the woman make herself drunk on the blood of God's people and on the blood of the witnesses of Jesus; and at the sight of her I stared in great wonder.

John now turns to a detailed study of the theme he has just announced in general terms. We have said earlier that John's sevens are his complete and panoramic views of divine judgment, and his unnumbered visions his close-up studies of detail (see on viii. 1-5). The seven trumpets led up to a general view of the great martyrdom, which was to be the means of destroying the new Jericho and releasing its inhabitants for the worship of the true God; and the three following chapters (xii-xiv) laid bare the true nature of the conflict. The seven bowls have led up to the announcement of the fall of Babylon, and the next two chapters will explain the causes of her fall.

Among the cities to which John is writing the first three are known to have had temples to the goddess Roma, and it is his purpose in these two chapters to expose this apparently digni-

1 fied and numinous figure as **the great whore.** He assumes that she may be identified with the Magna Mater, the Mother Goddess whose worship in one form or another was universal throughout the ancient world; and this enables him to draw on the strong repugnance expressed in the Old Testament against

2 **fornication,** literal or metaphorical.

In the Canaanite mythology, as elsewhere in the ancient world, one form of the creation myth has it that the world was brought into being by a divine act of procreation by male and female deities. With this myth were associated fertility rites, which certainly included prostitution. When Israel entered Canaan and learnt agriculture from the inhabitants, she was exposed to the seduction of these cults, and at times undoubtedly succumbed; so that, when she eventually fought free of them, she still retained much of their imagery. Israel was the bride of Yahweh, whom he had espoused in the wilderness, and every dalliance with paganism was **fornication** (Hos. ii. 5; Isa. i. 21; Jer. ii. 2; Ezek. xvi. 36 ff.; xxiii. 2 ff.). In other passages it is Nineveh or Tyre that is called whore, the one for her barbarity, the other for her worldliness (Nah. iii. 4; Isa. xxiii. 15). In the Book of Proverbs Wisdom is represented as the perfect hostess, the patroness of all gracious living, who pleads with the young man to regale himself in her salon and not to join the dissipation of the bawdy-house kept by Folly (Prov. ix). It has been plausibly suggested that the personification of Wisdom in the later Jewish literature was a deliberate attempt to offset the seductions of the Mother Goddess, whose pervasive influence must have been a source of anxiety to every Jewish community of the Dispersion, and especially to those in Egypt.[1] John, then, was using an image of great depth and power when he portrayed the unholy city as **the great whore,** who has seduced all nations to the worship of that which is not God.

The classic resistance to the encroachments of paganism in the history of Israel was that of Elijah to Jezebel. John has used the name Jezebel to designate the woman at Thyatira who was teaching church members to commit fornication (ii. 20; cf.

[1] See W. L. Knox, *St. Paul and the Church of the Gentiles*, pp. 57 ff.

2 Kings ix. 22), and he has also used Elijah as a type of the Christian martyr (xi. 6). It is therefore probable that Jezebel was the queen who sat for the portrait he is now painting. Stauffer has proposed Cleopatra as the model (*op. cit.* pp. 54 ff.), but Jezebel has prior claim, since she has actually been mentioned in the earlier passage. But John is also thinking of the personified Babylon of Isaiah xlvii and Jeremiah li. It was Babylon that was 'a golden cup in the Lord's hand, making all the earth drunk' (Jer. li. 7), and it was Babylon that sat **enthroned on many waters** (Jer. li. 13). In the original prophecy this last phrase was a reference to the elaborate irrigation system of Mesopotamia, on which the prosperity of Babylon depended; but in its present context it is a pointer to the mercantile empire of Rome, about which we are to hear more in the next chapter. It may be, too, that there is a secondary allusion to the ocean monster Leviathan; for the woman is said to be **enthroned on many waters** and also **enthroned on a scarlet monster,** 3 and we know that the monster had its origin in the primaeval ocean (xiii. 1). The ocean and the monster that emerges from it are the underlying realities on which rests the throne of imperial Rome (cf. xvii. 9).

The angel **carried** John **away in a trance into the desert,** not because that was where the whore was to be found, but because only from that place of security and detachment was it possible for him to see the seducer in her true colours (cf. xii. 1-6). Only there could he be safe from the lies of the dragon, the threats of the monster, and the seductions of the whore. One reason why John uses such violent and offensive language in this and other passages is his sense of appalling exposure to the charm and attractions of Rome. He saw her **robed in purple** 4 **and scarlet and bejewelled with gold and precious stones and pearls.** The colours are the colours of royalty; and, though her earthly finery is meant to seem a tawdry parody of the heavenly splendour of the other woman who was clothed with the sun, and her jewels a poor contrast with the richness of the heavenly Jerusalem, nevertheless we cannot escape the impression that he was sensitive to the grandeur that was Rome. Even in the detachment of the desert, he finds himself staring at her **in great wonder;** and the words he uses to 6 describe his own conduct are not very different from those he used when he saw the whole world gaping after the monster (xiii. 3). If he has to steel himself against the intoxicating draughts of the golden cup she holds, how easy it must have been for the people of Thyatira to make themselves drunk with the influence of their local Jezebel.

4   The cup in her hand is **full of obscenities and the filth of her fornication.** This is emotive language, by which John is trying to make an otherwise splendid figure appear utterly repulsive. But it is also language which expresses the traditional Jewish horror of idolatry and the corruption it entailed. The Greek word *bdelygma* (**obscenity**) is the same that is used in the phrase 'desecrating obscenity' (abomination of desolation), which Mark's Gospel borrows from Daniel (Mark. xiii. 14; Dan. ix. 27; xi. 31; xii. 11). **Filth** or uncleanness is an idea which attaches to immorality in general, but specifically to the realm of the demonic and therefore to the world of false gods. The two counts John has against Rome are the idolatry she diffuses throughout the world and her persecution of those who refuse to participate in it. She makes others **drunk on the wine of**
6   **her fornication** and herself **drunk on the blood of God's people.** The magic is broken; the fairy godmother, who has put her spell on the whole world through the brilliance of her appearance and the munificence of her presents, is revealed as the old witch, old in sorcery before ever Rome grew to be her
5   latest and most powerful incarnation, **mother of whores and of all the obscenity on earth.**

xvii. 7-18. THE INTERPRETATION OF THE WHORE AND THE MONSTER

(7) Then the angel said to me, 'Why do you stare? I will explain to you the symbolism of the woman and the monster she rides, with its seven heads and ten horns. (8) The monster you saw was and is not and is to rise from the abyss; and it goes to perdition. The inhabitants of earth whose names have not been written from the foundation of the world in the book of life will stare in

wonder when they see that the monster was and is not
and is yet to be. (9) This calls for a mind with wisdom.
The seven heads are seven hills on which the woman
is enthroned. (10) They are also seven kings, of whom the
first five have fallen, one now is, and the other has not
yet come; and when he comes his stay will be short.
(11) The monster that was and is not is also an eighth,
yet he is one of the seven and goes to perdition. (12) The
ten horns you saw are ten kings who have not yet come
to the throne; they are to receive authority for one hour
with the monster. (13) They are all of one mind, to yield
their power and authority to the monster. (14) They will
wage war on the Lamb, and the Lamb will conquer
them, because he is Lord of lords and King of kings and
his companions are called and chosen and faithful.

(15) Then he said to me, 'The waters you saw, where
the whore sat enthroned, are peoples and masses,
nations and tongues. (16) As for the ten horns you saw,
they and the monster will come to hate the whore; they
will make her desolate and naked, they will devour her
flesh, they will burn her to ashes. (17) For God has put it
into their heads to carry out his purpose, by being of one
mind and yielding their sovereignty to the monster,
until God's words have been carried out. (18) The woman
you saw is the great city that holds sway over the kings
of earth.'

In chapter xiii John has represented the monster as a travesty
of Christ: like the Lamb 'bearing the marks of slaughter', the
monster bore on one of its heads 'the deadly marks of slaughter'
(v. 6; xiii. 3); and like him who 'was dead' and is 'alive for
ever', the monster 'had received the sword-wound and had
come to life' (i. 18; xiii. 14). The explanation of **the symbolism 7
of the woman and the monster** begins with more in the same
vein. The monster bears a title which is a parody of the divine
title: God 'is and was and is coming' (i. 4); the monster **was 8
and is not and is yet to be.** The last of these three verbs
(*parestai*) is the one from which is derived the noun *parousia*,
commonly used throughout the New Testament to denote the

future advent of Christ. The monster is to have its sinister Parousia, when it **is to rise from the abyss**. In an earlier reference to the monster John has used this same phrase in the present tense—'the monster that rises from the abyss' (xi. 7)— thus giving the impression that rising from the abyss was a permanent attribute of the monster's character rather than a single episode in its career. This impression John confirms here by immediately reverting to the present tense: **and it goes to perdition.** It is a second permanent attribute of the monster that it is constantly heading for perdition. Whenever in human history the monster has appeared, it has come trailing clouds of smoke from the abyss which is its home and labelled with its destination. If John here speaks of its rising from the abyss as future, it is because he is thinking of that Parousia which will coincide with the outbreak of persecution. The fact that he can say it **is not** is the clearest possible indication that there was no open and organized persecution at the time when he was writing.

We have been assuming all along that John's many symbols for the enemies of God's people denoted the varying aspects of the one reality—the monster from the abyss, the great city, the monster from the sea, Babylon the great, the great whore (xi. 7, 8; xiii. 1; xiv. 8; xvii. 1); and that this reality was Rome. The justification for these assumptions becomes apparent in this chapter, in which John has brought together all these names, with unmistakable clues to their significance. **The seven heads are seven hills.** From the time of her sixth king, Servius Tullius, Rome had been known as *urbs septicollis*, and the festival of Septimontium was celebrated every year in December to commemorate the enclosure of the seven hills within her walls (Suet. *Dom.* 4). Latin literature is full of references to this well-known feature of Roman topography (Vergil, *Geor.* ii. 535; *Aen.* vi. 783; Horace, *Carm.* 7; Ovid, *Trist.* i. 5. 69; Mart. iv. 64; Cicero, *ad Att.* vi. 5; cf. *Or. Sib.* ii. 18; xiii. 45; xiv. 108). It has sometimes been thought that apocalyptic writers resorted to symbolism because they were writing tracts for the resistance movement and wanted to make their seditious contents undecipherable by the secret police. In John's case this explanation of his symbolic language is patently absurd, for any Roman soldier who knew how to read Greek could find the answer to a conundrum as easy as this one. But to make doubly sure John adds that **the woman you** 18 **saw is the great city that holds sway over the kings of earth.**

At this point the interpretation becomes more complicated. The seven heads **are also seven kings of whom the first** 10 **five have fallen, one now is, and the other has not yet come; and when he comes his stay will be short.** At first sight this seems to be as straightforward a statement as we could wish. All we need is a list of the Roman emperors, and a little elementary computation will tell us the name of the emperor in whose reign John had his visions:

44 B.C.	*Julius Caesar (died)
31 B.C.–14 A.D.	*Augustus
14–37 A.D.	Tiberius
37–41 A.D.	Gaius (Caligula)
41–54 A.D.	*Claudius
54–68 A.D.	Nero
68–69 A.D.	Galba
69 A.D.	Otho
69 A.D.	Vitellius
69–79 A.D.	*Vespasian
79–81 A.D.	*Titus
81–96 A.D.	Domitian

But difficulties soon multiply. With which emperor are we to start counting, Julius, Augustus, or perhaps Caligula, in whom the monster's tendencies first made their appearance? Are we to count all the emperors or only those who were deified by an act of the Senate (marked in the list with an asterisk)? Are we to include the three rival emperors, Galba, Otho, and Vitellius, who reigned briefly between Nero and Vespasian? If we start with Julius, as the Jewish author of the fifth book of *Sibylline Oracles* did, we seem to find ourselves in the reign of Nero; but Nero is surely the head with the deadly wound, and therefore not the reigning emperor. If we start with Augustus and omit the three pretenders, then Vespasian is on the throne, Titus is the king whose stay will be short, and Domitian is the

eighth, a second Nero who can therefore be described as **one of the seven.** But what then are we to make of the tradition preserved by Irenaeus that John wrote in the reign of Domitian (*Haer.* v. 30. 3)? We could, perhaps, conjecture that John was exiled on Patmos and had his visions in the reign of Vespasian, but did not come to write them down until two reigns later, when the eighth emperor was already on the throne; but there was nothing in Vespasian's attitude to religion to stimulate John's apprehension of a world-wide persecution. We can make Domitian the emperor who **now is** either by starting with Caligula, which means omitting the first two deified emperors, or by counting only the deified emperors, which means leaving out Caligula and Nero, the strongest candidates for demonic status; and how could Nero *redivivus* be the eighth if he was not one of the seven? A further objection to all these solutions is that they pass over Galba, Otho, and Vitellius, whom the author of the fifth book of *Sibylline Oracles* included in his list of emperors from Julius to Trajan.

Since our problems are not due to any lack of historical information, there is no reason to think that John's first-century readers would have been in any better case than we are. It is probable, therefore, that we have been looking for the wrong sort of solution. After all, John did not arrive at the number seven by counting emperors; the monster Leviathan had seven heads centuries before the founding of Rome. The number seven is a symbol which John does not scruple to apply to earthly realities without insisting on numerical coincidence. No one supposes that he wrote to seven churches because there were only seven in the province of Asia, nor even because there were only seven in his diocese, a diocese so erratic as to contain Ephesus but not Magnesia or Tralles, Laodicea but not Colossae or Hierapolis. How little John was concerned with arithmetical precision we have seen in his account of the two witnesses, who were also two lamps; for although the seven lamps belong to seven named churches, the two lamps are not two of these churches, but a limited proportion of the whole church (xi. 4 ff.). By the same token the **seven kings** are a symbolic number, representative of the whole series of emperors, and they would remain seven no matter how long the actual list happened to be. (There is a probable parallel in the Eagle Vision of 2 Esdras xi-xii. Ezra sees an eagle with twelve wings and three heads, all of which represent emperors. There can be little doubt that the three heads are the three Flavian emperors, Vespasian, Titus, and Domitian. The twelve wings can be made to correspond to the six Julian emperors from Julius to Nero by taking them in pairs. But this solution is possible only on the hypothesis of extensive later redaction of the text, which as it stands repeatedly declares that the twelve wings are twelve kings who are to reign one by one, beginning with Julius. Since the book was written by a Jew, the number twelve can be regarded as a symbol for totality rather than a real number.) The one point John wishes to emphasize is that the imperial line has only a short time to run before the emergence of a new monstrous Nero, **an eighth** who is **one of the** 11 **seven.** If we compare verse 8 with verse 11, it is plain that the emergence of the new Nero, and therefore the onset of persecution, is the time of the monster's Parousia, when it **is to rise from the abyss.**

The ten horns were the one recognizable feature of the 12 fourth of Daniel's beasts, and John has mentioned them primarily to show that his monster was a synthesis of all four of Daniel's. In Daniel the horns were the kings of the Seleucid dynasty; and, since John does not need the horns to symbolize the Roman emperors, he must find some other use for them. The number **ten,** therefore, is as traditional as seven, and we need pay it no further attention. It is in any case pointless to attempt to identify the **horns,** for they belong wholly to the future: **they are to receive authority for one hour with the monster,** and this must surely mean at the time of the monster's Parousia. They are not to be identified with the kings of the east who come across the Euphrates for the battle of Armageddon (xvi. 12), for they are part of the monster. On the other hand, since they **will come to hate the whore,** pre- 16 sumably they belong to the provinces. They are human agents who are to share first the monster's attack on the Lamb, then his onslaught on the capital city. Beyond that we are in the realm of conjecture. Perhaps they were to be the native rulers of client kingdoms, which still existed in the more backward or

troublesome parts of the empire. Perhaps they were to be a new
series of upstarts, like the three who had already appeared,
claiming to be Nero (see on xiii. 3). Perhaps they are simply a
device for completing the monster's caricature of the Lamb, to
whom alone belongs the title **King of kings.** What is more
important is that their reign is to be **for one hour.** This phrase
is repeated three times in the next chapter, like the strokes of a
passing bell tolling the knell of departed Babylon. In the present
context the one hour is occupied with war on the Lamb. The
repetition of this key phrase suggests that John saw a closer
link between the attack on the Lamb and the fall of Babylon
than mere chronological succession.

14   The only way in which earthly kings can **wage war on the
Lamb** is through his followers. The war is therefore yet another reference to the great persecution. Earlier John has described the victory of the Lamb from the point of view of the
martyrs, whose conquest is already implicit in his representative
triumph: 'they have conquered him (*sc.* Satan) by the life-blood
of the Lamb and by the testimony they bore; no love of life
caused them to shrink from death' (xii. 11). Here he describes
the victory of the conquerors from the point of view of the
Lamb, who is still the agent of victory: **he will conquer
them,** not only **because he is Lord of lords and King of
kings,** but also **because his companions are called and
chosen and faithful. He is Lord of lords and King of
kings** in virtue of the victory secured once for all on Calvary
(i. 5; iii. 21; v. 5). But that is not of itself enough to make the
victory final and complete. It must be re-enacted again and
again in **his companions,** the picked and faithful soldiers of
the Cross. Whichever way we look at it, final victory depends on
the inaugural victory of the Lamb together with the victory
which he makes possible for the whole vast throng of martyrs.

    The sack of Rome follows as a direct consequence of the
victory of the Lamb. John has told his readers that the death and
victory of the martyrs was responsible for the earthquake in
which a tenth of the city fell (xi. 13), and that the great vintage
prepared the cup of wrath with which Babylon was to become
drunk and reel to her doom (xiv. 17 ff.; xvi. 6; xvii. 6). Here he
links the persecution and the fall of Babylon by his favourite

device of verbal echo. Because the ten kings **are all of one 13 mind, to yield their power and authority to the monster,** they attack the Lamb; and **being of one mind and yielding 17 their sovereignty to the monster,** they destroy the whore. The savaging of the whore by the monster and its horns is John's most vivid symbol for the self-destroying power of evil. **God has put it into their heads to carry out his purpose,** the purpose mentioned in the opening sentence of the book, that every power which sets itself up against God shall in the end break itself on the Cross of his Son and the martyr witness of his saints.

xviii. 1-8. THE LAMENT OF HEAVEN

(1) After this I saw another angel coming down from heaven with great authority; and the earth became bright with his splendour. (2) With a mighty voice he proclaimed, 'Fallen, fallen is Babylon the great! She has become a den for demons, a haunt for every unclean spirit, a haunt for every unclean and loathsome bird. (3) For all nations have drunk of the wine of the wrath of her fornication; the kings of the earth have committed fornication with her, and the merchants of the earth have made their fortunes on her lavish wealth.'

(4) Then I heard another voice from heaven say, 'Come out of her, my people, or you will be partners in her sins and receive a share of her plagues; (5) for her sins are piled high as heaven, and God has a record of her crimes. (6) Pay her back in her own coin, repay her double for all she has done! In the cup she mixed for others, mix her a double draught! (7) Mete out to her torment and grief to match her lavish pomp! She says to herself, "I am queen on my throne! I am no widow, never shall I know mourning." (8) Therefore in a single day her plagues shall come, pestilence, mourning, and famine; and she shall be burnt to ashes. For mighty is the Lord God, her Judge.'

After his visions of Judgment, in which he saw the glory of the Lord abandon the temple and so leave Jerusalem to its fate, Ezekiel had a vision of restoration, in which he saw the glory return to the rebuilt temple to consummate the redemption of Israel (Ezek. xliii. 2). It is to this passage that John alludes 1 when he says of the angel that **the earth became bright with his splendour.** This angel, notwithstanding the gloom of his proclamation, is an angel of the gospel. He comes, not to gloat over the fallen, but to announce the triumph of God's purposes and the final liberation of God's people from all oppression.

The Old Testament contains dirges over many ancient cities, and, because Babylon the great is the epitome of all tyrannical empires, John weaves echoes of them all into his tragic sym- 2 phony. The angel's opening words, **Fallen, fallen is Babylon,** are the words with which the prophet on his watchtower announced to Jerusalem the news of the capture of Babylon by Cyrus (Isa. xxi. 9). The picture of a city reduced to utter desolation, the home of unclean spirits and unclean birds and beasts, is found in doom oracles of about the same period, one directed against Babylon, the other against Edom, but both treated as the representative of all the enemies of God (Isa. xiii and xxxiv). In the Hebrew text of these passages some of the names of the denizens of the ruined city are ambiguous, and it is not certain whether they should be translated as wild animals throughout or as a mixture of wild animals and **demons.** But the Septuagint translator had no doubt that **demons** were included, and John stands in the same tradition of exegesis. The peoples of the Fertile Crescent were always keenly aware of the battle between order and chaos which went on at the frontier between the desert and the sown land. God had set man in a garden to cultivate it, and the desert was territory where God's writ of order and civilization did not run (see on xii. 6 for the ambivalence of the desert in Old Testament imagery). The desert was therefore the fit **haunt for every unclean spirit** and **for every unclean and loathsome bird;** for the **unclean** was precisely that which could not be accommodated to the demands of the divine holiness. A city which **has become a den for demons** was one where the desert had returned irrevocably to claim its own, one which has vanished without a trace like Sodom and Gomorrah (Isa. xiii. 19; xxxiv. 9; Jer. l. 39). In the repetition of the word **unclean** there is no doubt a contrast intended with the holy city, into which nothing unclean may enter (xxi. 27).

The reason given for the total obliteration of Babylon is the now familiar one: **all nations have drunk the wine of the** 3 **wrath of her fornication** (xiv. 8; xvii. 2; see esp. notes on xiv. 8 for the peculiar difficulties of this phrase). But now John has a new disclosure in store for us. He has repeatedly warned his readers against the dangers of idolatry, particularly by the use of the offensive word **fornication**. He has seen men freely choosing to worship the monster (xiii. 4). But he has so far given barely a hint why men should have considered it reasonable to do so or what the precise nature of their **fornication** was. Now we are given the first hint, which will be enlarged on in the next paragraph: **the merchants of the earth have made their fortunes on her lavish wealth.** Rome has given peace and security to the world, thus making possible the growth of a vast luxury trade and bringing widespread prosperity even beyond the frontiers controlled by her legions. This, we are to understand, is the true nature of the seduction exercised by the great whore. **The kings of the earth** were guilty of an economic dalliance, which involved the idolatrous worship of Mammon. When the Roman Babylon, like the ancient one, boasts, **'I am queen on my throne'** (Isa. xlvii. 7-8), her fault 7 is not mere arrogance, but an unquestioning faith in her own inexhaustible resources, unaccompanied by any sense of a deeper lack (cf. iii. 17).

When the Old Testament prophet said, **'Come out of her,** 4 **my people'** (Jer. li. 45), he was addressing exiled Jews and telling them to make their escape from Babylon before it should fall to the invader. When John hears the same words spoken from heaven over the figurative Babylon, they mean something quite different. They cannot be addressed to the martyrs, for the great ordeal has already sent them to their death. They can hardly be addressed to the other faithful members of the church, for the church has long since been carried on eagle's wings to the security of the desert, beyond the contaminating range of Babylon's sins. The only inhabitants now left in the great city are those who, through all the pre-monitory plagues, have obdurately refused to repent (ix. 20; xvi. 9, 11). Yet even at this late hour it is still possible for men to prove themselves God's **people** and to escape their share in Babylon's **plagues** by dissociating themselves from **her sins.** To the bitter end the miracle of grace remains open, and God never ceases to say, 'My people', to those who before were not his people (Hos. ii. 23; Rom. ix. 25 f.; 1 Pet. ii 10).

6   The command to **pay her back in her own coin** is, of course, addressed not to God's people, but to the angelic agents of retribution. Vengeance is the prerogative of God alone (Deut. xxxii. 35; Rom. xii. 19; Heb. x. 30). Throughout John's theology there runs a consistent belief in the *lex talionis*, the law which demands that the punishment shall **match** the crime. But he qualifies this belief in two ways. Exact retribution there may be, but only for those who insist to the last on being given
5 their deserts and on refusing the offer of divine mercy. **God has a record of** (lit. has remembered) **her crimes.** There are books to be opened (xx. 12); but what those books contain is entirely a matter of what God chooses to remember and what he chooses to forget. When God forgives, he also forgets; and what God forgets is blotted for ever from the record (Jer. xxxi. 34). The **double** repayment is for those only who to the end refuse to come out from the doomed city, and whose sin is therefore part of her permanent record. The second qualifica-tion is that there is no arbitary connexion between crime and punishment. The punishment is simply the crime allowed to
6 take its destructive course. **The cup** from which Babylon must drink **a double draught** is **the cup she mixed for others,** to which God has had to add no other ingredient but his ratifying wrath.

xviii. 9-19. THE LAMENT OF THE EARTH

(9) 'The kings of the earth who shared her fornication and luxury will weep and wail over her, as they watch the smoke from her burning. (10) They will stand far

off in terror at her agony and say, "Alas, alas, for the
great city, the mighty city of Babylon! In one hour your
doom has come!" (11) The merchants of the earth also
will weep and mourn for her, because there is no longer
a market for their cargoes, (12) cargoes of gold and silver,
jewels and pearls, linen and purples, silk and scarlet;
scented woods and ivory work of every kind, and all
sorts of work in the most costly wood, bronze, iron, and
marble; (13) cinnamon and spice, incense, myrrh, and
frankincense; wine and oil, flour and wheat, cattle
and sheep, horses, chariots, slaves, and human lives. (14)
"The fruit you set your heart on is gone from you; all
your glamour and brilliance are lost, never to be restored." (15) The merchants of these wares, who made
their fortunes from her, will stand far off in terror at her
agony, weeping and mourning (16) and saying, "Alas,
alas, for the great city, that was robed in linen and
purple and scarlet, bejewelled with gold and precious
stones and pearls! (17) Alas that in one hour so much
wealth should be laid waste!" Then every ship's captain
and seafaring man, sailors and all who made a living
from the sea, stood far off (18) and cried out as they
watched the smoke from her burning: "Was there ever
a city like the great city?" (19) They threw dust on their
heads and cried out, as they wept and mourned, "Alas,
alas, for the great city, where all who had ships at sea
grew rich on her wealth! In one hour she has been laid
waste."'

Heaven has lamented the idolatrous materialism which led to
Babylon's fall. Now the voice from heaven goes on to tell how
earth will join the lament, because the bottom has dropped
out of the world market. **The kings of the earth** are said to 9
mourn **the mighty city,** the merchants the wealthy city; but
this is a distinction without a difference, for the kings have
shared her fornication and luxury, i.e. their sovereignty has
been based on the mercantile prosperity she provided.
   Three times we are told that the desolation is to be accomplished **in one hour,** and we are reminded of the one hour 10

of the ten kings' reign with the monster, during which they will wage war on the Lamb (xvii. 12-14). The one hour of persecution is balanced by the one hour of retribution, because the blood of the martyrs is not only the seed of the church but the ruin of the great whore.

As models for his lament John uses two dirges over the commercial city of Tyre found in Isaiah xxiii and Ezekiel xxvii, and most of the commodities he mentions are mentioned also by Ezekiel. The difference between the two cities was that Tyre had been the great middle-man of the east, whereas Rome was

11 the great **market for their cargoes.** In Ostia, the port of Rome, there was a colonnaded square where the companies of merchants, the *navicularii*, had their offices, and this must have been one of the biggest centres of power in the empire. The bulk of the trade that passed through Ostia was carried on within the empire, and the Semitic peoples—Syrians, Jews, and Aramaeans—were particularly active in it. But there was also a

12- vast foreign trade which is reflected in John's list: **jewels and**
13 **pearls** from India; **silk** and **cinnamon** from China; **gold, ivory,** and **costly wood** from Africa; **spice, incense, myrrh, and frankincense** from Arabia; **horses** from Armenia and beyond (cf. Ezek. xxvii. 14); and **slaves** from any country ready to supply them. According to the elder Pliny (*Hist. Nat.* xii. 84; cf. vi. 101) the annual cost of imports from Arabia, India, and China alone was not less than a hundred and ten million sesterces (four sesterces made one denarius, which was a day-labourer's wage in Palestine).

14- The **glamour and brilliance** of the great city is depicted in
16 terms which almost exactly reproduce the description of the whore, **robed in linen and purple and scarlet, bejewelled with gold and precious stones and pearls** (cf. xvii. 4). Throughout this chapter John never quite seems to have made up his mind whether he was speaking of a woman or of a city. There is also what Kiddle has called a 'temporal uncertainty'; 'a medley of tenses, present, future, perfect, preterite, testify to John's imaginative journeys from the present into a visionary future and back again'. But the future thus envisaged is a real future in the course of history. The fall of Babylon is the end to which all John's visions have been pointing, but it is not the

end of the world. When it has happened, men are still able to **stand far off** and **watch the smoke from her burning,** as 17 they had stood to watch the conflagration of A.D. 64. They can still regret the loss of **a market for their cargoes.**

With exemplary restraint John never shows us the fall of Babylon. Just as earlier he declined to describe God and allowed us to see him only through the hymns of the worshipping host of heaven, so now he allows us to see the fall of Babylon only through the laments of the heavenly and earthly spectators. But this is no mere literary or dramatic device. There is a sense in which the spectators speak for the author as well as for themselves. He has had to be told not to stare in wonder at the great whore (xvii. 6-7), for he too was able to appreciate the **glamour and brilliance,** however deeply aware he might be of their dangers. He was no Manichaean or eremite, contemptuous of the beauties and amenities of the civilized world. The cry, **'Was there ever a city like** 18 **the great city?'** is wrung from his own heart as he contemplates the obliteration of the grandeur that was Rome. The proof of this is to be seen in the thoroughly material splendours of the holy city, into which 'the treasures and wealth of the nations' are to be brought (xxi. 26). There was nothing sinful about the commodities which made up Rome's luxury trade, until the great whore used them to seduce mankind into utter materialism. Every object of worth which seafaring man had ever carried to Rome to grace the life of the imperial capital, whether in its natural state or enhanced by the craftsmanship of man, belonged to the order of God's creation which must be redeemed by the overthrow of Babylon, and would find its proper place in the new Jerusalem. In the meantime it is with infinite pathos that John surveys the loss of **so much wealth.**

xviii. 20 - xix. 4. THE JUDGMENT OF BABYLON

(20) But let heaven rejoice over her. Rejoice, saints, apostles, and prophets; for God has imposed on her the sentence she passed on you!' (21) Then a mighty angel

lifted up a stone like a great millstone and hurled it into
the sea and said, 'Thus shall Babylon, the great city, be
hurled headlong down, never to be seen again ! (22) Never
again shall the sound of harpers and minstrels, of flute-
players and trumpeters be heard in you; never again
shall craftsmen of any trade be found in you; never again
shall the sound of the mill be heard in you; (23) never
again shall the light of the lamp be seen in you; never
again shall the voice of bridegroom and bride be heard
in you. For your merchants were the magnates of the
earth, and through your sorcery all nations went astray,
(24) In that city was found the blood of prophets and
saints and of every victim of earthly slaughter.' (1) After
this I heard what seemed the roar of a vast throng in
heaven shouting: 'Alleluia ! Victory and glory and power
belong to our God, (2) because his judgments are true
and just. He has passed sentence on the great whore who
corrupted the earth with her fornication, and has avenged
on her the blood of his servants.' (3) Then a second time
they said, 'Alleluia ! The smoke from her goes up for
ever and ever !' (4) And the twenty-four elders and the
four living creatures fell down and worshipped God as
he sat on his throne and said 'Amen ! Alleluia !'

Superficially verse 20 belongs with what precedes, for it is
the end of the angel's speech, which begins at verse 4 and includes the whole prediction of world-wide mourning; but
structurally it is the introduction to the paragraph that follows.
The first half of the verse is a clear and deliberate echo of xii. 12:
there heaven was bidden to rejoice over the defeat of the
dragon, and earth was warned to expect the unprecedented
20 horrors attendant on his death-throes; here **saints, apostles,
and prophets** are bidden to share the heavenly joy, because
through their martyrdom the heavenly victory has now become
an earthly reality also. The jubilation can now be complete and
unqualified, because the Satanic woe has passed. The cross-
reference between these two passages is particularly interesting
because they are the two court-room scenes of John's book. In
the first scene, in a legal contest between Michael and Satan,

Satan appears in his traditional role as the accuser, the prosecutor who demands and is prepared to execute the death sentence; but, because the accused are those redeemed 'by the life-blood of the Lamb', he loses both his case and his standing in court, and Michael is able to drum him out of heaven. In this second scene the contest is between the martyrs and their earthly accuser Babylon.

Verse 20b is not easy to translate. Literally it reads: 'God has judged your judgment from her'. This very difficult expression has given rise to a great many different interpretations. Lohmeyer and many others have assumed that it is a condensed way of saying, 'God has judged her and vindicated you'; but it is not obvious how this can be got from the Greek. The RSV appears to take *krima* (judgment) as a cognate accusative and 'your judgment' as the equivalent of 'judgment in favour of you': 'God has given judgment for you against her'. The NEB takes *krima* as the equivalent of the Hebrew *rib*, which can mean either a lawsuit or the cause which a man submits to the arbitration of a judge: 'in the judgment against her he has vindicated your cause'. These renderings share the same two disabilities; they overload the final phrase, *ex autes* (from her), and they give to *krima* a meaning which it does not have anywhere else in the Revelation, in the New Testament, or indeed even in the Septuagint. In the New Testament *krima* means one of three things: (*a*) the right to act as judge (Rev. xx. 4); (*b*) the judicial act of passing sentence (John ix. 39; Rom. v. 16; Acts xxiv. 25; 1 Pet. iv. 17); and most frequently (*c*) the sentence passed by a judge. It is not hard to see that only the third sense will fit the present context. 'Your judgment', then, must mean either 'the sentence passed by you' or 'the sentence passed on you'; and the first of them is inapposite here because God is the judge. Thus your judgment must be the sentence passed on the martyrs in the Roman lawcourt. John has previously been invited to watch the passing of sentence on the great whore (xvii. 1); now he hears that this consists in the reversal of **the sentence she passed on you.** The phrase *ex autes* is best explained by two Old Testament laws—the law of bloodshed and the law of malicious witness. The law of bloodshed declares: 'I will require from a man the life of his fellow man.

Whoever sheds a man's blood, by man shall his blood be shed'
(Gen. ix. 5-6). The law of malicious witness adds: 'If a malicious
witness comes forward to accuse a man of crime, then both
parties to the dispute shall appear before the Lord . . . and if
the witness is found guilty of perjury and has accused his fellow
falsely, you shall do to him as he meant to do to his fellow'
(Deut. xix. 16-19; cf. Rev. xi. 13). John has produced a port-
manteau version of these two laws. **God has imposed on her
the sentence she passed on you.** Babylon has brought a
malicious accusation against the martyrs, which has resulted in
their death. But the case has been carried 'before the Lord', to
the court of final appeal, where judgments are true and just.
There Babylon has been found guilty of perjury, and God has
therefore required from her the life of her victims, exacting from
her the penalty she exacted from them.

With this forensic setting so clearly before us, we can now
the better appreciate why John has throughout called the victims of persecution witnesses (*martyres*). The Greek word
martys had not yet come to be a technical term, meaning a
martyr. It still meant 'one who gives evidence in a court of
law'. It had, of course, been used metaphorically of the mission-
aries of the church, who were witnesses to the truth and power
of the gospel (e.g. Acts i. 8). But John uses it more literally than
this, with an eye to its legal origins. He knows that no Christian
can be put to death for his faith without first being given the
opportunity of testifying at his own trial before a Roman judge
(cf. Luke xxi. 13). But he wishes to assure the prospective
martyr that his evidence, given in the earthly lawcourt and
leading to a sentence of death, is also evidence given in the
heavenly court, leading to the condemnation of Babylon. This
explains why John sees the fall of Babylon as an immediately
impending event; it is part and parcel of the same lawsuit in
which the martyrs are sentenced to death. It helps also to
remove the element of gloating from the song of triumph, since
the martyrs can be vindicated only by the reversal of Babylon's
sentence, so that Babylon's malicious witness recoils on her own
head.

21-
23   The **mighty angel** is the third to be given this appellation
(cf. v. 2; x. 1). Since the first was the angel of the great scroll,

in which was written the redemptive purpose of God, and the
second was the angel of the little scroll, which contained the
church's part in that purpose, the appearance of a third must
mark the consummation of the contents of both scrolls. His
symbolic act with the **millstone** and the words he speaks over
it are reminiscent of both Jeremiah and Jesus. Jeremiah wrote
his prophecies against Babylon in a scroll and was told to tie a
stone to it and throw it into the Euphrates, saying, 'So shall
Babylon sink, never to rise again' (Jer. li. 60-63). Jesus declared
that it would be better for a man to be thrown into the sea with
a millstone round his neck than to cause one of Jesus' disciples
to stumble (Luke xvii. 2). With the hurling of the millstone it is
as though a voice had cried 'Stop!' over all the multifarious
activities of a hustling metropolis, and here again we are
reminded of Jeremiah and Jesus. Jeremiah said of his com-
patriots: 'I will silence among them the sounds of joy and
merriment, the voices of bridegroom and bride, and the noise
of the mill; I will put out the light of their lamps' (Jer. xxv. 10;
cf. vii. 34; xvi. 9). And Jesus had warned their descendants that
the day of the Son of man would overtake them, like lightning
out of a clear sky, amid all the ordinary daily pursuits of peaceful existence—trade, agriculture, and building, banqueting and
marriage (Luke xvii. 24-30). For some of John's readers this
passage would have awakened more recent memories of that
August night in A.D. 79 when the lamps and gaiety of Pompeii
and Herculaneum were extinguished for ever by a pall of
volcanic ash. It is not, after all the heroic sins that bring the
downfall of cities, but sheer heedlessness of approaching disaster. Babylon's **sorcery** had bewitched all nations into a false
sense of security, leading them to believe that Rome was the
eternal city. On coins and in inscriptions *Aeternitas* had been
adopted as the motto of the Flavian dynasty.

There is yet another echo of the teaching of Jesus in the last
words of the angel. Jesus had warned his contemporaries that,
unless they dissociated themselves from the past by an act of
national repentance, their generation would 'be held accountable for the blood of all the prophets shed since the foundation
of the world' (Luke xi. 50). The nation's history was a record of
cumulative guilt. In the same way Rome is held responsible not

only for the atrocities of her own history, but for those of Babylon's history as well. Babylon is the type of every persecuting
24 empire, and therefore **in that city was found the blood of
prophets and saints and of every victim of earthly
slaughter.**

The scene of judgment ends with another very important
1 piece of recapitulation. John hears **the roar of a vast throng.**
They must be the same vast throng which before he saw in
white robes and with palms in their hands (vii. 9 ff.), for their
song of triumph is almost the same. Then they sang, 'Victory
to our God who sits on the throne and to the Lamb!' Now they
sing, **'Victory and glory and power belong to our God'.**
There is no need for John to repeat in full what he said in the
earlier chapter, but it is implied. The victory of God is the
victory won by the martyrs, and their victory is the victory of
2 the Cross. If God has now **passed sentence on the great
whore** it is because they have given in their sacrificed lives the
evidence which secured her condemnation. There is nothing
3 ghoulish or macabre about the shout of triumph: **'Alleluia!
The smoke from her goes up for ever and ever!'** John
may use the imagery of Sodom and Gomorrah to portray
Babylon as a perpetually smoking ruin, but the reality he is
thus expressing is the victory of love over all that stands in love's
way.

IX

THE REIGN OF GOD

xix. 5-10. THE REWARDING OF THE PROPHETS

(5) Then from the throne came a voice which said: 'Praise our God, all you servants of his, you who fear him, both great and small !' (6) And I heard what seemed the noise of a vast throng, like the roar of many waters and mighty peals of thunder, which said, 'Alleluia ! For the Lord God Omnipotent has entered on his reign. (7) Let us be glad and jubilant and do him homage, for the wedding of the Lamb has come. His bride has made herself ready, (8) and has been given a wedding-dress of linen, pure and shining.' (The linen signifies the sanctity of God's people.) (9) Then the angel said to me, 'Write this: "Blessed are the guests invited to the Lamb's wedding feast!"' 'These,' he said, 'are the very words of God.' (10) I fell at his feet to worship him. But he said to me, 'No, not that ! I am a fellow servant with you and your brothers who hold the testimony of Jesus. Worship God. For the testimony of Jesus is the spirit that inspires prophets.'

John now turns to a detailed exposition of the theme already announced by the seventh trumpeter (xi. 15 ff.), as he makes quite evident by the many verbal similarities between the two passages—the **servants . . . who fear him, both great and 5 small** (cf. xi. 18), the **peals of thunder** (cf. xi. 19), and above all the declaration of divine sovereignty (cf. xi. 15, 16). Then it was the choir of heaven that sang: 'the sovereignty of the world has passed to our Lord and to his Christ'; now the vast throng of martyrs joins in the **Alleluia** chorus, because it is through 6 them that God has broken down the last resistance to his universal and eternal **reign**. Then the elders declared: 'Now is the time . . . for rewarding your servants the prophets . . . for destroying the destroyers of the earth', and these are the two ideas which John now proceeds in turn to develop.

7   The servants of God are rewarded by an invitation to **the wedding of the Lamb.** At this point John weaves together no less than three strands of Old Testament thought, all of which have been used before in Christian literature, but not in a single context. The first is the picture of the reign of God as a great **feast,** which is first found in the Old Testament in a late passage in the Book of Isaiah (Isa. xxv. 6; cf. 2 *Bar.* xxix. 3 ff.; 2 Esdras vi. 52; Mark ii. 19; Matt. xxii. 1 ff.; xxv. 1 ff.; Luke xiv. 15 ff.), but which probably had its roots in the mythology of Canaan.[1] The second is the idea of Israel as the **bride** of Yahweh (Hos. ii. 5; Isa. i. 21; Jer. ii. 2; cf. Eph. v. 32). The third is the use of clean garments as the symbol for **sanctity** (Gen. xxxv. 2; Isa. lii. 1; lxi. 10; Zech. iii. 4; Rev. iii. 4; vi. 11; vii. 14). Jesus had turned the messianic banquet into a wedding feast, but in his wedding parables the central figure was the bridegroom. Here attention is focused on the **bride.** The wedding day has come because the **bride has made herself ready,** and her readiness is symbolized by her **wedding-dress.** This dress is not of her own making; like the white robes of the martyrs to which it is closely related, it is **given** to her (cf. vi. 11). It is made of a **linen** which **signifies the sanctity of God's people,** a sanctity achieved in the great ordeal by those who 'washed their robes and made them white in the life-blood of the Lamb' (vii. 14). It is martyrdom which has provided the prothalamium to **the wedding of the Lamb.**

    The bride is the church, but the members of the church are
8   guests at her wedding, and their deeds are her **wedding-dress.** We should be ill-advised to put this down to clumsiness in the combining of different images. John is far too meticulous an artist to lay himself open to such a charge. There are other examples of the same fluidity in the use of imagery: the Lamb is also the shepherd (vii. 17), and the woman robed with the sun is the church and the church members her children (xii. 1-6). These examples prove that John is master of his medium and not its slave, that he can use his symbols with complete freedom from any literalness or pedantry.

[1] See T. H. Gaster, *Thespis*, pp. 207 ff.

A more serious problem is presented by John's double eschatology. In most Jewish and Christian systems of eschatology the great banquet, the last battle, and the last judgment have their place, and John has been showing how in his visions he saw these expectations fulfilled. He has recounted at some length the judgment of the great whore, he is now dealing with the appearance of the bride for the wedding feast, and he is about to depict the last battle. But then follows the millennium, and after the millennium an entirely new set of fulfilments of the same expectations: Gog and Magog are defeated in battle, the dead are judged, and the new Jerusalem descends from heaven like a bride adorned for her husband. Even Charles, who thought the last three chapters so incoherent and self-contradictory as they stand that only radical rearrangement could make sense of them, did nothing to eliminate this threefold repetition. Some scholars have seen the root of the trouble in the millennium itself, regarding it as a piece of traditional eschatology which John felt bound to include, although it played no integral part in his own thinking, yet one which could not be accommodated to his vision of the future without causing violent dislocation. But we shall see that this cavalier treatment of the millennium is quite without justification. The only other possibility is that the dual fulfilment, with the intervening millennium, is a vital part of John's theology. Let us start from that entirely reasonable hypothesis and see where it leads us.

Since John believed that the world as he knew it was to continue for the long but indeterminate period represented by a symbolic thousand years, it follows that only the events which happen after that period can strictly be called eschatological. Yet it is beyond question that events anterior to the millennium have regularly throughout the book been described in eschatological language. We have seen the seven seals of God's scroll of history broken, heard the last trumpet sound, and listened to an angel pronouncing the doom of Babylon with the words, 'It is over!' We are bound, then, to conclude that John has deliberately used eschatological language and imagery to depict events which possess only a qualified finality, events through which in the course of history men are compelled to face the ultimate issues of life. More than once in this commentary we have found evidence to support such a conclusion. The warnings of the coming of Christ in the letters are couched in the traditional language associated with the Parousia, yet they are conditional and therefore cannot properly be taken to refer to a single, world-wide event beyond which nothing else could conceivably happen (ii. 5, 16; iii. 3; cf. iii. 20); and a similar warning occurs at the very height of the apocalyptic visions (xvi. 15). The seven trumpets which ushered in the day of God's judgment (xi. 18) were found to be related to the trumpets of Tishri 1, the day in the Jewish liturgy on which God annually judged the world. The seventh bowl, which completes the wrath of God and brings about the collapse of Babylon, is the end of an epoch, but it is in a different category from the dissolution of the physical cosmos which accompanies the final judgment (xvi. 17-21; cf. xx. 11).

We return therefore to the question raised by the very first sentence of the Revelation. What did John think was 'bound to happen soon'? Certainly not the End, which was at least a millennium away. He expected an event so important that it could properly be described in eschatological terms, an event in which the End was so embodied that through their involvement in it men would be committed to taking sides in the battle between good and evil and to being judged before the throne of God. That event was the persecution, in which he saw God's victory over Babylon, as surely as in the Cross he had seen God's victory over Satan.

If this is indeed the nature of John's eschatology, it raises the further question whether the same is not true of all eschatology. Could it be that no ancient writer (except perhaps the imitative pedants responsible for some of the pseudepigraphical literature) ever used eschatological imagery except to express his confidence that God was working out his purpose in the events of contemporary history? Dodd has coined the phrase 'realized eschatology' to explain certain aspects of the teaching of Jesus, and has been criticized for producing a paradox amounting even to a contradiction in terms. Is it possible that 'realized eschatology' is instead a tautology, because only literalists ever used eschatological language for any other purpose than to give a theological interpretation to the critical moment that is called Today (Heb. iii. 13)?

A different explanation is required for John's duplicated attempt **to worship** his angel guide (cf. xxii. 8-9). Here we are 10 not dealing with the traditional imagery of eschatology, and the episode must have been repeated simply for emphasis. We can dismiss out of hand any suggestion that John was in this way combating an outbreak of angel-worship (cf. Col. ii. 18), since there is no suggestion of this in the letters to the churches. In any case, John would not have included this warning once, let alone twice, if it had not been intimately related to his main purpose. The relationship is not far to seek: it is idolatry. John is recognizing that idolatry can infiltrate into the life and worship of the church by other means than the seductions of the whore, the coercions of the monster, or the Quisling behaviour of the Nicolaitans. Even such a fanatical upholder of pure religion as he himself was could be so impressed by the revelation that came to him and the scriptures which were its principal stimulus, by the liturgical forms and the imagery in which it found expression, and by the religious experience that it evoked, that, in the midst of his passionate appeal against idolatry, he found himself worshipping that which is not God. Idolatry is more than burning incense before a man-made statue. It is to accord to anyone or anything other than God an absolute worth and a controlling significance in the life of man. The angel's protest is a salutary warning to all crusaders not to mistake the cause they champion for the one true God.

Thrice already John has used the expression **the testimony of Jesus** (i. 2, 9; xii. 17), and in each case the context requires that the genitive be taken as a subjective genitive. 'The word of God and the testimony of Jesus' can only mean 'the word spoken by God and the testimony borne by Jesus', or, as we have translated it, 'the word spoken by God and attested by Jesus' (i. 9; cf. i. 2). 'The commandments of God . . . and the testimony of Jesus' must mean 'the commandments God has given . . . and the testimony Jesus has borne' (xii. 17). The first two instances were closely associated with the first of the titles given to Jesus, 'the faithful witness' (i. 5; iii. 14), which is to be repeated in the very next verse (xix. 11). **The testimony of**

Jesus, then, in the passages in which the phrase has occurred
hitherto, is the witness he has borne in his life and teaching, but
above all in his death, to God's master plan for defeating the
powers of evil by the sacrifice of loyalty and love. It is unlikely,
therefore, that here John should have used the same phrase to
mean 'the testimony that Christians bear to Jesus' (though this
is of course included in their holding his testimony). To **hold
the testimony of Jesus** is to stand by the principle which
governed his incarnate life, to confirm and publish the testimony
of his crucifixion with the testimony of martyrdom.

This conclusion is strongly reinforced by the angel's closing
sentence. It is unthinkable that John, who so obviously believed in his own prophetic inspiration by the Spirit of God,
should have committed himself to the view that the sole source
of his inspiration was his own testimony to Jesus, that he was
in fact self-inspired. **The testimony of Jesus is the spirit
that inspires the prophets.** It is the word spoken by God and
attested by Jesus that the Spirit takes and puts into the mouth
of the Christian prophet. At the end of the first century there
were many charlatans about, like the Jezebel of Thyatira, who
claimed to speak with authority in virtue of their prophetic gift,
and the church was under the necessity of devising tests to
distinguish the true from the false. The author of 1 John
insists that his friends shall 'test the spirits to see whether they
come from God' (1 John iv. 1), and the test he proposes is a
double one: a belief that in Jesus the redeeming love of God
has taken human form, and conduct conforming with that
belief. John the seer would agree with this test. As we have seen
in each of the letters to the churches, the Spirit speaks to the
churches in the accents of the crucified and risen Lord, summoning them to become conquerors in the name of him who
has conquered. It is the gospel of the Cross that gives to the
prophets the assurance of their mission and of its ultimate
success (cf. x. 7). To be a prophet in the streets of the great city
is to follow in the steps of the master (xi. 3, 10). And it is the
Spirit who introduces the harvest and vintage with his benediction on those who 'die in the Lord' (xiv. 13).

(11) Then I saw heaven wide open, and there before my eyes was a white horse; its Rider's name was Faithful and True, for with justice he judges and makes war. (12) His eyes flamed like fire, and on his head were many diadems. He had written on him a name known to none but himself, (13) and he wore a garment soaked in blood. The title given to him was the Word of God, (14) and the armies of heaven followed him, mounted on white horses and clothed in pure white linen. (15) From his mouth came a sharp sword with which to smite the heathen; for it is he who is to smash them with an iron bar, he who treads the winepress of the wine of the fury of the wrath of God Omnipotent. (16) On his garment and on his thigh he has this title written: King of kings and Lord of lords. (17) Then I saw an angel standing in the sun, and he cried aloud to all the birds that fly in mid-heaven: 'Come! Gather for God's great feast, (18) to eat the carcases of kings and officers and warriors, of horses and their riders, of free and slave, great and small.' (19) Then I saw the monster and the kings of the earth and their armies marshalled to do battle with the Rider and his army. (20) The monster was taken prisoner, and so was the false prophet who had worked miracles in its presence and thus deluded those who bore the monster's mark and worshipped its statue. These two were thrown alive into the sulphurous flames of the lake of fire. (21) The rest were killed with the sword that came from the Rider's mouth, and all the birds gorged themselves on their carcases.

At the beginning of his apocalyptic vision John saw an open door in heaven, and was called to enter it in order that he might be admitted to the secret council of God (iv. 1). With the sounding of the seventh trumpet he saw the Holy of holies in the heavenly temple open, to disclose the ark and to signify that the secret purpose of God was now accomplished (xi. 19; cf. x. 7). Now the revelation he was charged to communicate is

11 complete, heaven holds no more secrets, and all **heaven** breaks **wide open** before his gaze. The **Rider** on the **white horse** has, as we have seen, no connexion with the rider of the first seal, except that in each case the **white horse** is the symbol of victory. The other rider was part of a fourfold scourge, active only through the divine permission, fit company for Death and Hades. This **Rider** is the Christ, in whom the eternal purpose of God has come to full expression and achievement.

The first thing we are told about the **Rider** is that his **name was Faithful and True.** He is thus identified with the heavenly Son of Man in his address to the church of Laodicea, 'the Amen, the faithful and true witness' (iii. 14), and consequently also with the faithful witness of the opening salutation (i. 5). In turning warrior he has not deserted his original function of witness-bearing, on which all his other achievements are founded. He is armed, as we shall see in verse 15, with no other weapon than the good confession which he witnessed before Pontius Pilate (1 Tim. vi. 13). This is not some supernatural figure from the fantasies of Jewish apocalyptic, but the Jesus of history, whose final victory in the battle to come serves only to make plain to the world the victory seen by faith from the beginning in the Cross. Although the battle he fights is described for the most part in military imagery, it is also, as befits the faithful witness, the wordy battle of the lawcourt: **with justice he judges and makes war.** In the Old Testament the *locus classicus* for this mixture of legal and military metaphor is Joel iii. 1-16, where all nations are summoned to battle in the Valley of Verdict; and this is a passage to which John has alluded more than once. But a closer parallel is the war in heaven between Michael and Satan, which turned out to be a legal battle between defending and accusing counsel (xii. 7-12). It may seem illogical to us that the witness should be said to judge, but there are two reasons for this. One is that John is preparing the way for a reinterpretation of Isaiah xi. 1-5, where it is said of the Messiah that 'he shall judge the poor with righteousness and give a verdict that is fair to humble folk'. The second reason is that the verb *krinein* (judge) and even *katakrinein* (condemn) are used elsewhere in the New Testament to denote the part played in the lawcourt by the witness. When Jesus says that at the last judgment the Queen of Sheba and the population of Nineveh will condemn 'this generation', he does not mean that they will have a place on the bench, but that their evidence will secure a conviction (Matt. xii. 41-42; Luke xi. 31-32; cf. also Luke xi. 19—'therefore they shall be your judges'). Similarly, when Paul says that Gentiles who keep the law will judge Jews who possess the law of Moses but break it, he means that they will provide the necessary evidence to refute the Jewish claims to superiority (Rom. ii. 27). This usage probably goes back to the legal practice of the small town in ancient Israel, where disputes were settled before an assembly of townsfolk in the gate and every speaker was entitled to give his verdict. (The legal practice of the early Greeks was not substantially different, as may be seen from the picture of the peaceful town on the shield of Achilles in Homer's *Iliad* xviii. 497-508.) So here the witness judges because it is on his evidence that the legal victory turns.

Every phrase in the description of the Rider adds something important to our understanding of his character and function. If we have any doubts that the name **Faithful and True** was a deliberate cross-reference to the letters, they are removed when we are told that **his eyes flamed like fire** (cf. i. 14; **12** ii. 18). This is the Son of Man who was first seen walking among the seven lamps, with a vigilant care for his people and an omniscient knowledge of what they were doing. To this extent he is the same, but in the meantime something has been added to his dignity, for **on his head were many diadems.** There is a contrast intended between the seven diadems of the dragon and the ten diadems of the monster on the one hand and the many diadems of the Rider on the other (cf. xii. 3; xiii. 1). Here is royalty far surpassing any earthly sovereignty. But the vital fact is that it has been acquired since John last saw the Son of Man, when no mention was made of diadems. Yet at that time he was already king, he had conquered and sat down beside the Father on his throne, he was ruler of earthly kings (iii. 21; i. 5). Whence then come the diadems? They signify, no doubt, that 'the sovereignty of the world has passed to our Lord and to his Christ' (xi. 15), but this does not tell us how he

came by them. They are his neither by virtue of the initial
victory on the Cross nor of the final victory over the monster
which is still to be recounted. They must therefore be the token
of the victory he has won through the Conquerors. He had
promised: 'To the Conqueror I will grant a seat beside me on
my throne, as I myself conquered and sat down beside my
Father on his throne' (iii. 21). They have conquered the
dragon by the life-blood of the Lamb (xii. 11), have been made
'a royal house of priests to his God and Father' (i. 6; v. 10),
have won their freedom from the monster and his statue (xv. 2);
and now all the diadems of their newly won empire meet upon
his brow. He is in fact a representative figure, incorporating his
faithful followers in his own inclusive person; for they have died
'in the Lord' (xiv. 13). They have come to know him more
intimately than others, for they have been entrusted with his
new name (iii. 12), a name which none can learn except the
Conquerors who receive it, because it embodies the secret of
his suffering (ii. 17). They have learnt the victory song of
heaven, which none can learn except those who die for their
faith (xiv. 3). Yet there are depths of his being which pass even
their comprehension, for he has **a name written on him
known to none but himself.** When they have joined all the
glorious names that adoring wonder can ascribe to him, he still
confronts them with an ultimate mystery.

13   The heart of the mystery is that **he wore a garment
soaked in blood.** This is the second time that John has
drawn his imagery from the gruesome vintage scene of Isaiah
lxiii. There the vintager is God himself, who comes from
treading the winepress with his garments stained with the blood
of his enemies. It has commonly been assumed that John must
have kept close to his model, and that the blood here is the
blood of the Rider's enemies also. In that case the winepress in
verse 15 is a symbol for divine retribution synonymous with the
symbol of annihilation in battle; and this interpretation must
be adopted also in the parallel passage (xiv. 18-20). The obvious
and insuperable objection is that the Rider's **garment** is
already **soaked in blood** before the battle begins. Some commentators have seen this difficulty and have tried to find a way
around it. Charles, for example, has argued that the blood must

be that of the Parthian kings and their armies killed in the battle referred to in xvii. 14. But that battle is almost certainly identical with the one now being described. We are told three things about it: that the attacking force will be the monster and its attendant kings, that the victory will go to the Lamb and his picked followers, and that he will conquer because he is Lord of lords and King of kings. All three points are reproduced in the present narrative, the only difference being that the Rider replaces the Lamb; and if this difference is considered an obstacle to the identification of the two accounts, it is equally an obstacle to a theory which uses the Lamb's victory to explain the bloodstained clothes of the Rider. Another weakness of this theory is that it leaves the staining of the garments totally unrelated to the vintage, which Charles does not connect with the Parthians in either of the places where it is mentioned. Kiddle would have it that the stained robe is 'a sign of his mission' which 'points forward to the function he is about to fulfil'. But John's faculty for kaleidoscopic changes of metaphor stops short of sheer incoherence. The picture of the vintager carefully dipping his garment in grape-juice as a sign of his trade before beginning to tread the winepress is too ridiculous to be entertained; but it has the merit of every *reductio ad absurdum*, that it sets us looking for a new and more adequate hypothesis. The theory that the Rider's garment is stained with his own blood is subject to the same disability as Charles' theory, that it severs the link between the stained garment and the vintage. If we stubbornly maintain that link, then the vintage must be subsequent to the exaltation of the Son of Man, but already over before the present scene opens. Now in our discussion of xiv. 18-20 we have seen good reason for the belief that John has there used the vintage imagery to make a profound disclosure about the great martyrdom, to show that the bloodbath of persecution, which might appear to be the total defeat of the church, was to the eyes of faith the ingathering of the elect and the means whereby the Son of Man would turn the slaughter of his saints into the downfall of his enemies. This theory, as we shall find, now acquires the additional virtue of solving our present problems also. The Rider bears on his garment the indelible traces of the death of his followers, just as he bears on his body the indelible marks of his own passion (i. 7; cf. John xx. 20-27).

The title given to him was the Word of God. This title appears at first sight to have only a superficial likeness to the eternal Logos of the Fourth Gospel. The Rider more closely resembles the personified Word of the Wisdom of Solomon, leaping from the royal throne like a relentless warrior into the doomed land of Egypt, bearing the sharp sword of God's inflexible commandment (Wis. xviii. 15-16), or that living, active word of God which cuts more keenly than any two-edged sword (Heb. iv. 12). But we must recall the charge laid upon John according to the title of his book—to bear 'witness to all that he saw, the purpose (or word) declared by God and attested by Jesus Christ (i. 2). Because Jesus in his earthly existence had been the faithful witness to the divine purpose, he had won the right to open the scroll of destiny, and so both to disclose and to achieve the purpose written in it. But the final disclosure and achievement are no different in character from the earthly life in which they were already anticipated. The word to which Jesus bore testimony in his life and death is now recognized to be indistinguishable from the person of the witness: he is **the Word of God.** The difference between the fourth evangelist and John the seer is that, while both are interested in the relation of the human Jesus to the eternal word or purpose of God, the one is writing a treatise on the Incarnation and looks back to the beginning, and the other is writing an apocalypse and looks forward to the end.

14   We normally think of **the armies of heaven** as consisting of legions of angels (cf. Matt. xxvi. 53), but here they are the Conquerors. They follow the Rider now, just as on an earlier occasion they followed the Lamb wherever he went (xiv. 4). Like his horse, their **white horses** are the token of victory. They have 'washed their robes and made them white in the life-blood of the Lamb' (vii. 14; cf. vi. 11; xix. 8). Their **pure white linen** is in striking contrast to his blood-soaked garment. His blood has made their robes white, and theirs has made his red. In this respect, as in the secret name he bears, he remains unique, even when surrounded by those who have won the same victory as he.

The description of the Rider continues with a catena of Old
Testament references: to the Davidic king who is to judge the
poor with justice and smite the earth with the rod of his mouth
(Isa. xi. 4); to the anointed king who is to smash the nations
with an iron bar (Ps. ii. 9); and once again to the vintager (Isa.
lxiii. 1). But none of these references can be taken quite at its
face value. The Davidic king was expected by the prophet to be
a person of such authority that he could redress the grievances
of the poor and break the power of the unscrupulous 'by the rod
of his mouth', i.e. by the mere pronouncement of a judicial
verdict; but here the rod has given place to **a sharp sword.**
Now the sword as a symbol of judicial authority is a Roman 15
metaphor, not a Jewish one. It is possible that John has done
nothing more than substitute the Roman symbol for the Old
Testament one, in order to assert, as he did in the letter to the
church at Pergamum, that Christ, not the Roman proconsul,
held the *ius gladii*, the ultimate jurisdiction of life and death.
But it is more likely that the full significance of the **sword** is to
be sought in the Old Testament, the source of most of John's
figurative language. There the 'mouth like a sharp sword' is the
symbol of the prophet, whose utterance has a cutting edge to it,
because he speaks the word of God (Isa. xlix. 2; cf. Heb. iv. 12;
Eph. vi. 17). Thus the only weapon the Rider needs, if he is to
break the opposition of his enemies, and establish God's reign
of justice and peace, is the proclamation of the gospel. The
quotation from Psalm ii does not need any further reinterpretation here, for the reader is expected to remember that John
has already done this on two previous occasions. In the promise
to the Conqueror at Thyatira (ii. 27) and in his extended comment on the psalm in chapters xi-xiv (see esp. xii. 5 and xiv. 1),
he has shown that the only **iron bar** God needs to reduce the
rebellious nations to submission is the Cross of his Son and the
martyrdom of his saints. About **the winepress** much has been
said already, and three things only remain to be added. The first
is that John here switches suddenly from future to present tense
and thus provides no justification whatever for the assumption
that the treading of the winepress is a metaphorical description
of the imminent battle. The second is that there is a new element
in the definition of the winepress: it is **the winepress of the**

wine, i.e. the place in which **the wine of the fury of the wrath of God Omnipotent** is prepared. 'The two ideas of the winepress and the cup of wrath', writes Charles, 'are here combined, and mean that from the winepress trodden by Christ flows the wine of the wrath of God, of which his enemies are to be made to drink. It is a case of mixed metaphors.' But it is a case of mixed metaphors only if we jump to the conclusion that winepress and cup both denote divine judgment. If we study the present passage without prejudice, we shall certainly conclude that **the wine of the fury of the wrath of God** is John's symbol for judgment, and that **the winepress** represents something quite different, namely the means by which the wine of judgment is prepared. When we remember that the cup of wrath is the cup which Babylon herself mixed (xviii. 6), and that she was seen drunk with the blood of the martyrs (xvii. 6), it becomes reasonable to suppose that **the winepress,** like the Cross, is a place where God has turned the murderous acts of men into the means of their own judgment. The third point confirms this view; for, having mentioned the winepress, John at once reverts to the **garment,** which we have seen to be already soaked in blood before ever the judgment of God's enemies has begun.

16   The Rider has a second title, **King of kings and Lord of lords,** and this one is written **on his garment and on his thigh.** The title is ambiguous, perhaps deliberately so; for it may refer to his sovereignty either over the rulers of the earth (i. 5) or over those whom he has made a royal house of priests to his God and Father. For a reason which will appear shortly it is likely that it was the second of these ideas that John had in the forefront of his mind. But whichever explanation we adopt, the title is the ground, not the result, of the coming victory; he will conquer the monster and the kings because he is already **King of kings and Lord of lords** (cf. xvii. 14). The warrant for the title is the initial victory of the Cross. It is natural therefore that the title should be written on his **thigh.** All John's readers, Jewish, Greek, or Roman, would readily understand that the **thigh** was the place where the sword hung (Exod. xxxii. 27; Judg. iii. 16, 21; Ps. xlv. 3; Cant. iii. 8; Homer, *Il.* i. 190; *Od.* xi. 231; Vergil, *Aen.* x. 788). Since in this picture there were

reasons why the sword should not be in its usual position, the **thigh** must do service for the sword, the weapon with which the victory and the title had been won. But why was the title written also on his **garment?** Surely for exactly the same reason: the **garment, soaked** as it was **in blood,** was the symbol of that other victory by which the Conquerors had taken their seat beside Christ upon his throne, yielding up to him their many diadems and so constituting him **King of kings.**

The summons to **the birds** has a fourfold significance. **17 God's great feast,** to which they are invited as guests, forms a grim contrast to the wedding feast of the Lamb. It is the first part of the double fulfilment of Ezekiel's prophecy about the defeat of Gog and his armies (Ezek. xxxix. 17 ff.; cf. Rev. xx. 7-11). It is also a reminiscence of the saying of Jesus which concluded his discourse on the day of the Son of Man: 'where the carcase is there will the vultures be gathered together' (Matt. xxiv. 28; Luke xvii. 37). As T. W. Manson has said, '"vulture" for the Palestinian does not have the unpleasant associations which it has for us'. It is a noble bird, whose distinctive characteristic 'is the almost incredible swiftness with which it discovers and makes its way to its prey' (*The Sayings of Jesus*, p. 147). There is no need for a sanitary inspector in the desert to make provision for the disposal of corpses; that can safely be left to the vultures. There is no need for men to concern themselves with useless questions about the time and place of the day of the Son of Man; divine retribution is not less reliable than the birds. John uses the same illustration to give the impression of swift and certain doom. But more important than all this is the cross-reference, which picks up a vital thread in John's own discourse. The invitation is to **the birds that fly in midheaven.** This curious phrase has been used before to characterize the eagle or vulture whose screech gave warning of the three woes (viii. 13), and we noted in the sequel that, although John seemed to be creating an atmosphere of mounting apprehension, he never actually depicted the third woe (cf. xi. 18). Instead the seventh trumpet called forth a jubilant paean on the establishment of God's sovereignty and a promise that the time had come to reward God's servants and to destroy the destroyers of the earth. It appears, then, that now at last we have reached the third woe. **The birds that fly in mid-heaven** come to make good the final threat of the eagle that flew in mid-heaven.

19 This reminder of the eagle and its three woes helps us to answer the next question as well. Who were these **armies marshalled to do battle with the Rider?** They are the destroyers. When John used that expression (xi. 18), he had already given a number of clear clues to its meaning, and in the intervening seven chapters he has expanded those clues to give a full and detailed picture of the demonic powers which have dominated the idolatrous world of heathendom. Thus we know that **the kings of the earth** are not to be identified with actual historic persons: they are the ten horns who have yielded their authority to the monster, who are in fact as much a part of the monster as its seven heads (xvii. 12-14). Whether John envisaged their armies as consisting of demonic hordes or of the kings' human dupes is harder to say. He certainly believed that in the end the unrepentant worshippers of the monster would share his fate (xvi. 9-10). On the other hand, the armies do not here and now share the monster's fate, and the judgment which decides the fate of men is postponed until after the millennium (xx. 15). It may even be that John himself never asked the question. For his attention is focused not on the armies, which are here hardly more than 'extras' in his battle scene **(the rest!)**,

20 but on **the monster** and **the false prophet. These two were thrown alive into the lake of fire,** which, although they must share it with their human followers, to whom it means annihilation, means something different for beings seemingly incapable of death (cf. xx. 10, 14).

xx. 1-10. THE MILLENNIUM

(1) Then I saw an angel come down from heaven with the key of the abyss and a great chain in his hand. (2) He seized the dragon, that old serpent, the Devil or Satan, and put him in chains for a thousand years; (3) he flung him into the abyss, shutting it and sealing it over him, to prevent him from deluding the nations again, until the

XX. 1-2   THE MILLENNIUM

thousand years were over. After that he must be let
loose for a little while.

(4) Then I saw thrones and seated on them those to
whom judgment was committed, the souls of those who
had been executed for the testimony of Jesus and the
word of God, those who never worshipped the monster
and its statue nor received its mark on forehead or hand.
They came to life and reigned with Christ for the thous-
and years, (5) while the rest of the dead did not come to
life till the thousand years were over. This is the first
resurrection. (6) Blessed and holy is the man who has a
share in this first resurrection ! On such the second death
has no claim; but they shall be priests of God and of
Christ, and shall reign with him for the thousand years.

(7) When the thousand years are over, Satan will be let
loose from his prison, (8) and will go out to delude the
nations at the four corners of the earth, Gog and Magog,
to muster them for battle. Countless as the sand of the
sea, (9) they swarmed over the breadth of the land,
encircling the camp of God's people and the city he
loves. But fire came down from heaven and consumed
them. (10) The Devil who deluded them was flung into
the lake of fire, to join the monster and the false prophet,
there to be tormented day and night for ever and ever.

We come now to a passage which, more than any other in the
book, has been the paradise of cranks and fanatics on the one
hand and literalists on the other. It bristles with questions. Why,
once Satan had been securely sealed in the abyss, **must** he **be
let loose** to wreak further havoc? And what claim does he have
on God, that God is bound to give the Devil his due? Why the
millennium? And what blessings does it confer on the martyrs
that make it worth their while to wait **a thousand years** for the 2
greater bliss of heaven? Who or what are Gog and Magog, and
what part do they play in John's theology of history?

It is possible to give a highly perfunctory answer to all these
questions. These ideas, we may say, were already part of the
apocalyptic tradition that John inherited from Judaism. They
were as much an embarrassment to him as to his modern

readers. He included them because he felt obliged to do so, though they added nothing valuable to his message. His book would have been more consistent and persuasive if he had left them out, but he was inhibited by the models he was following. But we may accept such a solution only on two conditions: we must be convinced on general grounds that John was a foot-slogging imitator, to whom tradition was as effective a prison as the sealed abyss to Satan; and we must be able to show that this particular tradition was so dominant in the first century as to leave him no viable alternative. The first of these conditions may be debatable, but the second is demonstrably false. Jewish and Christian literature of this period shows the widest possible variation of belief about the ultimate future. According to the *Epistle of Barnabas* 15 (cf. Irenaeus, *Haer.* v. 28. 3; Justin, *Tryph.* 81; Lactantius, *Instit.* vii. 14; Augustine, *C.D.* xxii. 30.5), belief in a millennium had its origin in a combination of Genesis ii. 2 with Psalm xc. 4, whereby each of the seven days of creation becomes a thousand years of history, ending with the messianic sabbath and succeeded by the timeless new world of the eighth day. That this argument was not a Christian innovation is proved by 2 *Enoch* xxxii. 2-xxxiii. 2 (where, however, there is no mention of a Messiah) and by a single reference in the Talmud (*San.* 97^b). But this does not mean that it was ever a Jewish orthodoxy. The Apocalypse of Weeks (1 *Enoch* xci. 12-17; xciii) divides world history into ten weeks of indeterminate length, and singles out the seventh week as the period of apostasy. 2 *Baruch* xxxix-xl follows Daniel in maintaining that world history consists of five ages or kingdoms, of which the last will endure 'until the world of corruption is at an end'; and as late as the third century the Babylonian Rabbi, Abba ben Raba, was still arguing for a figure of five thousand years rather than seven thousand before the beginning of the new world (*San.* 97^b). In 2 Esdras vii. 28-30 the Messiah is expected to reign for four hundred years before dying along with the rest of his generation (the second Arabic version, Vatican MS. Ar. 462, gives the figure as a thousand, but this is certainly a deliberate scribal emendation). In the Apocalypse of Elijah (*c.* A.D. 261), which in many other ways resembles Revelation, the age of the Messiah is to last only forty years. In

other Jewish writings, for instance the Similitudes of Enoch
(1 *Enoch* xxxvii-lxxi), there is no intervening earthly kingdom
before the transformation of heaven and earth. When we turn
to the New Testament, we find no trace of belief in a millennium in any writer other than John. Paul, indeed, speaks of the
reign of Christ continuing until all his enemies are in subjection
to him, but this is the reign that begins with his exaltation to the
right hand of God (1 Cor. xv. 24-28; cf. Matt. xiii. 41); there
are no enemies to be subdued in the millennial reign.

In the face of this evidence the only safe inference is that
John included the millennium because it was an indispensable
element in his vision of the future. What it meant to him we can
determine only by resolutely following such clues as he has
given. The first of these clues is that Satan is confined **to 3
prevent him from deluding the nations again.** This
plainly implies that throughout the **thousand years** there will
be a considerable world population which would otherwise
be susceptible to the attacks of Satan, and therefore a population
over and above the Conquerors, who have proved themselves
impervious to these attacks. This impression is immediately
confirmed by the twice repeated statement that the Conquerors
are to reign with Christ, since it would be a singularly empty
recognition of their services if they were to reign over a world of
which they were the sole inhabitants. If we take these statements
seriously, as indeed we must, it inevitably follows that the
commentaries are wrong which treat the battle of the previous
chapter as the end of world history and the wiping out of all
members of the human race who have not lost their lives in the
great martyrdom. The battle is the end of something, but not
that sort of end; for **the nations** as a whole survive it. Now it
cannot be argued that in this respect the present chapter is
isolated from the rest of the book and at variance with it.
What is here declared as a fact is no more than has already been
promised. The Conquerors have been told that they are to be
kings and priests (i. 6; v. 10), to reign on the earth (v. 10), to
have 'authority over the nations . . . to smash them with an iron
bar' (ii. 27; cf. xii. 5). This last quotation reminds us that **the
nations** are those mentioned in the second psalm, who rise in
their wrath against the Lord and his Christ (xi. 18). They are

not some mysterious reserve of manpower brought in from beyond the edges of the known world to fill the gap left by the total obliteration of Rome. They are the peoples among whom Christians were living, from whom they themselves had been ransomed (v. 9; vii. 9), and by whom they were to be persecuted (xi. 2). They were the peoples made drunk and seduced by the great whore (xiv. 8; xvii. 15; xviii. 3, 23). But they were also the peoples to whom John was bidden to speak his prophetic message (x. 11), to whom the angel of the eternal gospel was sent (xiv. 6), whose conversion the martyrs have confidently celebrated (xv. 4), and who are now given the assurance of future freedom from Satan's deceptions. The smashing of the nations therefore cannot mean disappearance from the face of the earth, but rather the breaking of that political power which, with the undergirding of idolatrous religion and materialist seduction, has organized them in resistance to the sovereignty of God.

Literally translated verse 4 reads: 'Then I saw thrones and they sat on them and judgment was given to them and the souls etc.'. In spite of the eccentric syntax it is probably safe to 4 assume that the occupants of the **thrones** are **those who had been executed.** The conjunction of **thrones** and **judgment** shows that John had in mind the judgment scene in Daniel vii, though he has interpreted it in his own way. According to Daniel it was the Ancient of Days who sat in judgment, and the phrase 'judgment was given to the saints' meant that the verdict went in their favour, so that the imperial power was taken from the fourth bestial kingdom and given to Israel (Dan. vii. 9, 22). It is just barely possible that we ought to adopt the same interpretation here. But John seems rather to stand in a Christian tradition of exegesis (cf. Matt. xix. 28; Luke xxii. 29 f.; 1 Cor. vi. 2 f.), which argued that, since Daniel spoke of thrones in the plural, they must be occupied by a plurality of judges or assessors. Those who are seated on the thrones must then be those to whom the right has been given to act as judges, not those in whose favour judgment is given. What is much more important, however, is that in Daniel the judgment is not the last judgment, but one that happens in the course of history. In the earlier chapters of Daniel we have been told that 'the

Most High controls the sovereignty of the world and gives it to whom he wills' (Dan. iv. 17, 25, 32), and in the judgment scene God is simply taking the sovereignty from one nation and giving it to another. 'The court shall sit in judgment, and his empire shall be taken away. . . . The sovereignty . . . shall be given to the people of the saints of the Most High' (Dan. vii. 26 f.). The judgment committed to the martyrs is thus not the right to determine the ultimate destinies of men—this God reserves within his own authority—but the right to assume the empire of the defeated monster.

For this purpose **they came to life;** and here again we detect the influence of the book of Daniel. Far too little notice has been taken of the salient fact that throughout the formative period of Old Testament eschatology from Amos to Daniel the Jewish people had no expectation of an afterlife. When they looked forward to the intervention of God in human affairs, in which he was to vindicate his oppressed people and introduce the new age of righteousness and peace, they inevitably conceived that new age as a direct continuation of earthly existence. It might be described in highly idealized terms, but, even if they thought of it as paradise restored, it was still an earthly paradise in which there would be a place for the administration of justice (Isa. xi. 1-11). It never occurred to them that the wrongs of this present world might be redressed in a different world altogether. The only other world they believed in was Sheol, but this was a world of death, not of life, and its inhabitants were flimsy creatures, mere carbon-copies of living beings in the eternal filing system of the underworld. 'Life' to them was the life of this present world, raised to its highest power by an abundance of health, vigour, and active enjoyment. It is true that God was believed to be the fountain of life, and that communion with him was regarded as the fulness of joy; but even this joy was not something mystic and ethereal, for it expressed itself in thoroughly tangible forms. When therefore the Jewish people began to entertain hopes of life after death, they naturally envisaged it as a return to the solid joys of the only life they knew. And it was the author of Daniel who first clearly enunciated the doctrine that the saints of the past would be restored to life in order to participate in the glories of the new age (Dan. xii. 2-3). But once this belief in resurrection had taken hold, it must soon have become obvious that the life of resurrection need not be limited to any earthly habitat; all that was needed was a heaven more solid and lasting, and therefore more real, than earth.

John seems to want the best of both worlds. He believes that the ultimate destiny of the redeemed is in the heavenly city, but he also retains the earthly paradise, the millennium. He therefore 5 requires not one but two resurrections: **the first resurrection** restores the martyrs to life for their millennial reign, the second brings all the dead before the great white throne. Now we have already seen that John was under no compulsion from tradition to indulge in such complexities. If he had wished to take the martyrs straight to heaven, there was ample precedent for his doing so. If he has not done so, it is because, like the Old Testament prophets before him, he really believed in the importance of the life men lead and the history nations fashion on this earthly scene. God is the Creator, and he has a purpose, not merely for isolated individuals of the human race, brands snatched from the burning, but for his creation as a whole. His purpose is worked out in history and must be vindicated in history. There must come a time on earth when it is true to say: 'the sovereignty of the world has passed to our God and to his Christ'. Unless the world is moving to such a goal, Christ has won only a Pyrrhic victory which, whatever the theologians may claim, leaves the powers of evil in possession.

But what did John mean by **resurrection?** Did he really expect the martyrs to return to their fleshly bodies and resume a physical existence? All the evidence we have is against such a literal interpretation. For John does not believe that the martyrs have all this time been lying in the sleep of death, waiting for the rending of the tomb. They have already put off their mortal garment of flesh and received instead the white robe of immortality (vi. 11), the breath of life from God has already come into them, and a cloud has carried them up to heaven (xi. 11 f.). It is unlikely, too, that John should have used the word resurrection in two completely different senses, and the resurrection of the rest of mankind is clearly not to earthly, bodily life. The decisive point, however, is the parallel between the resurrection

of the martyrs and that of Christ. Since it is said that they
reigned with Christ, he and they must be supposed to share
a common mode of existence: if they returned to bodily life,
then he too must have done the same; if he did not, then
neither did they. But what is here asserted of the martyrs, that
they came to life, has been said of Christ long since. He has
addressed the church of Smyrna as the one 'who was dead and
came to life' (ii. 8). His resurrection had a double sequel, in
heaven and on earth: for in heaven he sat down beside his
Father on his throne (iii. 21), and on earth he began a new
activity, unbounded by limits of time and space, walking among
the seven lamps of the world-wide church, sending out the
seven spirits of God into all the world, gathering the martyrs out
of every nation for their battle on Mount Zion (i. 13; v. 6;
xiv. 1). Now the martyrs have been promised that they are to
share Christ's heavenly throne, and on their coming to life
again they have heard a voice from heaven say, 'Come up
here!' (xi. 12). It would seem, then, that John expected the
millennial reign of Christ and the martyrs to be different in
degree but not in kind from the reign which Christ had exercised ever since his own resurrection. For them, as for him,
resurrection means that they have been 'let loose into the
world'.

The first resurrection is not therefore a postponement of 6
heavenly bliss. Already the martyrs are **blessed and holy.**
Already they walk with Christ in white, already they are before
the throne of God and serve him day and night in his temple
(iii. 5; vi. 9; vii. 15). Condemned in a human lawcourt, they
have had their sentence reversed by the tribunal of heaven. For
them the great white throne holds no terrors, for they have
passed the most exacting of scrutinies; and **the second death,**
the annihilation which awaits those who fail the final test, has
no claim on them (cf. ii. 11).

One thing more needs to be added to the description of the
martyrs' reign. They are to be **priests** as well as kings, the
means whereby Christ's redemptive no less than his regal
activity is mediated and diffused throughout the world (cf.
i. 6; v. 10). Through them the nations are to be brought to God
and made fit to be presented to God. Whatever else may have

stopped, the work of the gospel must continue in each successive generation. For generations there must be. The world of the millennium is not a deathless world. Death and Hades are destroyed only when the thousand years are over (xx. 14).

7   The release of **Satan** is dictated by John's belief that the millennium must be followed by a recrudescence of demonic evil. Satan is the personification of evil, and wherever evil is there Satan will be found as its prompter. But why did John find it necessary to believe that **Satan will be let loose from his prison?** Why did he believe in the recrudescence of evil,

8 symbolized by the invasion of **Gog and Magog?** The simple but inadequate answer is that he found this event prophesied in Ezekiel xxxviii-xxxix, and prophecies must have their fulfilment. It is inadequate because there has already been one fulfilment of this prophecy in the banquet of the birds, and there was no need to introduce another, unless John had found in Ezekiel some truth of ultimate and abiding significance. From what source Ezekiel derived the names Gog and Magog we cannot be sure, nor does it matter. Magog is mentioned among the northern nations in the genealogy of Noah (Gen. x. 2), and Josephus identified them with the Scythians (*Ant.* i. 6. 1; cf. *Jub.* viii. 25). Ezekiel accepts this northern origin, but with him it is more a mythological than a geographical north, the source of an archetypal enemy of whom all historic foes from the north were but a shadowy imitation (see on ix. 14). It is equally immaterial that Ezekiel's 'Gog of the land of Magog' has in John become a pair of nations: the same transformation is found in the *Sibylline Oracles* (iii. 512) and frequently in the Talmud, where Gog and Magog are said to be the rebellious nations of Psalm ii (*Ber.* 7^b, 10^a, 13^a; *Shab.* 118^a; *Pes.* 118^a; *Meg.* 11^a; *San.* 17^a, 94^a, 97^b; '*Abodah Z.* 3^b; '*Ed.* II 10. It is of some incidental interest that in *Sanhedrin* 94^a we are told that God had decided that Sennacherib should enact the part of Gog, but was persuaded to change his mind by the arguments of the Attribute of Justice. Gog is here being treated as a true myth, applicable to different historic situations. Anyone whom Gog's cap fits may wear it.) What does matter is that already in Ezekiel Gog and Magog are symbols of a profound spiritual truth. The invasion has nothing whatever to do with the

punishment of Israel for her sins or with her subsequent redemption or with the retribution inflicted on her persecutors. It is only after all this has happened, when peace and justice have been restored to the earth, that Gog is to come, so to speak, out of a clear sky. Three times it is said that he will come upon Israel only when she is living in security (Ezek. xxxviii. 8, 11, 14), and this gives us the necessary clue to the meaning of the symbolism. The myth of Gog enshrines a deep insight into the resilience of evil. The powers of evil have a defence in depth, which enables them constantly to summon reinforcement from beyond the frontiers of man's knowledge and control. However far human society progresses, it can never, while this world lasts, reach the point where it is invulnerable to such attacks. Progress there must be, otherwise God is neither Lord of history nor Lord of creation. But even when progress issues in the millennium, men must remember that they still have no security except in God. This is, in fact, the mythical equivalent of the Pauline doctrine of justification by faith alone, which teaches that from start to finish man's salvation is the work of grace, and never at any time his own achievement.

The object of attack is **the camp of God's people and the** 9 **city he loves. Camp** is the word used in the story of the Exodus for Israel's wilderness home, and reminds us that **God's people** are still, even in the golden age of the millennium, the church in the wilderness, the church in pilgrimage. The mention of a **city** has been thought to present more of a problem, since John has not yet seen the holy city descend from heaven. For this reason Charles considered it necessary to undertake one of his major surgical operations, excising xxi. 9-xxii. 2 and xxii. 14-15, 17 from the contexts in which they stand and inserting them after xx. 3. But there is no need for surgery. The descent of the city is not a single far-off divine event but a permanent spiritual fact. Just as the monster is a rising-from-the-abyss kind of monster, so the beloved city is a descending-from-heaven kind of city. In whatever place and at whatever time God's people are gathered together, there is the city of God (cf. iii. 12; xi. 2).

John shows no sort of squeamishness about the destruction of the armies of Gog. **Fire came down from heaven and**

consumed them. His emotional attitude to them is very much that of the modern reader of science fiction, who can contemplate with equanimity the liquidation of Mars-men with a ray gun, because they do not belong to the ordered structure of human existence. Like the four earthly winds of an earlier vision (vii. 1), they come from the four corners of the earth, the outlandish territory beyond the bounds of civilization.

xx. 11-15. THE GREAT WHITE THRONE

(11) Then I saw a great white throne and One seated on it from whose presence earth and heaven fled away, leaving not a trace to be found. (12) I saw the dead, great and small, standing before the throne; and books were opened. Then another book was opened, the book of life; and the dead were judged by their deeds according to what was written in the books. (13) The sea gave up its dead, and Death and Hades gave up their dead; and they were judged, each by his own deeds. (14) Then Death and Hades were thrown into the lake of fire. This lake of fire is the second death; (15) and into it anyone is flung if his name is not found written in the book of life.

The first thing that John saw in heaven was a throne (iv. 2), surrounded by a heavenly choir whose hymns celebrated the sovereign purpose of God in creation and the redemptive victory of the Lamb. Now the choirs of heaven are silent, the created world fades into nothingness, the Lamb surrenders the sovereignty to God the Father that he may be all in all (cf. 11 1 Cor. xv. 24-28); the **great white throne** stands alone, with nothing to challenge, to qualify, or even to mediate its sole supremacy. Whatever else John may say about the judgment, its essence is this, that men must stand immediately before the **throne** and bear, if they can, the burning bliss. It is a commonplace of Old Testament theology that the eternity of God and the incontrovertibility of his purpose should be contrasted with the transience of created things (e.g. Isa. xl. 8; li. 6). But there is more at stake here. **Earth and heaven** did not merely vanish like a puff of smoke, they **fled;** they **fled** in dismay before the moral grandeur of God, because they were unfit for his continued presence, because they were contaminated beyond the possibility of cleansing. For the second time John uses a phrase from Daniel's description of Nebuchadnezzar's dream, where the statue vanished, **leaving not a trace to be found** (Dan. ii. 35). Since John first used the phrase of Satan's ejection from heaven (xii. 8), we must suppose that the vanishing of **earth and heaven** has something in common both with that event and with its Old Testament prototype, that it represents the removal not merely of the transitory, but of that which is an obstacle to God's purpose. Yet their removal does not leave a total void; they are to be replaced by a new heaven and earth. The old order must make way for a new creation (xxi. 1-5), into which, however, the peoples of the old order may come and bring whatever treasures they have that are fit to survive (xxi. 24-26). We are thus reminded that earth and heaven are in John's cosmology a unit, but a unit of religio-political rather than physical geography. The old earth is the spiritual home of those who are called the inhabitants of earth, who are unable or unwilling to see beyond its material seductions to the glory of its Creator; and the old heaven is the location of that sea of glass which is the reservoir of demonic evil (iv. 6; xiii. 1), the home of man-made gods; and together they represent that structure of organized society in which idolatrous worship is offered and accepted. Throughout all the plagues this society has been the object of divine attack, and now it disappears without trace before the onset of his judgment.

The judgment itself is described with a stark economy. The first **books** to be **opened** are the record books, containing all the 12 evidence that the court needs if men are to be **judged by their deeds.** But the judgment is no automatic affair, such as could be carried out by any angelic clerk with enough arithmetic to recognize who had a credit and who a debit account. What the record books contain is determined, as we have already seen, by what God decides to remember and what he decides to forget (xviii. 5; cf. Jer. xxxi. 34). And before ever the ledgers are scrutinized by the auditors, **another book** is **opened,** whose contents must be thrown into the balance. This is **the book of life,** in which names have been 'written from the foundation

of the world' (xvii. 8), and it belongs to 'the Lamb slaughtered
from the foundation of the world' (xiii. 8). Thus into the scale
in men's favour are set the gracious, predestining purpose of
God and the redemptive love of him who died to ransom men for
God (v. 9). John has allowed for the possibility that a man's
name may be expunged from the book (iii. 5), that human disobedience may in the end prove impregnable to the assaults of
love. For such people the presence of God could be nothing but
a horror from which they, like the earth they made their home,
must flee, leaving not a trace behind. For them there remains
only the annihilation of **the second death.** In justice to John
let it be noted that **the lake of fire** is not for men, as it is for the
demonic enemies of God, a place of torment. But John makes no
attempt to usurp the judgment seat of God, either by a dogmatic
universalism or by an equally dogmatic particularism. There
would be no point in a last judgment unless the final decisions
lay in the hands of the Judge; and John is content to leave them
there. We may be sure that he has a greater confidence in those
decisions than many of his modern detractors who have accused him of undue severity.

13   **The sea gave up its dead, and Death and Hades gave
up their dead. Hades** was the universal grave into which
men entered by burial. Those who died at sea, without burial,
had no access to Hades and were therefore regarded as the
victims of a peculiarly pitiable tragedy. John classifies them
separately to indicate the universal nature of the resurrection.
But incidentally he gives us a reminder that in his cosmology

14 **the sea** belongs with **Death and Hades** as a demonic realm
hostile to the true character of God. When we first heard of
Death and Hades they were being let loose upon the earth
along with the other demonic horsemen, because the Lamb's
victory had enabled him to use even the destroyers of the earth
as the instruments of an ultimate purpose of grace and mercy.
But now that the purpose has been fully achieved, they appear
in their true light as enemies of the living God and contra-
dictions of his nature and will. Here as in the theology of Paul,
Death is the last enemy, whose destruction leaves no further
obstacle to the establishment of the eternal reign of God (cf.
1 Cor. xv. 26, 54).

X

THE NEW JERUSALEM

xxi. 1-8. THE NEW HEAVEN AND EARTH

(1) Then I saw a new heaven and a new earth, for the first heaven and the first earth were gone, and the sea was no more. (2) I saw the holy city, new Jerusalem, coming down out of heaven from God, made ready like a bride adorned for her husband. (3) I heard a loud voice from the throne say: 'Now is God's dwelling with men! He will dwell among them, and they shall be his people; God himself will be with them (4) and will wipe every tear from their eyes. Death shall be no more; grief and crying and pain shall be no more; for the old order is gone!' (5) Then he who sat on the throne said, 'See! I am making all things new!' 'Write this,' he said, 'for these words are faithful and true.' (6) Then he said to me, 'All is over! I am Alpha and Omega, the beginning and the end. To the thirsty I will give without charge from the spring of the water of life. (7) This is the Conqueror's heritage; and I will be his God, and he shall be my son. (8) But as for the cowards, the faithless and polluted, murderers, fornicators, sorcerers, idolaters, and liars of every kind, their lot is the lake that burns with sulphurous flames, which is the second death.'

All through the long story of God's assault on the old corrupt order there have been intimations of immortality: the promises to the Conquerors, the white-robed multitude, the triumph song of Moses and the Lamb, the wedding feast of the Lamb and his bride. The clouds of glory have hung low over the camp of the true Israel in their wilderness wanderings. Now at last John stands on Pisgah and surveys the promised land. In some ways this is the most important part of his book, as it is certainly the most familiar and beloved. 'If only we knew', the martyrs have cried, 'where it is all going to end!'; and much of

John's vision, and much of the human history it depicts and interprets, becomes intelligible, credible, tolerable, when we know the answer. Here is the real source of John's prophetic certainty, for only in comparison with the **new Jerusalem** can the queenly splendours of Babylon be recognized as the seductive gauds of an old and raddled whore.

1   The first thing that John has to tell us about the **new heaven** and **earth** is that **the sea was no more.** As we might have expected, there are seven elements of the old order which he dismisses with the same formula: sea, death, grief, crying, pain, all that is under God's curse, and night (xxi. 1, 4; xxii. 3, 5). Literally or symbolically this list embraces the whole range of evil, and the first and all-inclusive term is **the sea.** We need not waste time with the notion that this reflects the ancient horror of sea-voyages in an age without chart or compass, for we have only to turn back to the description of Babylon's sea-borne luxury trade to be sure that John was not the sort of land-lubber to be easily scared by tales of Scylla or the Clashing Rocks. His horror of the sea is the product of myth and of myth's historic equivalent in human experience. The sea which vanishes with **the first heaven and the first earth** is the cosmic sea out of which that heaven and earth were made, the primaeval ocean or abyss which is an alias for the dragon Leviathan, a home for the monster, and a throne for the whore (iv. 6; xii. 3; xiii. 1; xvii. 1). Notwithstanding God's initial conquest of it in creation, it has remained, both on earth and in heaven, as the symbol of an incomplete victory and an incomplete sovereignty. It has been a barrier between man and God, through which the martyrs have had to pass in their new Exodus, and it has been poured from the bowls of God's wrath to engulf the throne of the monster. But in a world where all things are spontaneously obedient to the rule of God it has no place.

The disappearance of **the sea** is proof that the transformation he is about to describe is in John's mind a real future, an octave beyond the seventh day of the millennium to which the whole creation is moving. History must have a real end, temporally as well as teleologically. Yet there are constituents of his vision which are hard to explain if this is all he has in mind. Why, for instance, does the new order require **a new earth** as well as **a new heaven?** And why is it necessary for **the holy city** to descend from the one to the other? Once the 2 descent has been accomplished, the distinction between the two seems to be forgotten. John assuredly does not want us to think that in the eternal sabbath earth will continue to be the dwelling-place of men and heaven the dwelling-place of God, for the whole point of the descent is that **now God's dwelling is with men.** The answer, which will become more and more apparent as we proceed, is that this is a future which inter-penetrates and informs the present. **The holy city** is described as **coming down out of heaven from God** because this is the essential quality it already has in the anticipatory experience of the church. In Ephesus, Pergamum, and Philadelphia the eyes of faith have seen it come **down out of heaven,** and wherever else there has been a conqueror inscribed with its potent name (iii. 12). It has come down to be trampled underfoot by the heathen wherever God's witnesses have prophesied (xi. 2 f.). It has come down **like a bride adorned for her husband** for the victory celebrations of the Lamb's wedding (xix. 7-8). It has come down to grace the golden age of the millennium (xx. 9).

> 'The true thy chartered freemen are,
> Of every age and clime.'

The first support for this interpretation of the descent of the holy city comes from the **voice from the throne** which im- 3 mediately follows: **'Now is God's dwelling with men!'** The word *skênê* **(dwelling)** has a long and important theo-logical history. It is the word regularly used in the Septuagint for the Hebrew *mishkan* (tent), which was the symbol of God's abiding presence in the midst of Israel in the wilderness. John has thus chosen to use a term which implies that the promise of God's presence has already had constant fulfilments in the past wherever Israel has been true to her calling. Yet he cannot mean literally that the tent is to be restored to its place among God's people, for in the new Jerusalem there is no temple, and therefore *a fortiori* no tent (xxi. 22). In some passages of the Old Testament the word *mishkan* had been used in a derivative

sense to denote the divine presence, and one of these is clearly in
the back of John's mind: 'I will set my *mishkan* among you ... I
will walk among you and be your God, and you shall be my
people' (Lev. xxvi. 11; cf. Ezek. xxxvii. 27). In later Jewish
theology *mishkan* in this sense gave way to another derivative
from the same verb *shakan* (to dwell)—Shekinah, or in Aramaic,
Shekinta. In the Targums *Shekinta* was one of the three terms
(along with *Memra*, word, and *Yeqara*, glory) regularly used as
reverential insulators to prevent the sacred name of God from
too close verbal contact with men. When the Old Testament
writers say that God spoke to men, dwelt with men, appeared to
men, the Targums tend to say that the *Memra* spoke, the
Shekinta dwelt, and the *Yeqara* appeared, though variations and
combinations also occur. Thus the Targum of Jonathan on
Leviticus xxvi. 11, quoted above, reads: 'I will set the *Shekinta*
of my *Yeqara* among you'. In the Mishna and the Talmud
the word *Shekinah* occurs frequently to denote the presence
of God. Thus in *Pirke Aboth* iii. 9 it is said that the *Shekinah*
is present where ten men meet to pray, where three meet to
administer justice, or where two meet to study the Torah. The
Greek word *skênê* was ideally suited to convey the whole of this
complex of meaning, because it was the natural rendering for
mishkan, but also because it had the same consonants as
Shekinah. (This may be a pure linguistic coincidence, but it is
more likely that *skênê*, like a number of other Greek words, is a
loan word from some Semitic language closely akin to Hebrew,
probably Phoenician.) This development of Rabbinic terminology must have been known to John, as it was undoubtedly
known to the author of the Fourth Gospel, who included all
three of the Targumic insulators in a single sentence: 'The
word (*Memra*) became flesh and dwelt (*Shekinta*) among us,
and we beheld his glory (*Yeqara*)'. (John i. 14.) **God's dwelling,** then, is the *Shekinah*, and its final establishment among
men has been anticipated in many ways, but above all in the
Incarnation.

The same point is made a second and a third time in the two
succeeding promises. **'They shall be his people'** is the promise first made in the covenant with Israel at Sinai (Lev. xxvi.
12; Jer. vii. 23; xi. 4; cf. Hos. i. 9), renewed in the promises of

the prophets (Hos. i. 23; Jer. xxx. 22; Ezek. xxxvi. 28; xxxvii. 23, 27; Zech. viii. 8), and realized in the new covenant of Christ (Rom. ix. 25; 1 Pet. ii. 10). **'God himself will be with them'** is the assurance given to Moses at the burning bush (Exod. iii. 12), enshrined in the prophetic name Immanuel (Isa. vii. 14), echoed in the missionary hope of the restored nation (Zech. viii. 23), and ratified by him who made the title Immanuel his own (Matt. i. 23). Thus the voice from the throne gives the permanent guarantee of those privileges which have always been enjoyed by those who, refusing to be at home in the old order, have lived as citizens of the city whose builder and maker is God (Heb. xi. 8-16; cf. Gal iv. 26).

Further confirmation of this thesis comes from the double fulfilments of Old Testament prophecy to which we have referred above (see on xix. 5-10). The promise that God **will wipe 4 every tear from their eyes** has already been used in the vision of the victorious martyrs (vii. 17), and we noted in that passage the ambiguity of tenses, which suggested that John thought the reward of martyrdom to be both a present reality and a future hope. But these words are also a quotation from the Old Testament passage which provides the model for the hope of a messianic banquet (Isa. xxv. 6-8), a passage from which John also derives the promise that **death shall be no more.** But this prophecy has already received a fulfilment within the history of the first earth, the wedding feast of the Lamb; and on that occasion also the church appeared **like a bride adorned for her husband. The old order is gone** and the new has come; yet the change is not one of simple temporal succession, for all along the new has been present in the old.

The pastoral relevance of the new Jerusalem to the needs of the seven churches becomes still clearer when for the first time since the opening of the visions we hear the voice of God. John is told to **write this,** because this voice from the ultimate future has something urgent to say to the critical present: **'I am 5 making all things new'.** This is not an activity of God within the new creation, after the old has been cast as rubbish to the void; it is the process of re-creation by which the old is transformed into the new. In Smyrna and Thyatira, in Sardis and Laodicea, in all places of his dominion, God is for ever making all things new, and on this depends the hope of the world. Paul had spoken of a new creation in the lives of men whereby, behind the façade of the outer man, subject as it is to weakness and decay, there is being built up an inner man, daily transfigured into the likeness of Christ, but kept hidden with Christ in God until the day of his appearing (2 Cor. iii. 18; iv. 16-18; v. 16-17; Col. iii. 1-4). John envisions the same transformation on a cosmic scale. Blind unbelief may see only the outer world, growing old in its depravity and doomed to vanish before the presence of holiness; but faith can see the hand of God in the shadows, refashioning the whole. The agonies of earth are but the birth-pangs of a new creation.

The one Greek word which proclaimed the end of God's demolition work now proclaims the completion of his new 6 creation. This, in the full and final sense, is the end: 'All is over' (cf. xvi. 17). But at once John reminds us that, ever since we first heard the voice of God (i. 8), we have held in our hands the key to the complexities of his eschatology. If from time to time we have been puzzled because he has brought us to the end, which turned out after all to be less than final, we now see why. The end is not an event but a person. In much that has been written during the last thirty years on the subject of eschatology the debate has turned on the nature of the *eschaton*, the final event, and whether this *eschaton* can properly be said to have entered history in the person of Jesus Christ. But the word *eschaton* (neut.) does not occur in the New Testament. John knows only of the *eschatos* (masc.), a person who is both **the beginning and the end.** To anyone who shares the biblical faith it goes without saying that he is capable of entering history at any point he chooses, and this is John's faith also. When he calls God **Alpha and Omega,** he is no deist, placing God at the beginning and end of a cosmic process which is allowed to run mechanically without intervention. God is the living God; and whenever men find themselves in the presence of the living God, there they confront **the beginning and the end,** the ground and goal of their being. All that man has and is, but above all man's salvation, is from start to finish the work of God. He requires nothing of man but an emptiness ready to be filled, a thirst to be slaked **from the spring of the water of life.**

The whole passage is resonant with echoes of the Beatitudes. The **grief** of the mourners is to be comforted, the craving of **the thirsty** is to be assuaged. The Conqueror, the victim of persecution, is to enter into his kingdom and be called God's **son.** Those whom Christ has made a royal house of priests inherit with him the promise once made to the royal house of David: 'I will be his father and **he shall be my son'** (2 Sam. 7 vii. 14). But there is more in this word than the fulfilment of an ancient prophecy. It contains the very heart of John's vision of heaven. Before he attempts to summon up the full resources of language to depict what is beyond language and thought, he leaves us with this first indelible impression that heaven is belonging to the family of God.

Even on the threshold of unimaginable joy John cannot forbear a parting glance over his shoulder into the abyss. The modern reader is likely to experience a shock when he sees **cowards** leading the cavalcade of the reprobate. However 8 highly we value courage, we are not accustomed to think of cowardice as one of the deadly sins, let alone the first of them. The explanation is that John's mind is at all times so dominated by the prospect of persecution that no other virtues or vices enter into his calculations than those involved in a response to the conflicting claims of God and the monster. In this conflict of duties nothing counts but the heroic virtues of courage and loyalty and their ignoble opposites, cowardice and faithlessness. The other terms in the list denote complicity in the crimes of the monster and the whore. The word here translated **polluted** is from the same root as that used for the obscenities of Babylon (xvii. 4, 5). **Murderers** are the monster's agents in the killing of the martyrs (xiii. 15), who have filled the cup that made Babylon drunk (xvii. 6). **Fornicators, sorcerers, idolaters** are variations on the one theme of idolatrous worship (ii. 14, 20, 21; ix. 21; xiv. 8; xvii. 1-xix. 2). **Liars** are those who have committed themselves to that fundamental falsity which is the nature of the dragon and his earthly agents. Those who have chosen to be identified with the destroyers of the earth in their godless task are identified with them also in their godless fate.

By their own choice Babylon and not the new Jerusalem is their eternal home.

xxi. 9-xxii. 5. THE HOLY CITY

(9) Then one of the seven angels who held the seven bowls full of the seven last plagues came and spoke to me: 'Come', he said, 'and I will show you the bride, the wife of the Lamb.' (10) So he carried me away in a trance to a huge, high mountain and showed me the holy city of Jerusalem coming down out of heaven from God, (11) bright with the glory of God. It had the radiance of some very precious jewel, like a jasper, clear as crystal. (12) It had a huge, high wall with twelve gates, guarded by twelve angels; and on the gates were carved the names of the twelve tribes of Israel. (13) There were three gates to the east, three to the north, three to the south, and three to the west. (14) The city wall had twelve foundation-stones, and on them were the twelve names of the twelve apostles of the Lamb.

(15) The angel who was speaking with me carried a gold measuring-rod, to measure the city, its gates, and its wall. (16) The city stands foursquare, its length equal to its breadth; it measured by his rod twelve thousand furlongs, its length, breadth, and height being equal. (17) When he measured its wall, it came to a hundred and forty-four cubits, measuring by a man's forearm, that is, an angel's. (18) The fabric of the wall was jasper, while the city was of gold, bright as clear glass. (19) The foundations of the city wall were bejewelled with every kind of precious stone: the first foundation-stone was jasper, the second lapis lazuli, the third chalcedony, the fourth emerald, (20) the fifth sardonyx, the sixth cornelian, the seventh chrysolite, the eighth beryl, the ninth topaz, the tenth chrysoprase, the eleventh jacinth, the twelfth amethyst. (21) The twelve gates were twelve pearls, each gate being made from a single pearl. The streets of the city were of pure gold, translucent like glass.

(22) I saw no temple in the city, for its temple was the Lord God Omnipotent and the Lamb. (23) It had no need of sun or moon to shine on it; for the glory of God gave it light, and its lamp was the Lamb. (24) The nations shall walk by its light, and the kings of the earth shall bring into it their treasures. (25) Its gates shall never be shut by day—and there shall be no night there. (26) They will bring into it the treasures and wealth of the nations; (27) but nothing unclean shall enter it, nor anyone whose life is obscene or false, but only those who are written in the Lamb's book of life.

(1) Then he showed me the river of the water of life, bright as crystal, flowing from the throne of God and the Lamb, (2) down the middle of the city's streets. On each side of the river stands the tree of life, yielding twelve crops of fruit, one for each month of the year. The leaves of the trees were a cure for the nations, (3) and all that is under God's curse shall be no more. The throne of God and the Lamb will be there, and his servants shall worship him; (4) they shall see him face to face and bear his name on their foreheads. (5) Night shall be no more; they will need no light from lamp or sun, for the Lord God will give them light; and they shall reign for ever.

Having charge over one of **the seven bowls full of the** **seven last plagues** does not seem to be an obvious qualification for an angel who is to act as guide to the celestial city. Perhaps John believed that the demolition squad had also an interest in the reconstruction for which they had cleared the ground. What is clear is that these angels have a structural significance in the architecture of his own book. The angel is the counterpart of the guide who showed John the passing of sentence on the whore (xvii. 1): both were angels of the **bowls,** both carried him off **in a trance,** and both showed him a bejewelled woman who was also a city. **The bride** is the heavenly reality of which Babylon is the earthly travesty.

The **huge, high mountain** is not a viewpoint but the actual site of the city, as in Ezekiel xl. 2. John has already had his

Pisgah panorama and is now being escorted on a detailed survey.
The idea that the heavenly city is built on the summit of a
high mountain has a double ancestry: the ancient myth about a
mountain in the far north, which reached to heaven and was
the home of the gods,[1] and the ideal pictures of Mount Zion in
the Old Testament. In the myth the mountain was located in the
north because that was the point around which the constellations
appeared to revolve; and Heylel, the morning star, attempted to
scale its walls in order to become king over the other stars, only
to be vanquished by the appearance of the all-conquering sun.
In the Old Testament this myth is given two different historical
applications, in one of which the part of Heylel is played by the
king of Babylon (Isa. xiv. 12-14) and in the other by the king of
Tyre (Ezek. xxviii. 12-16). The second of these passages is
particularly important because it identifies 'the holy mountain
of God' with 'Eden, the garden of God', and also because it is
one of John's sources for his list of precious stones. That this
mythical mountain continued to play a part in Jewish thought
is shown by further references in the intertestamental literature.
Thus in 1 *Enoch* xviii. 8 (cf. xxiv. 1-3; xxv. 3) Enoch has a
vision of a mountain which is both the throne of God and the
garden in which the tree of life is planted. In Psalm xlviii. 2 the
myth had already been united with the prophecy that in the new
age Mount Zion was to be promoted to be the highest of all
mountains, with the power to attract all nations to its central
sanctuary (Isa. ii. 2; Mic. iv. 1; cf. Zech. viii. 23; xiv. 16); and
the mountain has become 'Mount Zion in the far north, the
city of the great King'. John therefore had ample precedent for
combining in a single vision the imagery of the high mountain,
the holy city, and Paradise restored.

To any brand of literalism it is a serious difficulty that John
now for the second time sees **Jerusalem coming down
out of heaven from God.** Charles, for instance, takes it for
granted that, since John saw the sight twice, it must have
happened twice. The whole of xxi. 9-xxii. 2, therefore, ought to
be transposed to a point before the millennium, from which it
must have been removed by a botching editor; and, since the

[1] See Bruno Meissner, *Die babylonische-assyrische Literatur*, p. 28; H.
Gunkel, *Schöpfung und Chaos*, pp. 133-134.

city has to descend a second time after the last judgment, 'its removal from the earth is presupposed'. But all this is unnecessary when we recognize that the descent from heaven is not a single nor even a double event, but a permanent characteristic of the city. There is no suggestion that, if John had arrived a little earlier or a little later, he would have missed seeing what he saw. To the crack of doom Jerusalem can never appear otherwise than **coming down out of heaven,** for it owes its existence to the condescension of God and not to the building of men. The very light with which it gleams, **like a** 11 **jasper,** is **the radiance** which John has already seen streaming from the figure on the heavenly throne (iv. 3).

Like the city of Ezekiel's vision (Ezek. xlviii. 30 ff.), John's Jerusalem has **twelve gates,** three on each side, corresponding 12 to **the twelve tribes of Israel.** The only difference is that Ezekiel regarded the gates as exits through which the tribes were to go out to their allotted land, and John thinks of them as entrances, open to the nations of the world. Attempts have been made to connect these gates with the twelve signs of the zodiac, the portals by which the sun, moon, and planets enter on their diurnal course. There is no doubt that Jewish and Christian writers of this period were as familiar as their pagan neighbours with astrological lore. The author of 1 *Enoch* xxxiii-xxxvi tells of a vision in which he saw twelve portals of heaven, three at each point of the compass; and above the eastern ones were small portals through which 'the stars of heaven pass to run their course to the west'. The author of 1 *Enoch* lxxii-lxxxii— almost certainly a different person with polemical intentions towards astrologers—has produced a calendrical system with a year of 364 days, based on twelve heavenly gates which are quite independent of the zodiac. Thus, if John had wanted to give the gates a zodiacal significance, there was no reason why he should not have done so. On the other hand, there is no need to look for an explanation beyond his Old Testament model in the pages of Ezekiel. The evidence seems to be that he was aware of the astrological possibilities, and, like the author of 1 *Enoch* lxxii-lxxxii, deliberately turned his back on them. In the first place there is the curious order in which the **gates** are listed—ENSW. It is true that for this, too, John had a 13

precedent in Ezekiel (xlii. 16-19), but why out of the many
possible Old Testament precedents did he choose the most
erratic? It is an order which no one in his senses would choose
if he were at all interested in the zodiacal cycle, but one which a
man might choose to discourage such an interest in his readers.
Secondly, John has taken the twelve precious stones, which he
must have known to have associations with the zodiac as well
as with the twelve tribes (Exod. xxviii. 17 ff.; xxxix. 10 ff.; cf.
Wis. xviii. 24), and has deliberately broken the association by
14 making them **foundation-stones,** bearing the **names of the
twelve apostles,** and by listing them in an order exactly the
reverse of that used in astrology. These facts seem to give
sufficient justification for Charles' dictum that John 'regarded
the Holy City which he describes as having nothing to do with
the ethnic speculations of his own and past ages regarding the
city of the gods'.

The addition of **the twelve apostles** to **the twelve tribes**
almost certainly means that John's city has no astrological
ground plan. It also means that **the twelve tribes,** as we have
already seen in the episode of the sealing (vii. 1-8), are the tribes
of the new Israel. But the apostles have a further theological
significance as well. A city which is built on the foundation of
the apostles (cf. Eph. ii. 20) is built on the apostolic tradition, the
revelation of God of which the apostles were eye-witnesses and
guarantors.

When John himself was given a measuring-rod and told to
measure the sanctuary, it was for the purpose of protection;
whatever he did not measure was left exposed to heathen
15 attack. The purpose of the angel's **gold measuring-rod** is to
convey information about the city which could not be imparted
by direct vision. Just as John formerly heard the number
144,000, but saw a vast throng beyond human computation, so
now he tries by means of the reported measurements to give
the impression of a city which in magnitude, symmetry,
solidity, and splendour transcends the power of man to en-
visage. He bursts the bonds of language in an attempt to hint at
what is essentially beyond imagination. Yet his symbols are not
16 therefore devoid of meaning. Like the city of Ezekiel's hope, this
city stands foursquare (Ezek. xlv. 2; xlviii. 20), but not even

Ezekiel with his soaring and surrealist mind had dared to contemplate a city that was a perfect cube. John has remembered the Holy of holies in Solomon's temple, twenty cubits each way, **its length, breadth, and height being equal** (1 Kings vi. 20). This cubic symbol of the earthly presence of God among his people has expanded before his mind's eye, so that it not only fills the whole templeless city, but embraces heaven and earth. Men had dreamed of building a Babel whose top should reach to heaven (Gen. xi. 4), or of scaling the northern mountain on which stood the city of the gods. But here coming down out of heaven was a city so sublime that before it human aspirations must dwindle into insignificance.

The measurements of the city show how much John cared for symbolism and how little for mathematics. Clearly the **twelve thousand furlongs** bear some relation to the twelve thousand sealed from each of the twelve tribes. But if we attempt to make the relationship an arithmetical one, we shall find ourselves in trouble. Since there is a tribe to each gate and three gates to each side, why do the sides of the city not measure thirty-six thousand furlongs? Or, if the city is a human square of twelve thousand, should we not expect the symbolic number of its citizens to be a hundred and forty-four millions? Such computations are quite outside John's range of interest. Lacking the figure zero, he would probably have been hard put to it to calculate a square of such dimensions. As before, he has simply taken the symbolic number twelve and multiplied it by a thousand, the symbol of vast magnitude. Similarly with the height of the wall. The criticism has often been raised that a **17 hundred and forty-four cubits,** if it is the height of the wall, is a surprisingly insignificant figure for the wall of so vast a city, and, if it is the thickness of the wall, represents a totally inadequate foundation for a wall fifteen hundred miles high. But this is to miss the point. The cubit was originally the distance from elbow to finger-tip; but, as with the foot measurement, the value of a cubit came to be standardized, though the standards varied from country to country. John explains that, when he says 'cubit', he does not mean the standard cubit, but the actual measure of **a man's forearm,** with the proviso that, as so often in apocalyptic vision, man here means angel (cf.

Ezek. ix. 2; Dan. viii. 15 f.; ix. 21; x. 5; xii. 7). By what calculus
then are we to compute **a hundred and forty-four** measures
of **an angel's** forearm?[1]

18 The unimaginable wonder of the city is further evinced by
its **fabric. The fabric of the wall was jasper,** the substance
which most nearly serves to convey an impression of the being
of God himself (cf. iv. 3). John no doubt recalls the prophecy of
Zechariah that the restored Jerusalem would need no wall, because the Lord would be a wall of fire about her and a glory
within her (Zech. ii. 5). We, recalling the same prophecy, might
be tempted to ask why the holy city needs a wall at all, now that
there can be no threat to its security from without. To the
ancient mind the possession of a wall was precisely what constituted a city. John cannot therefore dispense with a wall, but
he makes it clear that the fabric is nothing else than the radiance
of the divine presence which characterizes the city as a whole
(cf. verse 11). The fabric of the city itself is **gold,** but no
earthly gold; it is **bright as clear glass, translucent** at all
points to the omnipresent glory.

19-
20 The twelve gems which together make up the foundation of
the wall appear to be related to the twelve which decorated the
breastpiece of the high priest, each one bearing the name of one
of the twelve tribes (Exod. xxviii. 17 ff.; xxxix. 10 ff.), and to the
identical list of jewels worn by the king of Tyre (Ezek. xxviii.
13 LXX; the Hebrew text has only nine). It is true that five of
John's Greek words are different from those found in the
Septuagint of these three passages, but the reason for this is

---

[1] There is a remarkable similarity between this passage and that in which
Herodotus gives the measurements of the historic Babylon. 'The city stands
in a broad plain, foursquare, with each front a hundred and twenty furlongs,
so that the entire perimeter is four hundred and eighty furlongs. In proportion to the vast size of the city of Babylon, in magnificence it excels
every other city that eyes have ever seen. It is surrounded in the first place
by a moat, deep, broad, and full of water, then by a wall fifty royal cubits
in width and two hundred in height. (The royal cubit is larger by three
fingers then the common cubit.)' (Herod. i, 178.) Note that John also
describes a city which stands foursquare, uses the stade or furlong measure
for the perimeter and the cubit for the height of the wall, and explains the
size of the cubit measure he is using. If we were comparing his description
with a passage from the Old Testament or Jewish literature, such resem-
blances would be taken as demonstrative proof of literary dependence. Is it
possible that he had excerpts from Herodotus in his Greek reader?

not that John is using a totally independent list, but that he has
made his own translation from the Hebrew. Most ancient
writers were somewhat vague in their identification of precious
stones, so that a single Hebrew stone could easily be equated
with more than one Greek one. (The only systematic treatises
on this subject in ancient times were Theophrastus's *On Stones*
and Pliny's *Natural History*, Book xxvii. In English the best
treatment of the subject is still that by J. L. Myers in the
Encyclopaedia Biblica, IV. 4,799-4,812.) But even if we suppose
that John's stones are the same as those on the high priest's
breastpiece, it is certain that he does not enumerate them in the
same order. If we take the Exodus order as normal, then John's
order is:

$$6 \quad 5 \quad 4 \quad 3 \quad 2 \quad 1 \quad 10 \quad 11 \quad 12 \quad 7 \quad 8 \quad 9$$

The first and second rows are interchanged and reversed, the
third and fourth interchanged but not reversed. Now some
scholars have argued that John's order must be connected with
the curious order in which he enumerates the four walls of his
square city—east, north, south, west; and others have added that
there must be a similar explanation for the erratic order of the
tribes in vii. 5-8. A little reflexion will show that there is no
solution to be found in this direction, and for the following
reasons:

(*a*) Assuming the primacy of Judah and the substitution of
Manasseh for Dan (see notes on vii. 5-8), the deviation of
John's list of tribes from the expected normal could be re-
presented thus:

$$1 \quad 2 \quad 9 \quad 10 \quad 11 \quad 12 \quad 3 \quad 4 \quad 5 \quad 6 \quad 7 \quad 8$$

A glance at the two lists of figures will show that no system
of arranging tribes and precious stones around the walls of the
city could explain the peculiarities of both lists. (*b*) John
has deliberately broken the association of the precious stones
with the twelve tribes and has connected them instead with
the twelve apostles. For these two reasons we should be content to leave the tribes out of account here and concentrate
on the stones. (*c*) Let us suppose that John began by arranging
the stones clockwise round his square, beginning in the north-

west corner (see diagram). He could then start in the opposite corner and read them off in the order of the gates: east, north, south, west. But this would still not produce the required list, for the last two rows would remain in their proper order, instead of being interchanged. The list of stones requires the order: east, north, west, south. (*d*) In any case, what right have we to attribute to John a procedure so odd? Why should he be interested in arranging the stones in one order, only to read them off in another? Why not arrange them in the order east,

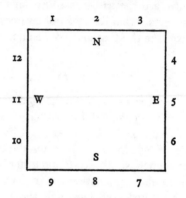

north, south, west to start with? (*e*) So far we have assumed that the order in Exodus is the norm. But Josephus gives a list of the twelve stones on the high priest's breastpiece which is in a different order from that in Exodus (*Bell. Jud.* v. 5. 7), and in a subsequent work goes out of his way to correct himself by giving a third list which is different again (*Ant.* iii. 7. 5). This would appear to make it doubtful whether in Hellenistic Judaism any list was regarded as standard. (*f*) The fact that John gives no list of the twelve apostles to be correlated with the stones on which their names were engraved strongly suggests that he was interested in the general symbolism of the city's structure, not in its detailed ground plan. (*g*) The final and decisive point is that there is an adequate explanation for the order of John's list of stones which is independent both of the high priest's breastpiece and of the order of the walls. According to both Philo (*Vit. Mos.* ii. 124) and Josephus (*Ant.* iii. 7. 7), the stones on the high priest's breastpiece were symbols of the zodiac.

Neither of these writers had any interest in pursuing the subject to the point of linking any particular stone with a particular zodiacal sign. Josephus was trying to prove to his Gentile reader that the Jewish religion was not indifferent to pagan cosmology, because the high priest's vestments symbolized the whole cosmos (cf. Wis. xviii. 24), and he offered two explanations of the jewels: they might mean the twelve months or they might mean the zodiac, the reader could take his choice. But according to Charles there is evidence from Egyptian and Arabian monuments from which the following table can be constructed.

1.	The Ram	Amethyst
2.	The Bull	Jacinth
3.	The Twins	Chrysoprase
4.	The Crab	Topaz
5.	The Lion	Beryl
6.	The Virgin	Chrysolite
7.	The Scales	Cornelian
8.	The Scorpion	Sardonyx
9.	The Archer	Emerald
10.	The Goat	Chalcedony
11.	The Water-carrier	Lapis lazuli
12.	The Fishes	Jasper

John's order therefore is the exact reverse of the astrological one. He must have derived his list not directly from Exodus, but from his knowledge of astrology; and he then deliberately reversed it to indicate his total disavowal of astrological interest.

With the list of foundation-stones John has for the time being deserted his primary Old Testament source, Ezekiel xl-xlviii. He now turns to a different description of the new Jerusalem in Isaiah liv. 11-12.

'I will . . . lay your foundation-stones with lapis lazuli,
I will make your pinnacles of agate, your gates of carbuncles.'

It is for this reason and not because he has suddenly become repetitive that he now turns back to the **gates**. The Hebrew **21** word *'eqdaḥ* (carbuncles), which does not occur elsewhere, he takes to mean **pearls,** and it is interesting to find that at least one of the Rabbis agreed with him. According to the Talmud, R. Johanan (early third century A.D.) told a disciple that God would make the gates of Jerusalem out of pearls measuring thirty cubits by thirty, in which he would cut a passage-way ten cubits wide by twenty cubits high (*Baba B.* 75ᵃ; cf. *San.* 100ᵃ).

The streets of the city were of pure gold. The Greek word *plateia* (**streets**) in xxi. 21 and xxii. 1 is a singular, and it is arguable that John envisaged a single main street running across his square city. If astrology were as dominant a source of his imagery as Farrer supposes, we should have to picture it as a golden Milky Way traversing the cosmic chart. But in the Septuagint the word is commonly used collectively or generically, much as in English we use the phrase 'in the street' without implying that there is only one. When Lot's angel visitors declare that they prefer to 'spend the night in the street', this tells us nothing about the town-planning of Sodom (Gen. xix. 2; cf. Jud. xix. 15, 17, 20). When, on the recommendation of Haman, Mordecai is made to ride 'through the street of the city', this is a procession which covers the length and breadth of the city, and not, as the RSV suggests, round and round a single central square (Esth. vi. 9, 11). Now John too has already used *plateia* in the singular in this generic sense when he said that the bodies of the witnesses would lie in the street of the great city (xi. 8); every city street in the world-wide Babylon that is the Roman empire is to display its evidence of the great ordeal. Johannine usage therefore favours the generic interpretation in the present context also.

22   The earthly **temple** had been the symbol of the presence of God in an otherwise secular or tainted world, and a reminder of two distinctions essential to Jewish religion, the one between the holy and the common, the other between the clean and the unclean. What was holy was set aside for the special service of God, and what was common remained available for the daily, secular use of man. What was clean could be either holy or common, dedicated to God or freely used by man; what was unclean could be neither. Thus from the large central area of the common and secular objects and persons were withdrawn in one direction by being sanctified and in the other by being

declared unclean. The temple was therefore the symbol of
God's claim on the secular world and of his abhorrence of the
unclean. But no such symbol is needed any longer. John sees
no temple in the city. The sphere of the holy has expanded
to include all that is capable of being offered to God, and all that
is unfit for God has been for ever excluded. The presence of
God, no longer confined to a sanctuary apart, pervades the whole
life and being of the city, which accordingly needs no created
light.   23

If John had been the ruthless and pessimistic rigorist that
many of his interpreters have supposed him to be, the elimina-
tion of the distinction between sacred and secular would have
been achieved simply by the abolition of the secular. But we
can now see that this is not what he meant by the disappearance
of the old heaven and earth. He did not believe that God would
be content to save a handful of martyrs and allow the rest of
mankind, along with all their achievements of culture and
civilization, to perish in the abyss. For into the holy city he now
brings **the nations** and **the kings of the earth.** To suppose 24
that by these phrases he means only the elect would be to run
counter to his consistent usage throughout the whole of his
book. **The nations** are the heathen, who had once been allowed
to trample the holy city underfoot, who were seduced by the
great whore, and who were finally reduced to subjection by
the armies of Christ (xi. 2; xviii. 3, 23; xix. 15). **The kings of the
earth** are those over whom Christ has asserted his authority
only at the cost of untold suffering to his faithful people (i. 5;
vi. 15; xvii. 2, 18; xviii. 3, 9). Those who once brought the
splendour of their luxury trade to deck the great whore now
bring their willing tribute to adorn the holy city. Nothing from
the old order which has value in the sight of God is debarred
from entry into the new. John's heaven is no world-denying
Nirvana, into which men may escape from the incurable ills of
sublunary existence, but the seal of affirmation on the goodness
of God's creation. The treasure that men find laid up in
heaven turns out to be **the treasures and wealth of the** 26
nations, the best they have known and loved on earth redeemed
of all imperfections and transfigured by the radiance of God.
Nothing is excluded but what is **obscene and false,** that is, 27

totally alien to the character of God. Nowhere in the New
Testament do we find a more eloquent statement than this of
the all-embracing scope of Christ's redemptive work.

At this point John returns to his two primary Old Testament
models, Ezekiel's new Jerusalem and the garden of Eden. In
1 Ezekiel's vision the life-giving **river** flowed from the restored
temple southward into the Dead Sea, which became fresh and
swarmed with fish; and along its banks grew trees bearing a
2 crop **for each month of the year** and with curative properties
in their **leaves** (Ezek. xlvii. 1-12). In John's vision the river
becomes the river of Eden, **the river of the water of life,**
and the trees **the tree of life** (cf. Gen. ii. 9-10). The river
flows **down the middle of the city's streets.** Here, as in
xxi. 21, the word *plateia* is a singular, and it is possible, as we
have said above, that John thought of a single street with the
river flowing along its length, and with an avenue of trees on
either bank. But it is more likely that he has in mind the 'river
whose canals are the joy of the city of God' (Ps. xlvi. 4), and
imagines every street with its tree-lined channel. Into this
Paradise restored come **the nations,** still bearing the wounds
of those battles by which their hostility to the Lamb has been
beaten down, smashed by the iron bar of his inexorable love;
3 but **the leaves of the trees are a cure for the nations. God's
curse,** pronounced over the whole creation because of Adam's
disobedience, is now abrogated (Gen. iii. 17; cf. Zech. xiv. 11),
for the whole creation has been renewed by the re-creating hand
of God; and no flaming sword bars the way to the tree of life.

John has now exhausted all the riches of Old Testament
imagery to describe the splendour of the new Jerusalem, but he
ends as he began with a reminder that the 'solid joys and lasting
treasure' which he has paraded before the mind's eye are the
symbol of a beatitude essentially personal and spiritual. When
all else has been said, the essence of heaven is to live eternally
in the presence of God. **His servants shall worship him;**
4 **they shall see him face to face.** The martyrs have protested,
'If only we knew how it was all going to end'. And this is the
true end of man, the beatific vision, which is also the trans-
forming vision; for those who enjoy it bear **his name** stamped
on their foreheads, because they have also come to bear the

impress of his nature on their lives (cf. 1 John iii. 2; 2 Cor. iii. 18; 1 Cor. xv. 49).

xxii. 6-21. EPILOGUE

(6) Then he said to me, 'These words are faithful and true'. The Lord God who inspired the prophets has sent his angel to show his servants what is bound to happen soon. (7) Be sure that I am coming soon!

Blessed is the man who heeds the words of prophecy that are in this book. (8) It was I, John, who heard and saw these things; and when I had heard and seen, I fell in worship at the feet of the angel who had shown them to me. (9) But he said to me, 'No, not that! I am a fellow-servant with you and your brothers the prophets and those who heed the words of this book. Worship God.' (10) Then he said to me, 'Do not seal up the words of prophecy that are in this book, for the time is near. (11) Let the wrong-doer still do wrong and the filthy remain in his filth; let the upright man still do right and the holy continue in his holiness. (12) Yes, I am coming soon, bringing my reward with me, to repay everyone for what he has done. (13) I am Alpha and Omega, the first and the last, the beginning and the end. (14) Blessed are those who wash their robes, so as to have the right to the tree of life and to enter the city by its gates. (15) Outside are dogs, sorcerers and fornicators, murderers and idolaters, all who love and practise falsehood. (16) I, Jesus, have sent my angel to give you this testimony for the churches. I am the Root and Scion of David, the bright morning star.'

(17) The Spirit and the bride say, 'Come!' Whoever hears, let him say, 'Come!' Come, if you are thirsty; accept, if you will, the water of life without charge.

(18) I solemnly declare to everyone who is listening to the words of prophecy that are in this book: if anyone should add to them, God will add to him the plagues that

are written in this book; (19) and if anyone should take away from the words of this book of prophecy, God will take away his share in the tree of life and the holy city, described in this book.

(20) He who gives this testimony is saying, 'Yes, I am coming soon!' Amen. Come, Lord Jesus.

(21) The grace of the Lord Jesus be with you all.

The splendour fades, and John is left alone with his guide, through whose lips there now come to him the words of Christ. For the guide is Christ's angel (cf. i. 1), and his words are the
6 words of him who sent him. **'These words are faithful and true.'** He whose name is Faithful and True (iii. 14; xix. 11) sets his imprimatur on the visions which John has been commissioned to write. The following sentence recalls the opening words of the book and reminds us that, however far back into the past or forward into the future the heavenly vision has carried us, John has never forgotten his avowed purpose of disclosing to God's servants the nature of their closely approaching ordeal, what is bound to happen soon. But now he adds that the source of this disclosure is **the Lord God who inspired the prophets.** Literally translated this phrase runs: 'the Lord God of the spirits of the prophets'. Since John can speak of the Holy Spirit as 'the seven spirits of God sent out into all the world' (v. 6), it is possible that he means: 'the Lord God who sends his Spirit to inspire his prophets'. But it is more likely that by 'spirits' he means the hearts of the prophets, open and susceptible to the influence of the illuminating and empowering Spirit (cf. 1 Cor. xiv. 32). In either case he is describing God as the source of all prophetic inspiration. But is he thinking of the Old Testament prophets or of Christian prophets? Since John normally uses 'prophet' as a title for the Christian martyr, and is about to do so in verse 9, it is natural to think that this is the sense he intends here. But in the present context the Christian prophet-martyrs are the **servants** to whom God **has sent his angel;** and it would be a mere tautology to say: 'the God who inspires his prophets has sent a revelation to his prophets'. Probably then the Old Testament prophets are meant. The God who inspired the prophets of the

Old Testament **has sent his angel** to **his servants,** on whom
the mantle of Elijah has descended, to warn them about **what
is bound to happen soon;** for what must happen is that they
are to prophesy not only with their lips but with their lives
(xi. 3). In the death and resurrection that awaits them they will
find their Lord keeping his tryst with them, reliving in his
Conquerors his own victory-in-defeat. **Be sure that I am** 7
coming soon! After all we have read it is no more possible to
think that John had a naïve attitude to this promise than it was
when we first heard it proclaimed in the letters to the churches
(ii. 5, 16; iii. 11; cf. xvi. 15). He will be there to meet them at
their own Calvary.

The benediction that follows is a repetition of that with which
the book began. But now it strikes differently upon our ears.
Now we know that in calling his book a **prophecy** John is
claiming more for it than that it foretells the future. The
function of the prophet is to declare to God's people, and
through them to the world, the whole counsel of God. John's
book is a **prophecy** because it reveals the true nature of the
conflict between the monster and the Lamb, between Babylon
the great and the new Jerusalem, and summons men to the one
victory that can overcome the world. At this point John
repeats the curious incident of xix. 10, in which he was forbidden to **worship** his escorting angel. Perhaps he was con- 8-9
cerned once again to remind his readers that the battle against
idolatry has to be fought on more than one front and may be
lost very near to home while it is being won against the obvious
enemy from without. But the warning serves also to show how
high a destiny John envisages for man, whose part in God's
service is second in importance not even to that of angels (cf.
Heb. i-ii); and it further serves to enhance the divine majesty
of Christ, to whom worship is paid without any sense of de-
traction from what is due to God alone.

When the author of the book of Daniel had his visions, he
was told to 'seal up the vision, because it is for many days
hence' (Dan. viii. 26; x. 14; cf. xii. 4, 9). Enoch, too, was given
to understand that what he saw was 'not for this generation,
but for a remote one yet to come' (1 *Enoch* i. 2). The device of
the sealed book was in each case forced on the writer because

he had chosen to adopt the name of a famous man from the past and had to explain why it was that the book had reference to his own day, centuries later than its presumptive date. John has abjured pseudonymity and can therefore dispense with the seal. Accordingly the command, **'Do not seal up the words of prophecy that are in this book'**, gives an added sense of urgency to his statement that **the time is near.** In case his readers have forgotten under the spell of his vast survey of history from creation to the end of time, he reminds them that the whole panorama may also be contracted to a span whenever a Christian is called on to testify to his faith at the cost of his life. In the Roman court-room, at the Roman scaffold, in the Roman arena, the ears that are attuned to the songs of Zion may hear the lament, 'Fallen, fallen is Babylon the great', and the eyes of faith may see both the monster rising from the abyss and going to perdition and Jerusalem coming down out of heaven from God. John knows that at last, far off, beyond the golden age of the millennium, the day will come when a voice will cry 'Stop!' and all earth's traffic will be halted in its track.

11 Then **let the wrong-doer still do wrong and the filthy remain in his filth; let the upright man still do right and the holy continue in his holiness;** for then it will be too late for any death-bed repentance. But he knows, too, that this eschatological moment of truth enters into and informs the lesser crises of historical existence and takes men unawares when they are compelled to face the claims of eternity on their lives. There is nothing determinist about these words. Rather they are a plain call to the reader to put his life in order while there is still opportunity for change.

12   When last John spoke of **reward,** it was at the blowing of the seventh trumpet; then and then only could it be said that the time had come for the dead to be judged (xi. 18). Here he takes up the same idea, but deals with it in a much more personal fashion. Here it is Christ who says, **'I am coming soon, bringing my reward with me'.** The words are derived from Isaiah xl. 10, but not the sense. The prophet had in mind a new Exodus, in which God, the good shepherd, would lead his people out of their latest Egyptian bondage; and the reward he brought with him was his flock, the recompense he had won

for himself by all his labours of redemption. Here the reward
is not that which Christ has won for himself, but that which he
gives, to repay everyone for what he has done; and, as the sequel
shows, the reward for the faithful is nothing less than access to
the holy city. Wherever and whenever Christ comes, this is the
reward he brings with him. He can do this because he shares
with God the title **Alpha and Omega** (cf. i. 8), and therefore 13
in his person **the beginning and the end** are eternally
present. The promise was made to the church of Laodicea that
anyone who opened the door to the imperious knocking would
find that he had admitted to his supper him who is 'the beginning of God's creation' (iii. 14, 20); and we can now add that he
would also find himself sitting at table with him who is **the
end,** in whom all the purposes of God and the aspirations of
man find their perfect embodiment. We have already been told
that Christ has 'released us from our sins with his own life-
blood' (i. 5), and have been shown the white-robed throng of
Conquerors safely installed in paradise, because 'they have
washed their robes and made them white in the life-blood of the
Lamb' (vii. 14); and now we can add that **those who wash** 14
their robes, that is, those who face martyrdom in the confidence
that the Cross is the sign of God's victory over evil without and
evil within, already see **the city** of God descending out of
heaven with its **gates** open to receive them, giving them immediate access **to the tree of life.**

If John had stopped at this point, we might have had some
lingering doubts about our interpretation of his eschatology. In
attributing to him a realized eschatology, in which the final
coming of Christ for judgment or reward is constantly anticipated in the crises of individual or corporate life, have we
modernized or spiritualized that which he himself took with
naïve literalness? Such doubts are for ever dissipated when he
adds that **outside are dogs.** For the dogs are pariahs (Deut. 15
xxiii. 18; Matt. vii. 6; Mark vii. 27) and are here defined as those
heathen who are indelibly marked with the qualities of the monster and the whore: **sorcerers and fornicators, murderers
and idolaters, all who love and practise** that **falsehood**
which is the basis of impenitent resistance to the rule of God.
But these are precisely the people whose lot is the lake of fire

(xxi. 8). When the new heaven and earth finally comes, there will be no **outside** for them to occupy; they will have disappeared into oblivion. It makes sense, then, to say that they are **outside** only if the city is considered to be a present reality at such time as they still exist. In the midst of the daily life of Smyrna and Pergamum, Babylon and Jerusalem exist side by side. Their citizens rub shoulders in the streets of Sardis and Philadelphia. The Conqueror in Ephesus may see an open gate in heaven giving him **the right to the tree of life** (ii. 7).

At the start of the book we were told that its contents were to be the testimony of Jesus which he would communicate by means of his angel to his servant John. Now that John has 16 completed his record, it can be said that the **angel** was sent **to give you** (plural) **this testimony for the churches;** the testimony is given to all who are prepared to make it their own in an act of self-sacrificing witness. For the vision needs more than artistry of word and image to make it credible. It needs the supporting evidence that only the martyrs can bring to it. Yet it comes from one about whom the most exalted claims can be made. He is not merely the **Scion of David,** the Branch, the messianic king sprung from the royal house of Judah (Isa. xi. 1; Jer. xxiii. 5; xxxiii. 15 f.; Zech. iii. 8; vi. 12; Ezek. xxxiv. 23; xxxvii. 24 f.; Hos. iii. 5; Amos ix. 11); he is **the Root** from which David himself sprang, the eternal, archetypal king. **The bright morning star** recalls the prophecy of Balaam, which was commonly taken to refer to the Messiah (Num. xxiv. 17; cf. *Test. Lev.* xviii. 3; *Test. Jud.* xxiv. 1-5; *IQM* xi. 6 f.). It also reminds us of the promise to the Conqueror at Thyatira (ii. 28), driving home the point already made in verse 12, that Christ himself is all the reward that the heart of man can desire. The title itself implies that, wherever Christ is present, 'the night is nearly over, and daytime at hand' (Rom. xiii. 12). In the realm of the spirit it is not the passage of time that brings daybreak and the end of darkness, but 'the morning star dawning in your minds' (2 Pet. i. 19).

The last verses have an unmistakably liturgical ring about them, beginning as they do with the invitation to communion and ending with the prayer of the expectant church. The first 17 **'Come!'** is addressed not to Christ but to all comers; and, since it is spoken by **the Spirit** that inspires the prophets and by **the bride,** the new Jerusalem, it is a summons both to join the ranks of the Conquerors and to enter into the Conquerors' reward. The invitation is to be echoed antiphonally by the earthly congregation of the faithful: **whoever hears, let him say, 'Come!'** That this worship is conceived as taking place in an earthly community is certain, for it ends with the eucharistic prayer, **'Come, Lord Jesus'.** It is therefore the more striking that what is offered in this eucharist, **without price** and without other qualification except the will to accept it, is that very **water of life** with which in the new Jerusalem God himself assuages the Conquerors' thirst (xxi. 6; cf. vii. 16-17). Thus it is above all in worship that the Christian may see the holy city descending out of heaven from God, and may enter it in response to the summons of **the Spirit and the bride.**

To the modern ear it comes as a shock when this solemn 18-
liturgy is interrupted by an equally solemn imprecation. But we 19
must remember that from the first John has intended that his book should be read in church and received with the status of scripture (cf. i. 3). To a Jew one of the characteristics of scripture was that its text should be regarded as inviolate. Deuteronomy twice declares that the Torah must be preserved intact without addition or subtraction (Deut. iv. 2; xii. 32; cf. 1 *Enoch* civ. 10; 2 *Enoch* xlviii. 7-8). An even closer parallel is provided by the Letter of Aristeas, which purports to describe the translation of the Pentateuch into Greek and its acceptance by the Jewish commune of Alexandria: 'As soon as the scrolls had been read, the priests, the eldest of the translators, representatives of the commune, and the rulers of the people stood up and said: "Forasmuch as the translation has been well and piously carried out and with complete accuracy, it is right that it should be preserved in its present form, without any further revision." When all had assented to this proposal, they gave a ruling in accordance with their custom that an imprecation be imposed on any who should revise the text by addition, by any alteration whatsoever of what was written in it, or by subtraction' (*Ep. Arist.* 310-311). According to Eusebius (*H.E.* v. 20. 2), Irenaeus appended to one of his lost works the following paragraph: 'Whoever you are that are making a copy of this

book, I adjure you by our Lord Jesus Christ and by his glorious advent when he comes to judge the living and the dead, that you compare your copy and correct it carefully by this original manuscript; and likewise transcribe this adjuration and set it in your copy.' What has seemed to some commentators to be evidence of John's unbending harshness of temperament turns out to be little more than a familiar literary, or perhaps theological, convention.

The reason why John feels it proper to include such an adjuration is that he does not regard himself as the author of the
20 book. **He who gives this testimony** is Jesus. For the third time in this epilogue the voice of Jesus is heard uttering the promise, **'I am coming soon'**. But here the promise has a new and distinctive note. It stands in the liturgical setting of the eucharist, and is answered by the eucharistic prayer *Maranatha* —**Come, Lord Jesus** (cf. 1 Cor. xvi. 22). Week after week that prayer was spoken and answered as the risen Christ made himself known to his disciples in the breaking of the bread. As they gathered to 'proclaim the death of the Lord until he comes' (1 Cor. xi. 26), the past event of the Cross and the future of the Parousia met in the sacramental moment of the present. But the prayer of the waiting church is to John something more than a liturgical response; for here, as at iii. 20, he is using liturgical language to express what transcends liturgy. No one who has read his book can have any illusions about what the prayer is asking. It is a prayer that Christ will come again to win in his faithful servant the victory which is both Calvary and Armageddon. It is the prayer which says, 'All I ask is to know Christ and the power of his resurrection, to share his sufferings and conform to the pattern of his death, if only I may arrive at the resurrection from the dead' (Phil. iii. 10-11). It is a prayer that the Christian, confronted by the great ordeal, may 'endure as one who sees the invisible' (Heb. xi. 27), and may hear above the harsh sentence of a Roman judge the triumph song of heaven.

THE THEOLOGY OF THE BOOK
OF REVELATION

THE Book of Revelation is not a handbook of systematic theology. John wrote as a pastor, to give courage and hope to men facing imminent persecution, and he wrote as an artist, giving to ancient images new life and meaning by combining them in the unity of a great work of art. We must not therefore complain if his book does not contain all that he himself ever thought or believed, let alone the whole of Christian theology. Yet it is a profoundly theological book; and, just because its ideas are expressed in symbols almost as old as the mind of man, they are capable of being applied to other needs than the one he particularly had in mind. So vividly did he apprehend the presence of God that he was able to make that presence real to others, and this no doubt is the reason why Christians in every generation have come back and back to his book, even when they imperfectly understood its symbols and were not entirely sure that they ought to approve of them. John's faith in God is all the more remarkable because he was at all points a realist. He was a realist in his appraisal of the churches with their little strength and their variegated weakness, so realistic that we can still recognize in them the churches to which we ourselves belong; yet he never doubted God's ability to clothe the church in the robe of purity and perfection which would make her a fit bride for the Lamb (xix. 7-8). He was a realist in his grasp of the power and splendour of imperial Rome and of her ability to crush the church, in his analysis of the real nature of the forces that were devastating the earth, so realistic indeed that his world, once we understand it, is very little different from our own; yet he never doubted that in the battle between the monster and the Lamb the ultimate victory would go to the Lamb. He himself had stood in a Roman court of justice, fortunate to escape with his life, and he believed that countless other Christians must stand where he had stood; yet he remained confident that every verdict of such a court must be either upheld or reversed before the superior court of the great white throne (xx. 11).

John conveys his sense of the reality of God with an economy which does nothing to dispel the divine mystery. He sees an enthroned figure 'like jasper or cornelian' (iv. 3), but he makes no attempt to describe him. When his readers come to the eternal city, then they will see God face to face (xxii. 4). Until then they may see him only as he is mirrored in the worship of the heavenly host. John has the best possible theological reason for this restraint. Like other New Testament writers, he believes that the glory of God has been seen in the face of Jesus Christ (cf. 2. Cor. iv. 6), that whoever has seen him has seen the Father (cf. John xiv. 9). He therefore portrays Christ at his first appearance in all the attributes of deity (i. 12 ff.); he is the Son of Man of Daniel's vision, but he has assumed the snow-white hair of the Ancient of Days, as well as the eyes, the voice, and the countenance of the Lord of glory. Like the throned figure before whom the elders lay their crowns, he is Lord of lords and King of kings (xvii. 14; xix. 16). He can lay claim to God's own title, Alpha and Omega, the beginning and the end (xxii. 13; cf. i. 8; ii. 8; xxi. 6). The heavenly choir addresses to him the same words as they have addressed to the Creator, 'You are worthy', and unites the Lamb in worship with him who sits of the throne (v. 7-9). Thereafter the names of God and the Lamb are regularly coupled (vii. 10; xiv. 4; xxi. 22), until at the last the very throne of heaven is called 'the throne of God and the Lamb' (xxii. 1, 3). Now we may hold that John is using all these devices to say something about Christ, invested with the insignia of Godhead; and so no doubt, incidentally, he is. But the more important fact is that he is saying something about God, once hidden from human sight, but now revealed in the known person of his Son.

John's Christology, and therefore his theology, is firmly anchored in the Jesus of history. This becomes clear when we turn from the character of God to his purpose. John repeatedly tells his readers that he has been commissioned to disclose to them 'what is bound to happen soon' (i. 1, 3; iv. 1; xxii. 6, 10, 20), and he makes it plain that the necessity arises not because of the state of world affairs but because the future has been decreed in the predestining purpose of God. It has been the thesis of this commentary that the one imminent event which John expected was persecution, and that everything else in his visions belongs, in Bunyan's language, to 'the backside of the wall', that framework of theological interpretation without which the imminent future would be meaningless tragedy. The prospective martyrs are to understand that their suffering is an essential part of the purpose declared by God and attested by Jesus Christ (i. 2), a purpose as old as the world and as ultimate as the crack of doom. Accordingly John's visions range over the whole of human history from creation to the new Jerusalem. Yet at the outset he gives us three indications that this vast panorama is but the backdrop to a drama of current affairs. (1) The revelation comes from God 'who is and was and is coming' (i. 4)—from him, that is to say, in whom the ultimate past and the ultimate future are comprehended in an eternal present, so that, wherever men are aware of his presence, they are confronted with the beginning and the end, the ground and goal of being (i. 8). (2) It also comes from 'Jesus Christ, the faithful witness, the firstborn of the dead, the ruler of earthly kings' (i. 5); and this is a reminder that the whole purpose of God had been contracted to a microcosm in the death, resurrection, and ascension of Jesus. (3) By his death Christ had appointed his followers 'to be a royal house of priests to his God and Father' (i. 6), to give new expression to his own kingship and priesthood. They are therefore called to share 'the ordeal and sovereignty and endurance' (i. 9), to reign in the midst of their martyrdom as he had reigned from the Cross. All this is to say that the secret purpose of God is known to John only because it has been revealed in the earthly testimony of Jesus, 'the faithful witness', and that it can be known to the world only if there are men like John prepared to hold to the testimony of Jesus, even at the cost of life or liberty.

The same point is made a second time when John takes us into the heavenly throne-room, where, like many an Old Testament prophet, he is allowed access to the privy council of God (ch. iv). The dominant symbols, the throne and the rainbow, introduce us to the central problem of all theology: how can God, in a sinful world, do equal justice to his sovereignty and his mercy? The sovereignty is emphasized by the lightning and thunder which issue from the throne, reminiscent of the law-giving at Sinai, by the four living creatures with their hymn to God's holiness, and by the elders who lay their crowns at the feet of the King of kings. The need for mercy is indicated by the presence of the sea of glass, the ocean of the creation myth, which God conquered in the process of bringing order out of chaos and light out of darkness, but which remains in heaven as the symbol of a universe still imperfectly subjected to the reign of God. This vision of the Creator thus poses the question: how does God intend to assert his sovereignty over his whole creation, so that in the new heaven and earth the sea may be no more (xxi. 1)? The answer to this question is contained in the scroll which God holds (v. 1). It is his redemptive plan. But although it is fore-ordained by him, he will not himself unseal it; he requires a human agent. Christ now appears as the Lamb, who by his sacrificial death has won the right to break the seals of the scroll and so both to disclose its contents and put them into operation. The comments of the heavenly choir remind us that the exercising of this right by Christ is to involve those whom he has made 'a royal house of priests in God's service' (v. 10), and that nothing less is intended than the bringing of the whole creation into the worship and service of God (v. 13). But apart from the Cross this purpose can be neither known nor implemented.

John has other ways of reminding his readers that the events they must live through are part of an all-embracing purpose. His constant allusions to the Old Testament imply an interpretation of history already foreshadowed in the prophetic writings. His use of typology, and especially of the Exodus story, points to an eternal pattern in God's ordering of history. His frequent references to the creation myth (iv. 6; ix. 1; xi. 7; xii. 3; xiii. 1; xv. 2; xxi. 1) serve to depict the imminent crisis as part of the agelong battle between good and evil, light and darkness. And his even more frequent use of eschatological language is an assertion that history has an end and therefore a meaning. But at every point we must remember that only the earthly life and death of Jesus provides the key to the divine purpose. The Old Testament leads John to expect a Messiah who will be the Lion of Judah, but the facts of the gospel present him with a Lamb bearing the marks of slaughter (v. 5-6). The Old Testament predicts the smashing of the nations with an iron bar, but the only weapon the Lamb wields is his own Cross and the martyrdom of his followers (ii. 27; xii. 5; xix. 15). The seven spirits of God can be let loose into the world only as the eyes of the Lamb (i. 4; iii. 1; iv. 5; v. 6). The Red Sea through which the followers of the Lamb must achieve their new Exodus is the bloodbath of their own martyrdom (xv. 2). The monster from the abyss can be conquered only by being allowed to conquer and so to burn itself out (xiii. 7); and the perfection of the holy city, into which nothing unclean is allowed to enter, is achieved by allowing evil to exhaust its strength in unavailing attacks on the people of God.

Because John has learned from Christ a high conception of human destiny, he has a criterion by which to measure the depravity of man's individual and corporate life. About the origin of evil he has little to say. It could be said of him, as was said of Jesus, that he was less interested in the genesis of evil than in its exodus. Yet it would be a mistake to suppose that, because John speaks of evil in vast cosmic symbols, he therefore believed in mythical demonic powers operating independently of human wrongdoing. He is told to write to the angels of the seven churches, charging them with faults and threatening them with punishment, but only because they are being held responsible for the earthly communities they represent (see on i. 12). The monster which the whole world worships is said to come from the abyss (xi. 7; xiii. 4, 8), yet the fault of its worshippers is that they 'did not renounce the gods of their own making' (ix. 20). It is human idolatry that corrupts the created order, turning the works of God into demonic powers. The abyss is a vast reservoir of accumulated evil, from which come many plagues to torment mankind; but it is fed from the springs of human sin. This is why the locust plague that issues from the abyss is said to have human faces (ix. 6); for though evil may assume a thousand disguises, in the final analysis it has a human face. Satan himself owes to human sin his right to appear in heaven and to thwart the merciful purposes of God by his accusations, for here, as in the Old Testament, he is the

Accuser, entrusted with the maintenance of divine justice; and only when Christ's redeeming work is done, and the charge against sinful men is dismissed, can Michael drum him out of heaven (xii. 7 ff.). Nothing in all creation is so sacred as to be beyond the distorting taint of evil; for even John, at the climax of his exposure of the heathen world's idolatry, needs twice to be warned against being so impressed by the revelation of God's truth and the means by which it has come to him as to worship that which is not God (xix. 10; xxii. 8-9; cf. Rom. vii. 7-13).

It is more directly to John's purpose to show that evil, once let loose into the world, has a cumulative effect and ramifies into titanic forms, far beyond the control of individual men. The two chief symbols for this are the monster and the whore, representing the political tyranny and the economic seductions of the omnicompetent state. John identifies both with the Roman empire of his own day, but each has a longer history than Rome. The monster has characteristics of all four world empires of Daniel's vision (xiii. 1-2), and the whore is Babylon the great, but also bears the allegorical names of Sodom and Egypt and the character of Jerusalem (xi. 8; xiv. 8; xvii. 5). Each in its own way has the power to delude the whole world, apart from those who are protected from such delusion by the seal of God (xiii. 8, 14; xiv. 8; xvii. 2; xviii. 3).

John uses the most offensive language he can to delineate his spiritual enemies (Balaamite, Jezebel, fornication, monster, whore), because he is aware that they present themselves to the world in a much more attractive light. No man chooses evil because he recognizes it to be evil, but always because, for the moment at least, it appears to be good. The essence of evil is deception and counterfeit. Satan is 'the deceiver of the whole world', who misleads men by telling lies about God. The monster is the Antichrist, the false Messiah, who makes blasphemous claims to deity. It bears 'deadly marks of slaughter', which are a parody of the marks on the Lamb, and its deadly wound has been healed in a mock resurrection (xiii. 3, 14). Its followers bear a brand which is a travesty of the seal of God on the foreheads of the martyrs (xiii. 16). Its title, 'was and is not and is yet to be', is a caricature of the name of God (xvii. 8; cf. i. 4). The whore, too, is decked in earthly finery which is made to look cheap by the heavenly splendour of the woman clothed with the sun, and with jewels which appear tawdry in comparison with those of the heavenly Jerusalem (xvii. 4; cf. xii. 1; xxi. 9 ff.). Chapter xviii shows how deeply impressed John had been by the grandeur and greatness of Rome and what an effort it must have cost him to free himself and his churches from her seductive power.

A further characteristic of evil is its self-destructiveness. It is the blazing mountain of Babylon, the 'destroyer of the whole earth', that pollutes the sea on which the Roman Babylon depends for its prosperity, and the star of Babylon's king that poisons the drinking water (viii. 8-11). The angel of the abyss, whether in Hebrew or in Greek, has the name Destroyer (ix. 12). The lies, blasphemies, and propaganda from the mouths of the dragon, the monster, and the false prophet become demon spirits which infect the nations beyond the frontiers of the Roman empire and unite them in alliance against it (xvi. 13 ff.). The cup which sends the whore staggering to her end is filled with the blood she herself has shed (xvii. 6). It is a permanent characteristic of the monster that it not only arises from the abyss but is headed for perdition (xvii. 8). And in the end the whore is destroyed by the very monster on whose back she sits enthroned (xvii. 16 f.). God uses this self-destroying power of evil to batter down the defences of those who try to find security in that which is not God. But he cannot give it full rein without assenting to the total destruction of the world he has made. He therefore limits its operation to give men every possible opportunity of repentance (vi. 1-8; viii. 6-12; xi. 13). It is at this point that John has to face his biggest pastoral problem. Why does God not cut short the suffering of his persecuted people? Sooner or later evil must be allowed to run its destructive course to a close. The answer is that God holds his hand, not willing that any of his creatures should perish, and as long as he does so, the martyrs must suffer. Martyrdom, like the Cross, is the cost of divine patience.

If John dwells on the magnitude of the world's need, it is only in order that his readers may fully appreciate the scope of God's redemptive plan and the significance of the part which they themselves are called to play in it. For unless God is to acknowledge defeat by abandoning his world to the destructive forces of evil, he must provide a way of stopping men from endlessly producing the means of their own destruction and must release them from the tyranny of demonic powers they themselves have brought into being. Since God 'is and was and is coming', it is hardly surprising that his plan of redemption also has three tenses: it is a past fact, a present duty, and a future hope. The salvation achieved once for all in the life, death, and resurrection of Jesus must be relived and proclaimed to the world by his faithful servants, until its full implications are realized in the individual and corporate life of men.

The fact of salvation is the source of all John's confidence and prophetic vision. Christ 'has released us from our sins with his own life-blood' (i. 6). He is 'the living one who was dead' (i. 18). He has conquered and sat down on his Father's throne (iii. 21). He has won the right to open the scroll of destiny (v. 5, 9). He has 'ransomed for God men of every tribe, tongue, people, and nation' (v. 9). He has won a victory for God over Satan, the Great Accuser (xii. 10). Although John at all times deals in heavenly symbols, it is important to remember that some things happen in heaven because earthly events have made them possible (see on iv. 1). John is chiefly concerned with the crisis of his own times, but his interest in and knowledge of the earthly Jesus may be gauged by the number of times he echoes the Gospel tradition (iii. 3; vi. 16; viii. 13; xi. 2; xiv. 4; xiv. 14, 20; xvi. 13, 15; xviii. 21-23, 24; xix. 17; xxi. 3-7). But more important than all this is the fact that Jesus has been the faithful witness (i. 5; iii. 14), and the parallel use of the phrase to describe the martyred Antipas proves that John has in mind the earthly testimony which led to the crucifixion. It follows that when John speaks of the testimony of Jesus (i. 2, 9; xii. 17; xix. 10; xx. 4) he is referring to this same historic testimony. 'The word of God and the testimony of Jesus' (i. 2, 9) have both the same content, for the purpose spoken by God is known only through being attested by Jesus in his earthly life, teaching, death, and resurrection. It is this same historic testimony that inspires the Christian prophets to witness to their faith and to confirm their testimony with martyrdom

(xix. 10). And because God's purpose of redemption has been translated into earthly fact in the lives of Jesus and his followers, the triumphant Jesus bears the title 'The Word of God' (xix. 14).

But the past fact of salvation must also be made contemporary in the experience of the church and the world. Each Christian is called to an *imitatio Christi*, a holding fast to the testimony of Jesus (vi. 9; xi. 7; xii. 11, 17; xix. 10; xx. 4). Each is called to be a Conqueror, repeating in his own life the archetypal victory of Christ (ii. 7, 11, 17, 26; iii. 5, 12, 21). He must wash his robes and make them white in the life-blood of the Lamb (vii. 14), and the white robe is the symbol of sanctity as well as of victory and everlasting life (xix. 8; cf. xiv. 4-5). John never allows his readers to forget that earthly conduct matters and matters eternally. For there are books to be opened, and men will be judged by their deeds (xx. 12 f.). Their names may be written from eternity in the book of life, but names may be erased (iii. 5; xvii. 8). The lake of fire stands at the end of the world's story as a proof of the dignity of man, whom God will never reduce to the status of puppet by robbing him of his freedom of choice. But more depends on the conduct of Christians than their own individual destiny. For the church has been appointed by Christ to be 'a royal house of priests' (i. 6; v. 10), to mediate his royal and priestly authority to the whole world. Through the church he is to exercise his sovereignty over the nations, smashing their resistance to his rule and releasing their subjects for a new and better loyalty (i. 5; ii. 26 f.; xi. 15 ff.; xii. 5; xv. 3-4; xvii. 14; xix. 11 ff.). Through the church he is to mediate God's forgiveness and lead the world to repentance (iii. 7-9; xi. 13; xiv. 6-7; xx. 1-6). And all this they may achieve only by following the Lamb wherever he goes (xiv. 4).

The Christian life is a duty, but a duty possible only because it is also a gift of God's grace. The white robe of sanctity is his gift as well as his demand (xix. 8). Christ is no absentee who has finished his work and bequeathed it to others, only to return at the end to see what they have made of it. He is continually present with his people. If they suffer, it is 'in Jesus' (i. 9); if they die, it is 'in the Lord' (xiv. 13). John regularly uses the simple name Jesus to denote the unity of believers with their Lord in human responsibility and suffering (i. 9; xii. 17; xiv. 12; xvii. 6; xix. 10; xx. 4). On two occasions (i. 13; xiv. 14) he speaks of Jesus as 'one like a son of man'; and, whatever modern critics may think about Jesus' own use of this term, John has no doubt that it is drawn from Daniel and indicates the representative character of Jesus and his involvement with his followers in the sufferings and ultimate triumph of 'the saints of the Most High'. Jesus is fully implicated in the life of the church: he walks among the seven lamps and holds in his hand the seven stars (i. 13, 16); he has an intimate concern for all their doings, and he comes constantly to them, either in discipline (ii. 5, 16; iii. 3) or in communion (iii. 20; cf. xxii. 17-21). As the Lamb he stands with his followers on mount Zion to share their ordeal and to win their victory (xiv. 1; xvii. 14), and even when he appears as a conqueror his robes are stained with the blood of their martyrdom (xix. 13). Though their outer life may be exposed to attack from worldly enemies, their inner life is secure under the protection of God (vii. 1-8; xi. 1-2; xii. 14).

Within the future hope of salvation John distinguishes two types of eschatology: the promise of eternal life for the individual and the promise of vindication for God's people within history through the triumph of the cause for which they have lived and died (vi. 9-11). He does not believe that heaven is only for martyrs. There are other faithful Christians who, like the Conquerors, are to be robed in white (iii. 5). The Conquerors are a chosen band, twelve thousand from each of the tribes of the new Israel (vii. 1-8), two lamps out of the seven which represent the whole church (xi. 4). It is one of their special privileges to participate in the first resurrection and to be thereby exempt from the second death, while the rest of the dead have their destiny decided at the second resurrection before the great white throne (xx. 4 ff.). The only limit that John is prepared to set to the saving power of God is that into the holy city nothing unclean may enter (xxi. 27); and even this is a limit which requires careful qualification. Men are judged by their deeds, recorded in the heavenly books. But what those books contain is decided not by a mechanical computer, but by

THE THEOLOGY OF THE BOOK OF REVELATION

the decision of God. It was said of Babylon that she 'was remembered before God' (xvi. 19), and that God had kept 'a
record of her crimes' (xviii. 5), as though this was a retribution
of special severity; and we are reminded of the promise of the
new covenant, that God would remember men's sins no more
(Jer. xxxi. 34). If God can remember, he can also forget; and
what God chooses to forget is blotted from the record. The
decision, moreover, is based not only on the record books, but
on another book—'the book of life of the Lamb slaughtered
from the foundation of the world' (xiii. 8). It contains the
names of all those for whom Christ died, unless indeed a man
has chosen to have his name removed from the roll.

But John is writing mainly for martyrs, and what he has to
say about heaven has a particular relevance to them. It is not
that there is a special heaven for them, but there is a special
and reiterated guarantee. It seems likely that John believed the
martyrs to enter on their reward immediately on death. They
receive the white robe of immortality while there is still a little
while longer to wait for the vindication of the cause for which
they died (vi. 9-11). After three and a half days a voice calls
them up to heaven and they receive a breath of life from God
(xi. 11 f.). But, if this is so, we cannot interpret the first resurrection as a physical return to earth for the period of the
millennial reign. Resurrection must mean for them what it
meant for Christ: both the beginning of a heavenly existence
and the beginning of a new activity on earth, freed from bodily
limitations (xx. 4-5).

The salvation of individual souls is not, however, enough to
vindicate the purposes of God. God is the Creator: 'You have
created the universe, by your will it was created and came into
being' (iv. 11). Merely to destroy what he has made would be a
confession of failure, a negation of omnipotence. It is the
enemies of God that are 'destroyers of the earth' (xi. 18). The
purpose of the Creator can be complete only when 'the whole
creation, everything in heaven and on earth and under the
earth and in the sea', joins in the worship of the heavenly
choir (v. 13). The world must not be abandoned to the final
control of demonic powers. There must come a time on earth
when it is true to say: 'The sovereignty of the world has passed

to our Lord and to his Christ' (xi. 15). It is for this reason that John looks forward to a millennium, a period when the rule of Christ will be established over those very nations which have resisted God and persecuted his people (ch. xx). From this it follows that the repeated attacks upon the ungodly world order by all the armament of heaven, which occupy so large a part of John's book, are designed not to destroy or to punish, but only to penetrate the defences which the world has erected against the rule of God. The dethronement of the monster and the fall of Babylon are necessary parts of God's redemptive plan, if the vast populations they have deluded and seduced are to be set free for the kingdom of God. And the secret weapon by which God means to achieve this end is the death of his martyr servants. Only in this way can the nations be liberated from the deceptions of Satan (xx. 3). John knows, of course, that even the millennial reign must come to an end; and the invasion of Gog and Magog is a reminder that man can have no abiding home or security among the things that are temporal and transitory (xx. 7-10). The old order must give way at last to a new heaven and earth. But there is here a final proof that John believed in a purpose for history as well as for individual souls. Into the new Jerusalem are brought not only the souls of the faithful but the wealth and glory of the nations; and down the middle of the city's street are avenues of the tree of life, whose leaves provide healing for the nations. Any achievement of man in the old order, however imperfect, provided it has value in the sight of God, will find its place in the healed and transfigured life of the new Jerusalem.

John's doctrine of salvation, like that of the New Testament as a whole, is in three tenses. But it is characteristic of his visions that the tenses are constantly interfused. Already when the Lamb receives the scroll of destiny, the whole creation joins in the worship of heaven (v. 13). No sooner are the Conquerors sealed for martyrdom than they are seen to emerge from it into their heavenly reward, and the tenses leave us in doubt whether John is describing the present or the future (vii. 9 ff.). The victory of the martyrs is already included in the victory of the Cross by which Satan is ejected from heaven (xii. 11). The fall of Babylon is already accomplished at the moment when the martyrs meet their death (xiv. 8). Christ comes like a thief in the crisis of Armageddon (xvi. 15). And the new Jerusalem descends out of heaven from God not only before and after the millennium, but wherever the martyr wins his crown (iii. 12; xix. 7; xxi. 2, 10). To anyone who believes that biblical eschatology is an ordered sequence of events leading inexorably to an *eschaton*, a final event beyond which nothing can conceivably happen, all this must be puzzling and frustrating. But there is no puzzle if we share John's faith that the end is not an event but a person, the first and the last (xxii. 13). John's book begins on the Lord's day and ends in eucharistic worship; and it is in the setting of worship that his eschatology is to be understood. He and his fellow Christians had no difficulty in believing that the end could come to meet them in the midst of time. For week by week their prayer *Maranatha*, Come, Lord Jesus, was answered as they kept their tryst with him who was Alpha and Omega, the beginning and the end.

INDEX OF BIBLICAL REFERENCES

OLD TESTAMENT

THE REVELATION OF ST. JOHN THE DIVINE

Jeremiah—contd.
li. 42 114
li. 45 223
li. 57 193
li. 60-63 231
Lamentations
i. 15. 189
Ezekiel
i. 4-21 64
i. 7 25
i. 26-28 63
ii. 9-10 129
ii. 9–iii. 3 71
ix. 1 ff. 97
ix. 2 274
xiii. 11, 13 143
xvi. 36 ff. 212
xvii. 1-8 192
xxiii. 2 ff. 212
xxvi. 7 122
xxvii 226
xxvii. 14 226
xxviii. 12-16 270
xxviii. 13 274
xxix. 3 150
xxxiii. 3 ff. 109
xxxiv. 23 . . . 102, 286
xxxvi. 23 52
xxxvi. 28 265
xxxvii. 23 265
xxxvii. 24 f. 286
xxxvii. 27 . . . 264, 265
xxxvii. 27-28 52
xxxviii–xxxix . . . 122, 256
xxxviii. 6, 15 122
xxxviii. 7-10 123
xxxviii. 8, 11, 14 257
xxxix. 2 122
xxxix. 17 ff. 247
xl–xlviii 277
xl. 2 269
xlii. 16-19 272
xliii. 2 . . . 25, 222
xliv. 4 200
xlv. 2 272
xlv. 20 109
xlvii. 1-12 . . . 194, 280
xlviii. 20 272
xlviii. 30 ff. 271
Daniel
ii. 19 205
ii. 28 11
ii. 35 259
iii. 5-6 177
iv. 17 . . . 162, 164, 253

iv. 25, 32 . . . 162, 253
vii. 1 ff. 137
vii. 2-3 68
vii. 2-7 162
vii. 8-11 127
vii. 9 . . . 25, 252
vii. 13 18
vii. 22 252
vii. 26 ff. 253
viii. 10 149
viii. 13 f. 127
viii. 15 f. 274
viii. 26 f. . . . 253, 283
ix. 21 274
ix. 24-27 105
ix. 27 . . . 127, 165, 214
x. 5 274
x. 5-6 25
x. 14 283
x. 20 10
x. 21 154
xi. 31 . . . 165, 214
xi. 31-35 127
xii. 1 154
xii. 2-3 254
xii. 4 283
xii. 6-7 127
xii. 7 . . . 159, 210, 274
xii. 9 283
xii. 11 . . . 165, 214
Hosea
i. 9 264
i. 23 265
ii. 5 . . . 212, 234
ii. 23 224
iii. 5 286
vi. 11 189
viii. 1 117
x. 1 192
x. 1-8 89
x. 8 90
xiii. 15 94
Joel
ii. 1 109
ii. 13 146
ii. 15 109
ii. 28–iii. 3 90
ii. 30 113
iii. 9 179
iii. 9-14 189
Amos
iii. 7 . . . . 12, 60
iv. 6-11 109
vii. 2-3 146
viii. 2 210

306

INDEX OF BIBLICAL REFERENCES

INDEX OF BIBLICAL REFERENCES

INDEX OF BIBLICAL REFERENCES

INDEX OF NON-BIBLICAL REFERERENCES

GREEK AND LATIN BOOKS

INDEX OF NON-BIBLICAL REFERENCES

316